STAGING THE PEOPLE

STAGING THE PEOPLE

THE PROLETARIAN AND HIS DOUBLE

Jacques Rancière

Translated by David Fernbach

V

VERSO

London • New York

First published in English by Verso 2011
© Verso 2011
Compiled from articles originally appearing in *Les Révoltes logiques*
© *Les Révoltes logiques* 1975 to 1981
Translation © David Fernbach 2011

1 3 5 7 9 10 8 6 4 2

Verso
UK: 6 Meard Street, London W1F 0EG
US: 20 Jay Street, Suite 1010, Brooklyn, NY 11201
www.versobooks.com

Verso is the imprint of New Left Books

ISBN-13: 978-1-84467-697-2

British Library Cataloguing in Publication Data
A catalogue record for this book is available from the British Library

Library of Congress Cataloging-in-Publication Data
A catalog record for this book is available from the Library of Congress

Typeset by Hewer Text UK Ltd, Edinburgh
Printed in the US by Maple Vail

Contents

Preface to the English Edition

Collected in this book and its companion volume, *The Intellectual and His People*, are almost all the articles I wrote between 1975 and 1985 for the journal *Les Révoltes logiques*, and for the books later published by the collective of the same name. It is doubtless today necessary to explain the nature of this publication and the intellectual and political dynamic in which it was located. Its starting-point was the desire to draw conclusions from the time around 1968. The May explosion, in which student action acted as the detonator for a mass strike, had overturned Marxist schemas of class consciousness and action. The great Althusserian project of a struggle of science against ideology clearly turned out to be a struggle against the potential strength of mass revolt. The inability of the far-left groups to build a new revolutionary workers' movement in the wake of the May revolt forced us to measure the gap between the actual history of social movements and the conceptual system inherited from Marx. It was on the basis of this twin situation that I embarked in 1972 on a research project that aimed to retrace the history of working-class thought and the workers' movement in France, in order to grasp the forms and contradictions that had characterized its encounter with the Marxist ideas of class struggle and revolutionary organization. This was the basis on which I set up in 1973, along with Jean Borreil and Geneviève Fraisse, a 'Centre de Recherches sur les Idéologies de la Révolte', which two years later gave birth to the periodical which we initially conceived as a place for publishing our work.

But the intellectual and political landscape was changing rapidly at this time. And our critical stance towards Marxist dogmatism found itself confronting in 1975 two forms of struggle against the same dogmatism that were each far more influential but also equally removed from our own perspective. On the one hand, distancing oneself from the great beliefs and enthusiasms of Marxist activists found expression in the rediscovery of a people that was both more firmly rooted and more light-hearted, more playful, than the austere proletariat of Marxist theory. This was the period in which a new enthusiasm for popular culture made itself felt in France, with a profusion of monographs on folkloric customs and biographies of men of the people who were proud of their trade and their traditions. This new tendency marked the cinema as well as academic history, with the success of 'retro' films. The break with forms of activist authority was also expressed in the ubiquitous praise for traditional festivals and the evocation of popular carnivals and plebeian leisure activities. The article I jointly authored in the first issue of *Les Révoltes logiques*, 'Off to the Exhibition', thus echoed a successful play of that year, *En r'venant d' l'Expo*, which itself took its title from a popular song of 1900 and re-immersed the glorious proletarian body in a world in which machines were a magical spectacle as well as the embodiment of Marxian 'productive forces', and the worker's identity was a matter of imagery and song as well as for the science of class struggle. Depicted in this way, in place of the strict proletarian of Marxist science we had a noisy and colourful people, reminiscent of what leftist activists glimpsed in their efforts to plumb the depths of the *pays réel*, but also a people that conformed well to its essence, well rooted in its place and time, ready to move from the heroic legend of the poor to the positivity of silent majorities. These people, in fact, was the imaginary correlate of the socialist intelligentsia that was about to take power in 1981.

As opposed to this 'soft' liquidation of proletarian rigour, however, there was also the start of a far more radical operation. At the time we were preparing the first issue of the periodical, French intellectual opinion was noisily celebrating the conversion of André Glucksmann, former spokesperson for the '*enragés*' of May 1968 and the Maoists of

La Gauche Prolétarienne, who published under the title *La Cuisinièr et le mangeur* (The Cook and the Cannibal) the first manifesto of those 'new philosophers' who went on to build their fame on denouncing 'concentration-camp Marxism' and identifying with its victims. From this side, the revolutionary people was liquidated en bloc, turned into pure embodiment of the Marxist dream of mastery, pure justification for the mass crime of the gulag. On the one hand, the denunciation of 'master-thinkers' simply revivified the old reactionary discourse for which dreams of purity and social justice necessarily lead to the crimes of totalitarianism. But, on the other hand, the purity denounced immediately resurfaced in a new guise when Glucksmann and his colleagues opposed to 'concentration-camp Marxism' a plebs endowed with a constitutive virtue of resistance to the assaults of that leviathan power whose final avatar was the Soviet state. The new embodiments of the popular body that the supposed 'new philosophers' opposed to Marxism actually reconstituted the same dubious alliance between positive and negative on which Marxism itself lived. And once again the celebration of the suffering and struggling people served to benefit its self-proclaimed representatives. The 'proletarian' intellectuals speaking in the name of the builders of a new world were replaced by the new 'dissident' intellectuals speaking in the name of the victims of that 'new world'.

It was not enough at this point to oppose proletarian dogmatism with the complexities and contradictions of actual movements of social and popular struggle. The issues at stake in these transformed figures of the people and the plebs had also to be grasped. In the guise of a critique of Marxism a strange operation was carried out, keeping all the dogmatism of *a priori* oppositions and the power of self-proclaimed vanguards, while simply dropping the struggles and emancipatory project to which these had been attached. The turns and shifts that *Les Révoltes logiques* proposed thus followed a demand that was simple in principle, even if it implied in practice a battle on several fronts: to prevent the liquidation of a certain way of thinking about revolution from dispensing with an understanding of the issues, complexities and contradictions of two centuries of struggle.

This project implied a different way of understanding words, and a different use of history. The former can be summed up in the shift that the very title of *Les Révoltes logiques* expressed. Revolt or rebellion is traditionally opposed to revolution, an opposition which doctrine ritually assimilates to that between spontaneity and organization. The point about reclaiming this suspect word was not to extol the virtues of spontaneity, but rather to undermine this very opposition by subverting the idea of time that underlies the contrast between the supposedly continuous 'process' of revolution and the scene of rebellion that is said to be momentary. This is why the word 'revolt' could be linked with a 'logic' that is seemingly opposed to it. There is also logic, the construction of a particular assembly of reasons at a specific place and time, when no process justifies in circular fashion its necessity by its continuity and its continuity by its necessity. 'It is right to rebel' was the great slogan of the Cultural Revolution, taken up in May 1968. The title of *logical revolts* declared less imperiously that what is called rebellion or revolt is also a scene of speech and reasons: neither the eruption (often celebrated in those years) of a popular unruliness irreducible to the disciplines of power, nor the expression of a historical necessity and legitimacy. It rather gave this reason a particular twist, since the expression was itself ironically lifted from Rimbaud's poem, in which the 'conscripts of good intention' say: 'We will destroy all logical revolt'.[1] It proclaimed, via the poet of 'Jeanne-Marie's Hands', a fidelity to the Paris Commune that was the very archetype of rebellion. But this was via the detour of a 'we' that inverted the usual function of the first person: that of attesting to the presence of the person speaking, ensuring the embodiment of the meaning that activist discourse presupposes.

This twisting of words implied a use of history that was itself multiple. On the one hand this functioned as a reality principle. To the controversies between Marxist schools, as well as the anti-Marxist imprecations of the 'new philosophers', *Les Révoltes logiques* opposed the need to enter into the quick of the contradictions that

---

1   'Democracy', in Rimbaud's *Illuminations*. [Tr.]

had constituted working-class history and the revolutionary scene, knowledge of which was the only way to help understand the vicissitudes and disillusions that doctrinaires exhausted themselves in deducing from principles – or from unfaithfulness to principles. To the conveniences of an 'anti-historicism' which, by disdainfully dismissing empirical facts, cleared the way for dogmatisms of all kinds, we replied that it was right to seek to know the reality of the practices, ideals and conflicts that made up working-class and revolutionary history.

But there are several ways of practising such a resort to history, several ways of appealing from concepts to realities. There is that which makes history into a living tradition and seeks to identify its legitimate transmission. This vision was doubtless still present at the origin of the historical studies presented in *Les Révoltes logiques*. But those who represented it did not themselves offer any activist subject claiming a right of inheritance such as even the tiniest left groupuscule insisted on. And the research process itself soon put paid to any idea of a continuous glorious legacy of workers' revolution. The magnetic digressions of the workers of 1840, the pronounced anti-feminism of the workers' delegates of 1867, the quarrels of the revolutionary syndicalists after 1914 and the transition of some of their number into the camp of collaboration in 1940, are all scenes that spoil the image of an authentically working-class and authentically revolutionary tradition, which those nostalgic for anarcho-syndicalism had opposed to Marxist confiscation. Working-class history was studied here in the interval separating two newspapers both called *L'Atelier*, both claiming in the same fashion an authenticity of workers' speech and thinking. The first, in the 1840s, placed the full weight of this authenticity in the service of the anti-socialist republican fraction that was to direct the repression of June 1848. The second, in the 1940s, celebrated collaboration and the Service du Travail Obligatoire[2] as the fulfilment of old working-class and socialist dreams. The history

---

2   The 'compulsory labour service' for young French men in Germany that Pierre Laval agreed with the Nazi occupiers in 1942. [Tr.]

practised in *Les Révoltes logiques* emphasized that there is no single 'voice of the people'. There are broken, polemical voices, each time dividing the identity they present: a *Tribune des Femmes* born out of the Saint-Simonian cult of woman and in reaction to the exploitation of this cult, as the expression of women in general and a school set up by advanced women for their less fortunate sisters; an *Écho de la Fabrique*, expressing the legendary revolt of the glorious Lyon silk-workers, yet bent on the seemingly futile task of finding a scientifically correct term to replace the insulting nickname *canut*. And so on.

But this deconstruction of traditional history had also to be distinguished from the other major form of resort to history, constructed on the ashes of disappointed activist hope: one that opposed solid and obscure realities to brilliant names and episodes, the great continuities of the social body to apparent revolutionary breaks, or its slow and irreversible changes to the false continuities of activist traditions. Disdainful as it may be towards the short cuts of activist history, academic history is political as well. It too needs a body of identification to assure the stable relationship of bodies to meanings. It has to found on this the play of categories that distribute relationships of high and low, stable and movable, contingent and necessary, which it uses to conceive both an intelligibility of history and a rationality of the social organization. This was indeed what historians of the Annales school did when they confined themselves in the microcosm of a traditional Breton village, or related the Cathar heresy to the traditions of a rural mountain community.[3] The scientific study of these peasant microcosms in the *longue durée* was just as political as the heroic representations of the Communard legend.[4] If the history that *Les Révoltes Logiques* sought to apply had an activist aim, it was not only by using work on the past to cast light on the problems of

3   Cf. André Burguière, *Paysans de Lozevet*, Paris 1975, and Emmanuel Le Roy Ladurie, *Montaillou*, Aldershot 1978.
4   Cf. Jean Borreil, 'Des politiques nostalgiques', in *Les Révoltes logiques*, no. 3, autumn 1976 (reprinted in *La Raison nomade*, Paris 1993), and J. Rancière, *The Names of History*, Minneapolis 1994.

political struggle today. It was also by questioning the practices of identification common to the discourse of both activist vanguards and academic historians.

What then had to be challenged in both Marxist and anti-Marxist dogmatisms was not a fine tradition of the revolutionary movement or a certain knowledge of the realities of the world and of workers' movements. It was not a history of voices from below against one of discourse from above, a history of individuals against that of the collectivity, or of spontaneous movements against that of organizations and institutions. It was a history that questioned the very functioning of these pairs of opposites, and also those that opposed realities to representations.

First of all, histories of borders and barriers. The 'pleasure at the *barrière*' that serves as the title of one of these articles expresses a point of view that inspired them all. In the nineteenth century, the '*barrière*' was the site outside the Paris gates where people gathered to buy wine not subject to excise, and where the dominant imaginary located the fantasized theatre of workers' orgies. In the mid 1970s, this sense was deliberately reversed, and these *barrière* orgies seen as the persistence of a popular tradition of resistance to the disciplines of the factory and bourgeois moralization. To take a certain distance from this simple reversal of the bourgeois fears of yesterday meant shifting the barrier and its signification. The real barrier operating in the social symbolic was not that dividing popular pleasures from bourgeois strictness or the pleasures of the rich. It was rather one that had no physical form yet was felt on all sides, a contention at the very heart of an undifferentiated space. This barrier did not divide spaces but linked them together, opening them to a community of contention. What disturbed the nineteenth-century censors were not the bars of the *barrière*. It was the theatres at the heart of the capital, where an imprecise line separated the bourgeois audience in their seats from the people standing in the 'little places'. The spatial distribution of these 'little places' that were not 'real' places, just like the time wasted and the collective mood acquired in the queue to obtain them, muddied the relationship between words and things, between fiction and a reality that itself required a stable relationship between the stage and the hall, the hall and the outside world.

To the grand themes of the enforced disciplining of popular work and pleasure, which at that time filled many studies inspired by a rather hasty reading of Foucault, my article opposed the trial and error of a repression aware of not controlling the spatial and temporal coordinates that connected inside and outside, the theatre and politics, the everyday life of the commercial street and the extraordinary life of the demonstration. To the activists with their haste to distinguish voices from below from voices from above, or forms of power from forms of resistance, *Les Révoltes Logiques* replied more generally that there are only ever indistinct barriers, at which shifts in the relationship of words to the 'real' that they represent define fragile productions of meaning and movable plays of identification. This was the case with the use that the theatre audience might make of the words of a cheap melodrama, but also that which one or other fraction of the working-class elite might make of the forms of existence of a social class and the traditions of a movement. Between resistance and collaboration, as I wrote in 'From Pelloutier to Hitler', the choice was less a matter of doctrine than one of sensibility to the spectacle that the street occupied by the foreigner presented. A doctrine can justify anything, depending on the protocol of application provided for the particular case, depending on what is designated as visible and conceivable. What then remains is the division between the tolerable and the intolerable, which defines the imaginary of a consensus or the reality of a revolt.

To scholars concerned to separate realities from representations, processes from manifestations, the economic structure, the political stage and the forms of ideological consciousness, *Les Révoltes logiques* replied in the same fashion that the reality denoted by the terms 'worker', 'people' or 'proletarian' could never be reduced either to the positivity of a material condition nor to the superficial conceit of an imaginary, but always designated a partial (in both senses) linkage, provisional and polemical, of fragments of experience and forms of symbolization – a division of the perceptible, as the author of these lines would later put it, a polemical configuration of ways of acting, ways of seeing and ways of speaking. Factory, street and theatre are forms of this division, in which the economic, the political and the ideological constantly exchange roles, defining in this way a certain conflictual relationship of space and time, ways of being and ways of acting, the visible and the expressible. This is also why there are always several kinds of workers in the factory, several forms of movement in the street, several audiences in a theatre: meaning not several different sub-categories but rather several ways of occupying the site and symbolizing its 'normal' functioning or its interruptions and metamorphoses – when the factory closes and the worker there becomes a spokesman for his or her class, when the street becomes theatre (whether with the spectacle of popular demonstrations or the cheap luxury of shop-windows and café terraces), when the theatre becomes tribune or shows itself to be a factory, subject to calculations about its audience and its own social problems. The 'people's theatre' studied in one of the present articles is the story of a long-term project that amounts to the archaeology of our present: the dream of a theatre that would be the site of a rediscovered communication between art and people, of social peace and collective energies. But this is also the site of confronting logics that constantly oppose several peoples in both minds and halls.

The people's theatre, like the people's revolution, has always had several peoples, equally irreducible to the simplicity of the Marxist proletarian, the trade unionist or the plebs that intellectual fashion formerly celebrated. A 'people' of this kind is not an assemblage of social groups and identities. It is a polemical form of subjectification that is drawn along particular lines of fracture, where the distribution of leaders and led, learned and ignorant, possessors and dispossessed, is decided. Such are the ideas that these pages sought to oppose to old dogmatisms or new scepticisms that reduced historical experience of domination and emancipation to an overly simple lesson. These texts are thus located at the intersection of two perspectives, one of which we might could call archaeological and the other polemical.

The two volumes of the English edition make it possible to display the articulation of these two perspectives. It is undoubtedly the archaeological perspective that dominates the first volume, devoted to the proletarian and his double. The texts collected here mark a number of key figures and moments within transformations that stretch from the singularities – even extravagances – of the emancipated worker of the 1840s to the constitution of the figure of the Communist proletarian and the perversion of the revolutionary syndicalist ideal in the service of wartime collaboration. I have sought to pin down some of the tensions between the ethical figure of labour, the sociological figure of the worker and the political figure of the proletarian that marked in turn the thinking of the emancipated worker, the revolutionary syndicalist and the Communist proletarian. But this genealogical work on the forms of working-class political subjectivity, which also lies at the heart of my book *Proletarian Nights*, links up with the reflection on 'the intellectual and his people' that gives the second volume its common theme. The analysis of the way in which the intellectuals of my generation sought to adopt for themselves, for their own fame, the virtues that they had initially conferred on the fighting people, was extended in *The Philosopher and His Poor*, where I showed how the modern ideas of labour and working-class revolution continued figures of thought that had their origin in the Platonic hierarchy of conditions of souls.[5] In the same way, the study of the historical project of a people's theatre and the analysis of the adventures of left culture in the wake of May 1968, as conducted in the second volume, are articulated with the genealogical study of the 'barrier of pleasures' conducted in the first, which opened the way to my later work on the relationships between politics and aesthetics. And the analysis of 'heretical knowledge' offered here led to studying the distribution of knowledge that

---

5   Cf. J. Rancière, *The Philosopher and His Poor*, Durhan, NC 2004; *Proletarian Nights*, London 2012 (published originally as *Nights of Labor*, Philadelphia 1989); and *The Ignorant Schoolmaster*, Palo Alto 1991.

gave rise both to *The Ignorant Schoolmaster* and to my critique of Bourdieu's sociology of reproduction.

What these articles amount to is thus a study of the various forms of what I later came to call the distribution of sensibility. The issues involved in such an inquiry presuppose, in fact, an articulation between genealogical study and its polemical presentation. As Foucault said, we have to hear the rumble of battle. Hearing the rumble of battle beneath the history of institutions or discourse also means letting it echo actively in the here and now, shifting the way in which discussions are formulated. The polemical articles reprinted in the second volume, devoted to the 'new philosophers', working-class sociology or new forms of debate about culture, expand on what is already supported by the 'historical' studies presented here. To analyze the tortured reasonings of collaborating trade-unionists meant not so much lifting the veil from shadowy zones of the workers' movement as intervening in a contemporary intellectual landscape in which a dubious rise of interest in the theme of 'voluntary servitude' made it possible to suspect in every form of struggle for emancipation a secret desire for servitude. Studying the ambiguities of the 'barrier of pleasures' meant responding to those studies that showed us the irresistible disciplining and domestication of untamed popular energies. Recalling the pedagogic and political project that underpinned the appearance of sociology, or presenting the singularity of Jacotot's intellectual emancipation, would lead to an attempt to find a way to escape the symmetrical blind alleys of both the sociological perspective and the 'republican' vision of the School. Rather than constituting an encyclopaedia, the studies conducted in *Les Révoltes Logiques* aimed to shift the terms of present debate, to intervene at the juncture between activist opinion and the university stage where the forms of decomposition and recomposition of the figure of the revolutionary worker were being determined.

Major figures of identification never vanish without trace. The decomposition of the scientific-activist figure of the Marxist proletarian gave rise to new identity figures that reincorporated its torn-off limbs and scattered features. At that time, this recomposition took two main forms. On the one hand there was Glucksmann's plebs, a proletariat dispossessed of its capacity to transform the world and transformed into an ethical instance of resistance to the infinite evil of power, but always sustaining – with its fleshy positivity and the ideal strength of its refusal – the authority of its intellectual spokesmen. On the other hand, a socialist people in the process of recomposition, borrowing its motley colours and rough manners from the leftist rehabilitation of the turbulence and carnivals of the past, but also increasingly adapting these leftist colours to the modernized figure of the working and unionized people: the 'sociological majority' that Mitterrand celebrated on the evening of his victory, and in whose name a newly painted Marxism was dispatched to the oubliettes just as swiftly as it had been revived, while the rationalized forms of return to intellectual order were established on the base prepared by the 'new philosophers'. As early as 1980, it was no longer the resistant plebs that *Les Révoltes Logiques* argued against, but rather the good governments of the elites whose progressive right and reason prevailed against the inertia and backwardness of the common people.

I would certainly not claim that these pages were exactly prescient about the forms that the great intellectual restoration of the 1980s would take. I simply want to explain the role that words today seen as awkward – people, poor, revolution, factory, workers, proletarians – and wielded by outmoded characters play in this process. To insist on the overly broad words of people, worker and proletarian is to insist on their inherent difference, on the space of dissenting invention that this difference offers. The intellectual restoration of the 1980s claimed to restore the dignity of a 'politics' freed from social identifications. It did the exact opposite: by championing political purity against the ambiguities of the social, it supported the tenacious efforts of governments both right and left to conjure away the dissenting appearances of political conflict, to reduce politics to the management of the economic and social interests of a supposedly homogeneous community. Any constitution of an egalitarian contention on the stage of social conflicts could then be denounced as an archaic insistence on outdated 'corporatist' privileges, while the whole history of emancipatory movements was gradually criminalized. 'Populism', a word borrowed from the Leninist dictionary, became a catch-all concept that enabled our governments and their thinkers to discredit all resistance to this management of economic necessity, whose principle they also took over from the Marxist tradition. Perhaps the republication of these texts, which sought to discern the new 'paths of power' in the fluid relationships of the intellectual stage to that of political struggle, will help an understanding of this rampant Marxism transformed into liberal raison d'état. Perhaps it will contribute to re-opening the space that supplies the contingency of revolts and their logics with the necessities from which the dominations of both yesterday and today fuel themselves.

1

The Proletarian and His Double, Or, The Unknown Philosopher

I would like to explain here why I am presenting to philosophers and historians a work that is not really philosophy and yet not exactly history either; to explain why, instead of developing a philosophical thesis, I am telling these stories about workers from the last century; why, finally, I have taken up working-class history not where we can see it being created – in factory struggles, in organizations and movements – nor where we can seek its roots – in the formation of the working-class population, its ways of life or its cultural practices – but rather in certain exchanges of arguments and fantasies, real and imaginary trajectories, passions and frenzies, that a few dozen workers, a few hundred at most, had with one another from the 1830s to the 1860s, some of their number playing a role in working-class and political history, but whose activity seems here much closer to what is generally viewed as the agitation and chattering of intellectuals.

To explain this means saying how the subject of this essay is hidden between its original title 'The formation of working-class thought in France' and its final title 'The proletarian and his double'.

My first intention was to track down the initial identity of the specific thinking of the working class that the overlay of Marxist discourse had covered up. I had been involved in a movement that maintained that all the ideas of Marxism could be summed up in a single one: 'It is right to rebel.' Unfortunately this movement soon exhausted itself in trying to give the pure negativity of this subjectless assertion the face of proletarian positivity, and discovered that the reasons for rebellion were rather more complex than they appeared at first sight. It seemed necessary then, in order to understand the wall that had arisen between empirical proletarians and the proletarian discourse we had lent them, to go back to the point of origin at which Marxist discourse first came to graft itself onto the voices of working-class protest – voices of a workers' movement 'as it was in itself', to be found precisely where Marxism had rejected archaism, spontaneity and utopia. There was thus a critique of class consciousness as conceived in the Marxist fashion, in terms of maturity or immaturity in relation to the development of the productive forces. But there was still the shared assurance of a class-subject, developing the unity of its combat in the interaction between practices of struggle and forms of cultural identity, which I hoped to find in the fabric of working-class sociabilities and utopian religions.

In place of this cultural unity, however, my investigation came across two apparently distinct and separate realities: on the one hand, a chronicle of struggles that were countless but on each occasion confined to the particularity of their actors – from the pin-makers of Rugles to the paper-makers of Annonay, from the miners of Anzin to the cloth-shearers of Lodève. On the other hand, there was the generality of those workers' pamphlets and papers that expressed well what I was looking for in terms of words that asserted a working-class identity. It was simply that this assertion was completely tied to a denial of the identity imposed by Others. The workers spoke in order to say that they were not those Others, those 'barbarians' that bourgeois discourse denounced, and whose positive existence we subsequently sought to discover. And this speech, far from being rooted in the soil of utopian culture, showed an indifference towards, or rejection of, extravagance or utopian immorality.

It is true that this disappointment could be turned around. The very gap between the wide dissemination of practices of struggle and the grand Sunday speeches about workers' dignity authorized a different definition of working-class identity: a strategic identity in which this discourse of denial crowned the everyday guerrilla of practices of resistance, the discourse of the norm expressing a counter-legality rooted in the battle between the bosses' regulations and the workers' counter-regulations, as in the multitude of illegal popular actions. The very formalism of this speech and the claiming of a good image made it possible to conceive these as instruments in an overall strategy of labour reappropriating itself and asserting its place. And in the same way, the rejection of utopia could be read as the class prescience of a strategic perception denouncing the promise of utopian happiness as an avant-garde version of the bourgeois prospectus. In the Fourierists' 'attractive work', 'short shifts' and 'variegated practice', working-class thinking could sense the offensive of fragmented labour, deskilling, and forms of incentive geared to raising productivity. It rejected the lack of distinction this also made between working and leisure time, as heralding an offensive of total subjection of life to production. And in the face of theories of sexual emancipation, it defended the family as a cell of resistance to the invasion of life by the capitalist and state order. There was here the positive existence of a subject that deployed its forms of identification around a solid core: labour, the struggle of labour to maintain its ownership and appropriate its space. It was possible then to trace a straight line running, by way of working-class association and revolutionary syndicalism, from the striking tailors of 1833 who decided to manufacture on their own account, through to the Lip strikers of 1973 who combined taking over the bosses' factory with an identical discourse of love of their work and working-class dignity: the autonomous path of a socialism and workers' revolution raised against the strategy of dispossession that ran from the philanthropic enterprises of employer paternalism in the nineteenth century down to the great manoeuvres of industrial barbarism – Marxist and anti-Marxist – of the twentieth.

The problem was that this workers' discourse never functioned so well as it did in the logic of others or to their advantage. The solid class discourse that *L'Atelier* opposed to the interventions of philanthropy turned out in 1848 to be simply the discourse of workers ready to serve the 'honest and moderate' Republic. The reports of the workers' delegates to the 1867 Exposition, maintaining the irreplaceable role of women in the home, in which I tried to capture the perspective of an overall working-class counter-offensive to the bourgeois strategy of organizing life from birth through housing to death, have in fact to be seen as a more modest proposal: nothing more than Jules Simon[1] copied for the needs of a more mediocre cause, i.e. reducing the supply of hands on the labour market. And even the great idea of a civilization of producers that underlay revolutionary syndicalism turned out likewise to be wedged between the official hymn to the civilization of labour and the petty practices of corporative Malthusianism. Not to speak of that bit of the road when a portion of its heirs managed to drag a whole swathe of this great tradition of revolution and working-class socialism behind Vichy's 'national revolution' and collaboration. It seemed, therefore, that this discursive class identity was in actual fact something indeterminate, that the dual relationship that defined it was perhaps never more than an alibi for a certain politics.

From this point on, however, the spirit of the time provided the means for placing back on its feet the dual relationship necessary to the quest for identity. All that was needed was to redistribute the camps, to place the avant-garde worker/spokesman and the utopian activist on the same side, that of master-thinker, as against the plebeian-proletarian. It was at this time that I scoured the reports of Saint-Simonian missionaries sent into the popular quarters, and it was easy to recognize, in the practice of the activist serving the people, not only the philanthropic gaze of the visitor to the poor and the filing of the police commissioner, but above all the thirst for paternal – or maternal – power to sustain the apostolic devotion. It was equally easy to return to the story of Cabet's Icarian community and show its founder's paranoid discourse as a prefiguration of the dictatorships of our own century – the discourse of a power all the more pure in that it had in this case no other weapon than that of speech; easy again to discover the indestructible resistance of plebeian derision in the attitude of the Icarian who read his newspaper while the Father of the Community was 'exhausting himself' delivering a speech on Fraternity; or to show the continuation of

---

1   Republican politician and French prime minister in 1876–7, associated in particular with educational reform. [Tr.]

workshop resistance not in the grand discourse of the producer-king but in the improvisation of those disabused Icarians who used the community's timber to make bits of furniture for their wives or toys for their children. But the question then raised was: Isn't this makeshift carpenter, improvising his family life with material recovered from the great activist undertaking, at bottom the same character as the proud carpenter demanding, in the name of his skill and his love for fine workmanship, a place for producers in the social order; the character that intellectuals and politicians posited around the insistent fantasy of proper identity and proper place – labourers whose activity is to labour, plebeians whose nature is to resist? The self-accusation of the master-thinker, and the regard for mute resistance expressed in the smile of plebeian derision, both offer fine examples of the command prescribed in all these positive existences, as openly expressed in the advice of the established poet, Victor Hugo, to the apprentice worker-poet: 'Be always what you are' – to which the latter added the tacit implication: 'so that we can remain what we are'. In the contemporary conjuncture of philo-sophical homage to the plebs, historians' enthusiasm for oral history, and the enthusiasm of the intellectual and political class for popular memoirs and cultures, for ordinary working people and the anti-heroes of '*la France profonde*', this stubborn insistence on 'making the mute speak', could we not always see on the horizon the figure of a single character: that unknown soldier whose habit-ual silence and occasional speech underpin the ability of political discourse to confer collective identities, giving history the weight of its acting subjects and reserving for philosophy the lightness of its thinking ones?

At this point in my reflection, I had the good fortune to meet not a mute person but a talkative one: a carpenter equally indifferent to work on the black and to the glory of a masterpiece. I had gone to the Gauny collection on the basis of an article indicating that, as well as his somewhat 'exalted' poetry and letters, this Saint-Simonian carpenter-poet had left various texts on working-class labour and conditions of life. The collection, however, supplied something quite different: the only direct first-person experience that remains of what it really did mean at that time to be a worker. Not a chronicle of work, but the commentary of a genuinely philosophical experience: how to live the working-class condition philosophically. The experience of a working-class identity lived in the mode of a split, an absolute rift, denouncing with the robust strength of the proud labourer the sheer nervous tension of despair produced by the basic reality of labour being simply the abstraction of hours in the workshop, the reality of time stolen, with skill and the possible attraction of labour providing at most a diversion from one's own pains – a description that challenges the supposedly natural road from exploitation to emancipation by the workers 'becoming conscious' and reappropriating their identity. The path of emancipation far rather appears as passing by way of the capacity to become different: not by becoming conscious, but by dizziness and loss of identity. Hence the irreplaceable role of the encounter with the Other: only the words of the poet, the apostle, the young Saint-Simonian bourgeois coming to meet the proletarians, can express reasons for revolt that are not those of egoism, preserving a rebellious energy distinct from the nervous tensions of servile labour, and opening for the proletarians the path of an association which would be a community of the freed and not one of discontented slaves.

In this way, experience also led them to pour derision on speeches that almost invariably dragged on about the activist ideal, conceived in categories of sacrifice as opposed to pleasure, and paid in the surplus value of power. There appeared in place of these a spiral that included with the same necessity both desertion of the working-class space and obligation to spread the apostolic word, the pleasure of personal emancipation and the echo in oneself of the pains of others.

On this basis it was possible to gather fragments of discourse on working-class identity and recognize on all sides the mark of this split: the sense of proletarian exile, the indifference to the much vaunted skill of labour, the absolute solitude in relation to those workers who were spoken about or depicted, and the fascination for what happened on the other side of the barrier. Behind the vainglory of masterpieces, or journeyman Perdiguier's *tours de France*, there was execration of those shavings and splinters that a more discreet pamphlet detailed.[2] Behind the grand polished discourse of *L'Atelier*, the lost dreams of a little shepherd who believed himself inspired by God and could only recognize himself – and call on his fellows to recognize themselves – in the image of the soldier-worker at the price of surreptitiously taking the portrayer's place.[3] The same intimate split also governed the failed encounter between the proletarian and the utopian. For the Saint-Simonian missionaries whom it was convenient to present as students 'in the service of the people' were in reality workers or former workers whose whole drama lay in being sent out by their apostolate to the same egoistic workers whom they had sought to escape from by becoming Saint-Simonians. And behind the parade of Cabet's paranoid discourse and the symbolic parricide that put an end to it, there was the internal rift of these ungrateful sons to explore, the way in which they had lived the impossible equation between the Icarian promised land and the American new world.

The object of this study was thus the story of two processes that are in reality one and the same: the trajectory of an identification, and the chronicle of the misfortunes of devotion. And if a 'thesis' had to be extracted for discussion, it could be this: that at the root of forms of identification and 'typical' discourse that underlie the idea of working-class emancipation, the idea of a class and its combat, there is the singular phenomenon of a production of meaning that is neither the consciousness of an avant-garde instructed by science nor the systemization of ideas born out of the

2   The 'Compagnons du Tour de France', who still exist today, are a quasi-guild organization of craftsmen, with the *tour* undertaken by apprentices lasting a number of years. Agricol Perdiguier (1805–75), trained as a carpenter, became a writer and republican deputy. His *Memoir d'un Compagnon* is a classic of French working-class history. See Jacques Rancière, *Proletarian Nights*, Chapter 2. [Tr.]

3   This is an allusion to the locksmith Jérôme-Pierre Gilland, editor of *L'Atelier* and a deputy in the National Assembly of 1848. He related his dreams and childhood experiences in novelistic form in *Les Aventures du Petit Guillaume du Mont-Cel*; see *Proletarian Nights*, chapters 1–5. [Tr.]

practice of the masses; a pure product not of the activity of a group but rather of a network of individuals who, by various paths, found themselves in a position of spokesman, at the same time central and outside the game: not people who carried the word of the masses, but just people who carried the word; individuals separated from their supposed fellows by what they had grasped, caught up in the circuit of a speech that came from elsewhere, and who were able to reconcile themselves in a common identity only by making themselves spokesmen in an opposite sense from that ordinarily understood: by taking speech *to the masses*.

But this necessity comes up against a double impossibility. First of all, in relation to the proletarians themselves. For the dream of a philadelphian association, free from the pettiness of working-class interests, could never be identified with the association of workers united to defend those same interests. Workers can overcome the 'egoism' inherent to their condition individually, but not collectively. The apostle never manages to transform his 'brother' workers into labourers in God's vineyard. He will never succeed in making them like him or making himself like them. There is the same impossibility in relation to those Others who alone are capable of expressing the reasons for rebelling, universalizing the intervention of the spokesman. As soon as the pure relationship of friendship that underlies the joy of individual encounters with the missionaries or Father Cabet becomes a collective relationship in which the workers are addressed as such, it enters into the system of service and demand, returning the worker to the position of his 'egoistic' identity. A double impossibility, in other words. And the argument would be that it is in this spiral of impossibility that a certain image and identity could develop, giving body to the discourse of workers' emancipation; that this would be the discourse of the working class or workers' movement, matching the actual inability of its bearers to find the principle of their own identification.

We can then understand how the discourse that seeks to account for this spiral finds itself in a limit position in relation to both philosophy and history. What in fact does philosophy find itself faced with here if not the very phenomenon that a subheading in

Budé's translation of Plato's *Republic* dramatizes as 'philosophy beset by unworthy sectarians'? A collapse of the arrangement, implicit or explicit, that classically underlies its existence, the division between three categories of individuals. First, there are the artisans – or proletarians – who express their identity in the production of useful objects or the conduct of effective struggles. Second, the philosophers who borrow paradigms from them in order to weave together their reasons or lay the bricks of their edifice, and end up by presenting them in return with a science of their production and their struggle. And finally, the false philosophers and false workers – portrayers, sophists, ideologists – who reduce production to semblance and consciousness to illusion.

What can then happen if proletarians, instead of expressing their identity in their products or their struggles, start to reflect this on the painter's canvas or in the sophist's mirror? What if this reflection leads them into the giddiness and verbiage of speculation? If they start not only offering but also practising – with ascetic joy or wrenching pangs – those speculative truths that may well be revolutionary but do not upset too much the academic existence of those who profess them: that being is identical to nothingness, the finite to the infinite, and – in the last analysis – sacrifice identical to pleasure? What then happens may be described as a certain deterioration of the philosophical instrument. The identity of opposites is something that should not be put in the hands of everyone, and these sophist artisans do indeed seem incapable of bringing it to a higher unity, or holding together constraints otherwise than in the spiral of non-resolution, that bad infinity that gives ideology its scholarly name. What is at issue in this invasion, however, is something different from a collapse of the philosophical ground on the side of irrationality. It is rather the path of a radicalization of the question: What does it mean to think?

This 'outside' of philosophy is not for all that the place of historians. What indeed can they make of this discursive trajectory? Are they not necessarily caught in an alternative? They can take the discourse of identity in its finished state and treat it as a cultural fact. In other words, they can note in the sequences of this discourse a certain number of distinctive features, which can be contrasted with other cultural traits belonging to technological culture, lifestyles, and working-class sociabilities. But will they able to do anything more on this path than the simple operation that relates the elements of this discourse to the predicates of a subject, or enriches a collective subject with new properties? They will undoubtedly be able to rise above the political naivety that immediately refers back to the properties of an already given subject, the working class or its movement. They will be able to enrich this subject with a series of fine determinations: marks of the time or of the gap between different temporal rhythms; marks of a territory or of a trajectory across several territories; distinctive traits of this or that group or sub-group – occupational, cultural, political, etc. But a detailed anthropology or sociology will always refer us to habitus, a working-class ethos that confirms in the last analysis that things could not be otherwise than how they are, thus cancelling out what is singular in this production of meaning, in this speech that relates the encounter with the impossible. Or else they take the other path, the one that seeks to concern itself with working-class practices while leaving aside ideology and the supposed subject of working-class discourse. But making this choice, saying that we are concerned with practices and not with ideology, means massively confirming, beneath the seeming honesty of a good methodological principle, the initial division that is rightly challenged in this discourse of the impossible: the division between those whose lot is production and struggle, and those whose lot is discourse and ideology.

The singularity of this discourse, therefore, is no easier for the discourse of history to appropriate than it is for that of philosophy. To the very extent that it provides the possibility of its identifications, or lends history its material, it finds itself excluded and rejected into what is not historical. It has to disappear from history, not as repressed, forbidden or unthought, but rather as insignificant: mere verbiage that cannot be counted on any of the registers where speech is deemed to lead to action. Hence the necessarily labyrinthine and evanescent form of this account, which restores voices not in the nakedness of their popular belonging but rather in the suspense of their impossible quest. These trajectories and discourses whose materiality has to be verified by the procedures of the historian must also have their status of impossibiiity restored. Their existence both within and outside of history has to be made palpable, to appear in its fleeting character, and can only be appropriated by the historian's discourse at the price of vanishing into this. An allegory might be the final episode in the life of that former seamstress, in her eighties and an unrepentant utopian, whose last word was to say that she would only be able to return to real life when she became blind – and who died before experiencing this.

The mode of existence that I have been compelled to give these silhouettes and words cut loose from their anchorage is thus similar to what a contemporary poet, speaking of Baudelaire and in particular of his 'Swan', defined as 'the act and the place of poetry':

> Baudelaire substituted for a classical archetype a distant passer-by, a real woman, poorly known but respected for her essential fragility, her non-necessity, her mysterious pain. Baudelaire did not create this Andromaque, he 'thought' about her, meaning that that there is being outside of consciousness and that this simple fact is worth far more, in its chance existence, than the dwelling of the spirit. Here, moreover, around this injured woman and in the sympathy that she arouses, we see how the world, instead of cancelling itself out or vainly proliferating as it formerly did, opens up the perspective of all lost creatures, the captive, the defeated, as Baudelaire writes, all those whose very exile renders their presence yet less explicable and less reducible.[4]

The perspective opened up here is not the same as the expansion I was offered in the first philosophy lecture I attended, a lecture by Jean Wahl titled 'Defence and expansion of philosophy: a resort to poets?' The poet that year was Rainer Maria Rilke, and an

4   Yves Bonnefoy, 'L'acte et le lieu de la poésie', *L'Improbable*, Paris 1959, p. 160.

allegorical geography could be drawn from him that would not be totally irrelevant to our present purpose. We know that Rilke, when he came to Paris, lodged in a small hotel on the rue Toullier – which is reached, if you come from the Sorbonne, through a little side gate. Thinking back to this, it was hard not also to evoke the adage of Georges Canguilhem that has so often been both used and abused:

> When you leave the Sorbonne through the rue Saint-Jacques, you can go up or down: if you turn upward, you come to the Panthéon, which is the conservatory of a few great men, but if you go downhill you are surely heading for the Préfecture de Police.[5]

There was a time when it was tempting to turn this invective of philosophy towards psychology and the human sciences in general back on philosophy itself, to question its devotees about the road they themselves took when they left the Sorbonne. But perhaps it would be more interesting to take a different path and leave by the little side gate into the rue Toullier where, at the beginning of the century, a young poet in exile also meditated on the trajectory of the rue Saint-Jacques. Except that this was not for him the crossroads of paths of philosophy but rather the enigmatic path of proletarian existence, followed from its origin in the lying-in hospital of Port-Royal to its end in the Hôtel-Dieu. A trajectory in thrall to people's faces, and above all to that face which a woman of the people held in her hands: 'As soon as I saw her,' said the poet's alter ego, 'I began to walk softly. When poor people are thinking of something one should not disturb them. Perhaps it will occur to them'.[6]

Not disturbing the reflections of poor people is perhaps also the condition for acceding to the poetic pantheon. For myself, not being bound by the same obligation, I have been happy to disturb this woman of the people, to mingle our thoughts with hers for a

---

5   Georges Canguilhem, 'Qu'est-ce que la psychologie?', *Cahiers pour l'Analyse*, no. 1–2, p. 83.
6   Rilke, *The Notebooks of Malte Laurids Brigge*, Urbana-Champaign, IL 2008, p. 4.

moment; to pursue, across the twisted streets of the quartier Saint-Jacques, the path already taken by the Saint-Simonian missionary, who went out to recruit workers for the new world, up to the dwelling of the unknown poet and the unknown philosopher of the Faubourg Saint-Marceau. The main hero in this adventure, in fact, is one of those children from the Faubourg Saint-Marceau whom Diderot mentioned when he raised the question, in relation to painters, of what exactly is expressed on such a canvas in the way of a social and moral identity:

> I saw at the end of Faubourg Saint-Marceau, where I lived for a long time, children who had charming faces. At the age of twelve or thirteen, those eyes full of sweetness became intrepid and bold; that pleasant little mouth twisted strangely; that rounded neck was swollen with muscle; those wide smooth cheeks were marked by harsh ridges. They had acquired the physiognomy of the market halls. By dint of irritation, injury, fighting, shouting, putting themselves out for a farthing, they had contracted for their whole life an air of sordid interest, boldness and anger.[7]

The story related here is that of a child who did not want to change his face, who recognized quite precisely in the robust strength of the labourer and the dark eye of the rebel, to which homage is paid, the three attributes of proletarian degeneration: sordid interest, boldness and anger. The story of a vain attempt to rediscover a lost face. But it seemed to me important in a way for thought to present this hollowness at the heart of what our discourse readily recognizes as most positive: the order of productive labour and proletarian pain. Perhaps the notion of this hollowness touches the heart of the question of what we are and what we are doing.

---

7   Denis Diderot, *Essay on Painting* (1759).

2

Heretical Knowledge and the Emancipation of the Poor

The name 'canut'

As every school student studying social history knows, in November 1831 the proud *canuts* of Lyon brought the working class onto the stage of world history. The emblem of this arrival was a slogan on a flag: 'Live working or die fighting'. Later on, a rousing chorus would link it with contrasting images of gold chasubles, rags, and the shroud of the old world. The outlines of the scene have been sufficiently well drawn to make it unnecessary to read the organ of its protagonists, *L'Echo de la Fabrique*.

And yet such a reading places the slogan on the flag in a more authentic linguistic context, and a surprising one at that. A few months after the insurrection, the newspaper organized a competition. The object was to find a generic name for the class of workers in the Lyon silk factories, who were divided into various specialities. The only word that then existed was in fact *canut*, which was an insulting nickname. Some people had already taken the initiative of replacing it with the name of *ferrandiniers*, after the name of a particular material.

But this replacement was far from winning unanimous approval. It even aroused open indignation on the part of one correspondent in the paper:

'In the century of progress in which our heroic people has raised itself above all nations,' he wrote, 'I believe that this people should not be demeaned in its language any more than it has weakened in its actions, and I think that the title that a worthy class of workers of our town has recently adopted does not respond to our epoch of regeneration. In fact, the name *ferrandiniers* does not leave in the mind any trace that suggests it relates to silk-weaving.'

He therefore proposed, after the Latin *sericarius*, the name *séricariens*, which at least 'would leave a correct idea in the minds of those who wish to analyse it'. This question, he concluded, 'is not as frivolous as certain people might think; for if all innovators acted in this way, the great philosophical problem of the language of nations would soon be resolved'.[1]

Almost everyone agreed that the question was not a frivolous one. But this is also why this honourable correspondent's solution was likewise discarded. *Séricarien*, in fact, has a suffix that is unsuited for names of trades. A competition was therefore organized, and for a few months philologist workers and grammarian friends of the people argued over the name best suited to displaying the full activity of the silk-worker. *Soierifèvre*, which some preferred to *séricarien*, was rejected, as its suffix was only suitable for those who worked with a hammer; *polymithe*, *bombixien*, *pamphilarien* and *arachnéen*, as well as some thirty or so other words designed to make clear the work in question, or draw attention to its divine origins, also came under consideration. *Canut* was in fact rehabilitated by a foreign correspondent, as having been a name honourably borne by several Scandinavian kings. *Turquetnariste* was finally proposed in homage to the founders of the Fabrique Lyonnaise, and a sign that gratitude was also a working-class virtue. This last proposal was accompanied by a vigorous call to order, demanding that the newspaper's commission should respond to the need for a name that was 'a result of the progressive and universal movement'.[2] It seems that the commission could not agree on such a name. And after a final meeting in January 1833, nothing more was heard of it.

---

1   Letter from Méziat, *L'Echo de la Fabrique*, no. 43, 19 August 1832.
2   Letter from J. H., a proletarian, *L'Echo de la Fabrique*, 23 December 1832.

More would often be heard, on the other hand, of its inspirer, the republican lawyer Marius Chastaing. In 1846, for example, as editor-in-chief of *La Tribune Lyonnaise*, he welcomed the arrival in Lyon of the director of *Le Journal du Magnétisme* with a vibrant speech:

> Magnetism is knowledge of the vital spirit that, coming from God himself, inspires all beings and, through an uninterrupted chain, although our senses cannot perceive all its links, connects them to the supreme author of all things . . . magnetism is the universal medicine, of which what is taught in the universities is only a crude imitation.[3]

We should not believe that this former activist for the workers' cause took refuge in magnetic arcana. The magnetic digressions of the pre-1848 period, following on from the linguistic digressions of post-1830, accompanied the idea of social justice, which had passed from the terrain of language and struggles for recognition to that of life and hopes for solidarity. In 1848, Marius Chastaing wrote an *Astréologie ou Solution du problème social*, dedicated not to the stars but to Astrea daughter of Themis, and devoted to the realization of justice in the prosaic form of national education, funds for retirement and for victims of industrial accident.

I have chosen to begin with this singular socialist trajectory because it seems exemplary to me of the relations that developed between the 1830s and 1850s on the boundary between scholarly and popular space. Encounters proliferated, both of people and ideas, sometimes in the context of more or less recognized institutions (Société pour l'Instruction Élémentaire, Association Polytechnique, Société des Méthodes . . .), but also in an informal way around eccentric theorists, industrialists who wanted to help their fellow workers profit from the young social science, heretical medicines and pedagogies, even local grammarians delivering to random pupils notions of universal language and divine justice along with French measurements. By way of these

---

3   *Le Journal du Magnétisme*, 1846, p. 205.

encounters between semi-schooled proletarians and semi-proletarian scholars, the idea of emancipation took shape between two poles: that of a theory of language and that of a science of life. The former involved the nomination of the proletarian as social actor, the latter defined the space of his activity. The idea of social emancipation passed by way of certain forms of popular appropriation of the intellectual universe, or – if you like – a certain idea of science, responding to a double requirement: the constitution of a plebeian 'care of self' that was at the same time a care for others, an idea of the human individual that was also an idea of solidarity between beings.

The sign of intelligence

I want now to examine some striking features of these forms of plebeian appropriation of knowledge. The term 'plebeian' is more suitable here than 'proletarian', to avoid ambiguity. Some people, in fact, insist that 'proletarian' should simply be used for workers in a certain kind of industry. It should be clear, on the other hand, that 'plebeian' denotes a symbolic relationship and not a kind of labour. The plebeian is the individual excluded from the speech that makes history. This archaeological meaning was quite contemporary during the period I am discussing. In 1829, in *La Revue de Paris*, Ballanche gave an exemplary account of the plebeian secession on the Aventine. This rebellion was characterized by the fact that it recognized itself as a speaking subject and gave itself a name. The Roman patrician power refused to accept that the sounds uttered from the mouths of the plebeians were speech, and that the offspring of their unions should be given the name of a lineage. This was because 'invasions of property on earth are the actualization of invasions of property whose boundaries are marked in heaven',[4] while conversely, the agrarian law was first of

4 P.-S. Ballanche, 'Essais de palingénésie sociale. Formule générale de l'histoire de tous les peuples appliquée à l'histoire du peuple romain. Deuxième fragment', *Revue de Paris*, June 1829, p. 146.

all a symbolic revolution, the inscription of a name in heaven. The plebeians recognized that they had 'the sign of intelligence that is speech'.[5] Conscious of this property, they dared to give a name to their leaders, thus conferring on them the power to impose on the patricians the reciprocal speech of a contract.

The importance of the inaugural scene sketched here cannot be exaggerated. We need only change the names to recognize the scenario of the conflicts over recognition that form the material of workers' pamphlets and newspapers after 1830. Social rehabilitation was effected by way of an intellectual rehabilitation that was first of all a battle for names. This intellectual demand linked up with the question of popular education in a very particular fashion. Contemporary problematics of teaching present this as a means of integration that is more or less suited to reducing social tensions. Some people question the respective share of *instruction* that enlightens the people and *education* that keeps them in their place. Others privilege 'useful knowledge', determining the division of knowledge according to the economic model of harmonization of interests. Alongside these problematics a far more acute concern is developed: that of a social rehabilitation of the proletarians effected by the transformation of their material universe into a universe of intellectual determinations.

'Learn something and relate everything else to it.' This was the great precept of Joseph Jacotot's method of intellectual emancipation.[6] This 'something' had a very profound echo in the experience of the artisans whom he made it his priority to address. The theoretical indifference of the point of departure relates to the practical hazards that made one thing or another the clinching point in the decision for intellectual emancipation. The person who emancipates himself is the one for whom anything at all can be made into writing, and any writing at all into a textbook. Recognition in oneself of the 'sign of intelligence' was correlative with an

5   P.-S. Ballanche, 'Troisième fragment', *Revue de Paris*, September 1829, p. 89.
6   Rancière discusses Joseph Jacotot's educational theories at greater length in *The Ignorant Schoolmaster*. [Tr.]

intellectual redepiction of the surrounding universe. I commented elsewhere on the fine text that shows Gauny as a child transforming the bags used for packing lentils into fragments of an impossible encyclopaedia.[7] This should be compared with other texts by Gauny that likewise mark this concern to appropriate intellectually the plebeian framework of life – which in the converse sense means taking physical possession of the determinations of the intellectual universe.

There is first of all the constitution of what I shall call the natural history collection of the poor. Thus Gauny describes the 'scientific study projects' that he conducted with a friend of his own age:

> Without any funds to conduct our research, we threw ourselves into mineralogy, botany, numismatics, archaeology, and seized on the fossils we could glean from the quarries . . . starting from collections of pebbles; we sought the reasons for their colours and shapes, losing ourselves in wild conjecture in the attempt to discover these. These spiral, perforated, punctuated, multicolour stones, containing agglomerations, pyrites, shells, crystals, and the heterogeneous unions produced by seemingly erratic analogies, were sometimes enhanced by a fold of agate that enchanted us.[8]

The mineralogy and botany of the poor have as their common foundation the interest in natural history that was part of the thinking of the Enlightenment and the illuminist tradition of analogy, the lessons of things and the 'wild conjecture' that vests the proletarian's roadside pebbles with the dignity of objects of knowledge. The thing is enhanced because it becomes writing. And reciprocally, the language of scholars is made available to the poor in so far as it can be grasped and described as a thing. It was in this way that Gauny was initiated by a young soldier into

---

7   Jacques Rancière, *Proletarian Nights*, p. 50.
8   Gabriel Gauny, *Le Philosophe plébien*, Paris 1983, p. 25.

the world of language: 'A linguist and a psychologist, he explained to me the roots and connotations of words from which the splendours of a sentence arose. We loved to linger on the structure of letters, noting their oratory sounds, and from the infinitive we headed out to the universal, asking it to explain its immense unknown!'[9]

Between the structures and sounds of letters and the folds and analogies of the flint, between a natural history and a geography of language, an activity of material appropriation of the intellectual universe is at work. Emancipation takes place by the establishment of translatability between the world of everyday material experience and the world of science. This idea of translatability can be understood on two levels.

On translation: Analysis and analogies

On the first level, translatability defines an egalitarian conception of intellectual apprenticeship, founded on a philosophy of common sense and an analytical conception of language. Thus Jacotot's idea of the equality of intelligence corresponds to a theory of intelligence that conceives this as essentially translating. In the context of this conception, three paradigms can help to define the material paths of apprenticeship that the emancipated individual embarks on.

There is first of all the paradigm of the mother tongue. All knowledge must be capable of being acquired in the same manner as the mother tongue, in other words without the intermediary of an explaining schoolmaster. For Jacotot, explanation, or the ordinary routine of pedagogic practice, was above all a display of inequality: if explanations were necessary for acquiring knowledge, that meant for the poor the double impossibility of learning for themselves and of teaching their children. The necessity of paying the explainer was only a small symbol of this limitless symbolic debt. The mother tongue, on the other hand, was a

9   Ibid., p. 31.

paradigm of the ability of the parents of poor families to teach their children themselves.

This privileged role of the mother tongue, however, does not imply any privilege for 'oral culture' as some people understand this, opposing the good culture specific to the poor to its perversion by semi-literate culture. On the contrary, the second feature or paradigm of this apprenticeship was that of writing. The method was, starting from what the individual knew by heart – a song, a prayer, no matter what – to find in his surroundings a 'lettered' person able to write this down and have him compare the text he knew with what he saw. This recognition involved a manipulation of letters, an attention to their form, their dimension, and everything that could be said about them. This was the practice of the locksmith much favoured by Jacotot, at grips with the first word ('Calypso') of the Book par excellence of princes and paupers alike, *Télémaque*, which he spelled by calling 'O' the circle and 'L' the square. (Proudhon perhaps remembered this when he wrote his alphabet of labour . . .)

This first writing was the decisive step. Every written text that the pupil has assimilated is fit to serve as a dictionary and encyclopaedia on the basis of which it is possible to learn everything else. The 'method' was first of all a philosophy. Jacotot opposed the inegalitarian philosophy of Plato's *Phaedrus* all along the line. Plato condemned writing as the death of thought, in a letter presented for the use of non-initiates.[10] Jacotot, conversely, privileged writing, mnemonic techniques, the material manipulation of the sign, as suited to breaking the monopoly of any school or explainer, capable of cropping up anywhere to be gathered by the hands of those whose 'business' was not that of thinking.

This is precisely the third paradigm: that of the thing. 'A material thing,' he wrote, 'is the only communicating bridge between minds'.[11] Opposed to the word of the explainer is the

---

10 *Phaedrus*, 274c/277a. See also Jacques Rancière, *The Philosopher and His Poor*, pp. 39–42.

11 *Journal d'Emancipation Intellectuelle*, 3rd year, 1835/6, p. 263.

entry into a universe of language provided by the lesson of generalized things, where one appropriates the art of orators of all views, and where a learned schoolmaster himself may be used, but only on the condition of being precisely treated as a thing: 'A learned teacher is a fact full of instruction: listen, look, watch closely, dissect; *faciatis experimentum in professore*. Learn him, check him, imitate him, translate him; he has done scientific work, do your own.'[12]

The idea of translation thus involves the idea of a correspondence between words and things. But this may be understood on two levels. Jacotot understands it according to the reason of the Enlightenment and the analysis of the Ideologists. The underlying assumption of his 'method' is that the logic of all apprenticeship is identical to the logic of invention. Both things depend on the rationality of analysis. Jacotot's 'ignorant schoolmaster' sets in motion a scholar's logic, one that peruses the world of knowledge on the basis of a small number of fundamental data, those of a human mind that is identical in each speaking subject. But if Jacotot's lesson can be received, it is because this reception is rooted in an experience and thought of symbolic appropriation that no longer depends on the simple logic of the Enlightenment: a universe in which 'everything speaks', where reason is inscribed in the folds of the flint, analogous to the curve of destinies. The relationship of word and idea is surpassed in the raw resemblance of words and things, signature of a reason that assists the speaking subject by discovering the omnipresent inscription of his supraperceptible destination. The act of knowing then acquires the figure of an initiatory relationship, and the universe of the knowable that of a world of revelation.

'God speaks incessantly,' said Ballanche, 'it is only a question of recognizing his voice.'[13] Some commentators have seen here the assertion of an 'occult socialism', a black mass or obscurantist necromancy that would be the dark side of the humanist and

---

12   Ibid., p. 136.
13   *Revue de Paris*, art. cit., April 1829, pp. 147–8.

socialist aspirations of the foolish nineteenth century.[14] Illuminism, as well as the Enlightenment, would be its shadowy truth. But this couple can be seen in a rather less simplistic logic. It is true that the socialist theory of equality linked a notion of common sense and rational nature with archaic visions of relationships between life, language and history, a rationalism of analysis with a super-rationalism of analogies. This discordance is above all the mark of a dissymmetry: not the simple contradiction between scholarly and popular logic, but rather the difficult conjunction of a practice of distribution of knowledge by the most generous of those endowed with a practice of appropriation by the most insistent of those excluded. The super-rationalism born at the boundary between scholarly and popular space, which gave this socialism its rickety philosophy, attests to this fundamental symbolic relationship for those whose business – as Plato put it – is not that of thinking, so that they have no natural entry into the world of natural reason, only an entry that is forced. The super-rationalist 'this-sided' return of the simple reason of the Enlightenment defines symbolic access and practices to the Enlightenment for those whom this had left out in the cold. The right to reason was forced by wild reasoning about flints.[15]

The science of individuals

It still remains that this untutored practice of intellectual appropriation had echoes that were understandably disquieting for minds sensitive to the iniquities of the political theme of 'two sciences'. The years from 1830 to 1850 were a time of declarations of war against official science on several fronts: the front of basic apprenticeship, particularly with Jacotot's method; the medical front that was particularly sensitive since alternative sciences proliferated here (homoeopathy, Raspaillism, magnetism, Leroy

14   See Philippe Muray, *Le XIXe siècle à travers les âges*, Paris 1984.
15   It is evident that expansion of these remarks would require discussion of the explanatory schema put forward in *The Order of Things*, but this would go beyond the context of the present work.

medicine, etc.), while established science could use the arm of the law against its competitors. We could add to this table a number of more or less challenging innovations: the musical method of Galin and Chevé, the gymnastics of Amoros, and a hundred other new procedures for acquiring the arts, science or health, either under the aegis of the Société des Méthodes or conveyed by popular educational associations. The violence of the attacks against a monopolizing science (the Université, the Académie de Médecine, etc.) highlighted an opposition between the management of privilege justified in terms of the 'difficulty' of science, and a popular science that delivered the secrets of these 'monopolists' to all, the means for dispensing with their services, and eventually the principles of the true science of body and soul that they did not understand.

But do we have here, for all that, an opposition between popular science and bourgeois science, rather than some occult basis of socialist reason? Attempting a response to this involves highlighting some characteristic features of this battle. I shall introduce three main ones, concerning the acquisition, transmission and use of heretical science.

First of all, the battle was over the modality of apprenticeship. It privileged the knowledge that the individual acquires for himself as against that which he receives from others – whether in the gentle form of a lesson or the brutal form of surgical intervention. The same knowledge experienced by the poor also serves as support for modes of institutional valorization of the learned, in which advancement and social privilege overshadow disinterested research and humanitarian commitment. It was not a question here of opposing the knowledge of the people to that of elites. Rather, it began by obliging each person to take independent charge of their instruction and their health.

This individual dimension of self-emancipation was constantly emphasized by Jacotot. He rejected all institutions that proposed a mass application of his 'method'. Everywhere, he sighed, the poor are taught to read; but nowhere are they taught that they can learn by themselves. The duty of Jacotot's disciples was merely to tell the fathers of poor families that they were able to instruct their children on the simple condition that they emancipated themselves, i.e. became aware of who they were and what they were doing in the social order. 'Know yourselves,' said Ballanche's plebeian oracle; 'mortals who know themselves are quite close to being men.' Emancipation was not the result of instruction, but its precondition.

With Raspail we find the same call for individuals to take responsibility for themselves. Each must make an effort to acquire 'rational ideas that are accessible to good sense' about the causes of sickness, to contribute the 'inner sense' that enables them to point out to the doctor the seat of a sickness that he would be hard pressed to divine just by taking the invalid's pulse.[16] Some days besieged by 150 or 200 patients, Raspail reproached those proletarians who were able to read for not studying medicine for themselves. Ideally, he should only have to give those who came to see him the *Manuel-annuaire de la santé* that he had written for the use of the poor, study of which would enable each person to become his own doctor. Thus in Lyon, where the working class 'devotes itself to the culture of intelligence with a praiseworthy emulation', he assures his readers that there is 'not a single worker who does not have his *Manuel* and is able to make up his own medicine'.[17] This ability presupposes first of all that the individual acquires an independent concern for his health. The heteronomous action of disease that is the triumph of official science must be answered by an autonomous practice of health, as the work of emancipated individuals.

It cannot be too greatly emphasized that the idea of intellectual emancipation gave the idea of social emancipation its principle and model. The reflex of workers' self-emancipation was formed here, in the proletarian's effort to become aware of himself, to name

16   *Revue Élémentaire de Médecine et de Pharmacie*, no. 1, 15 June 1847, p. 12.
17   Ibid., p. 74. On the success of Raspail's work in Lyon, see the *Mémoires et Souvenirs* of the former *canut* Sébastien Commissaire.

himself, to give both himself and others the science needed by
every free being. This self-emancipation was not that of a group,
based on collective values. It was the obligation of each person to
transform himself from 'mortal' to 'man'.

Emancipation in the family

From this point of departure, the propagation of knowledge took
two basic paths. It initially privileged the one-to-one relationship.
People went to see Jacotot or Raspail individually to be shown
how to learn by themselves and enable others to learn languages or
medicine. The teacher here had a dual role. He supported the
desire for emancipation on the basis of which the ignorant made
themselves the basis for the emancipation of others. He also gave
object lessons, providing the book with which the learner had to
get by. This very particular teaching relationship thus falls into a
figure of propagation that was quite characteristic of the time: that
of initiations (Ballanche again) that transform a social identity.
These initiations spread chain-like in the friendship of emancipated proletarians, or even in the philadelphian excursion that
scatters seed haphazardly to the wind.[18] Propaganda is not a relationship of a single person to a multitude; it is the dialogue and
promise of one individual to another.

But above all, it is a relationship placed in a key position: the
family. Jacotot never tired of repeating that his method was a
method for 'family fathers', as against the 'social' method provided
by learned explainers in the context of institutions. This privilege,
moreover, was not at the expense of the mother. For Jacotot, she
had the same mission as the father: both were to give the children
knowledge they did not themselves possess. The author of the
'official' refutation of his method himself emphasized this point: 'A
touching discovery! Women, mothers, the finer half of the human
race, will themselves be the schoolteachers of their children . . .
We can see how there will be enough universal education for

18   See *Proletarian Nights*, chapters 4 and 5.

everyone'.[19] Raspail also asked the mother to transform the concern she had for the health of her children into an independent competence, whereas the 'learned' homoeopaths criticized 'popular' homoeopaths for placing science 'under the protection of skirts'.[20]

Via the appeal to the father, therefore, it was the family as such that was valorized as the natural place for the appropriation of knowledge and emancipation of the poor. The conceptual role ascribed to it here differed a bit from what has been said about the role of 'familialist' ideologies in the popular milieu. The over-valorizing of the family in nineteenth-century working-class discourse has generally been explained in two ways. Some people have seen it as the assertion of a male power, compensating for the worker's abasement and dispossession in the world of work. In this perspective, the intensification of exploitation or the deskilling linked with the growing division of labour produced a reactive stress on the family as the site of the male worker's restoration of power and the recomposition of his self-image. Others have seen it as the inculcation in the popular milieu of a bourgeois ideology of the family order, suited to restraining popular subversion and perversion.

The poor family appears here in a different role, involved in the process of emancipation. In order to analyze it, we have to look once again at the major text of Ballanche and the very definition of the plebeian or proletarian. The proletarian was a person who made children and must content himself with *making* them without being able to transmit to them any *family name*.[21] Excluded from the legitimacy of marriage, he was without either ancestors or

---

19   Lorain, *Réfutation de la Méthode Jacotot.*
20   *Journal de la Doctrine Hahnemannienne*, 1840, vol. II, p. 152.
21   On the definition of *proletarius*, see Cicero (*De Republica*, II, 40), and in particular Aulus Gellius, *Notes Atticae*, XVI, 10: '*a munere officioque prolis edendae appellati sunt; quod, cum re familiari parva minus possent rem publicam juvare, subolis tamen gignendae copia civitatem frequentarent.*' ('They received this name from their work and duty of progeniture, in the idea that, if the mediocrity of their inheritance rendered them less fit to serve the Republic, at least they would people it by the abundance of their descendants.') We can see in the same chapter of Aulus Gellius how, by the second century CE, the word seemed to have lost its meaning in the course of time.

descendants. The claim of a 'sign of intelligence' thus went hand with hand with the claim for family legitimacy. In this model, the family is the place of instruction because it is the place of a certain sense of self. The self-belonging of the rational being comes to be defined in terms of common family membership. Jacotot sees the family father as faced with the contradiction of giving his children food for their bodies while being deemed incapable of giving them food for their minds. He emancipates himself by an act of self-knowledge that is the inventory of what he knows: his mother tongue, the skills of his trade, and the rhetoric of protest. On this basis, he can serve as 'ignorant schoolmaster' for his son.

The link between individual autonomy and family power assumes dramatic form in the popular experience of sickness and death. Raspail sees the mother as focus of this contradiction; the care that she takes for the health of her loved ones should expand into a medical skill. Yet this is the weak link on which official medicine exerts its intimidation. The 'new method' was to provide the up-to-date clinical knowledge needed for the sick person and those who in everyday life have the greatest concern for him. This clinical knowledge is defined in opposition to the fortress of the monopolizers of medical knowledge and exploiters of the popular body: the hospital. This is frequently described as a site of dispossession of the proletarian self that coincides with a separation from his family. Removed from the space where he is the object of affection, the poor becomes simply an object of experiment, 'good material for the instruction of students, on which all experiments can be happily performed'.[22]

---

22 Extracts from a letter found in the Hamel papers (Archives Historiques du Ministère de la Guerre, June 1848, dossier 3669 bis) and published in part in A. Faure and J. Rancière, *La Parole ouvrière*, Paris, 1976. Hamel, a former worker who became a language teacher, illustrates this thesis very well. He came to culture and Saint-Simonian (later Fourierist) socialism by way of the lectures and theory of Greek roots of the Le Havre grammarian Andreu, also the teacher of the worker-poet Constant Hilbey. In 1848 he edited a number of social-Bonapartist newspapers and was a member of the commission for the 'Banquet du Peuple'.

This dispossession reaches an extreme with the profanity of autopsy ('instead of coming to claim a father or a husband, you are simply given a shapeless mass of flesh'), and without being able to pay the 27 francs owed to the administration it was impossible to recover the dead body. Suzanne Voilquin describes the pain of the young mother who sees her hospital bed surrounded by medical students,[23] while Raspail's diary regularly expands on the theme of medical mutilation in entries of the kind: 'Legs to be severed according to traditional practice, and preserved according to the new method.' Improvement in family clinical knowledge, and the return of the sick person to their domestic space, were thus conceived as taking back possession from a medical science based on the seizure and mutilation of the popular body.

The poor family is thus the site of science to the extent that its reproductive activity spills over into social activity, the father no longer remaining content just to provide food but also teaching, while the mother no longer simply watches but also heals. This expansion was opposed to the classical division between a function of instruction vested in the schoolmaster and a task of education vested in the family. In the classical schema, the family was the principle of ethical objectivity, recalling the pupil to the social function that instruction risked leading astray. It taught the 'knowledge of self' of the artisan who reinvested all his knowledge in the practice of his trade and the performance of his family and social duties. Here Jacotot reverses the Platonic logic that commands the artisan to stick to 'his own business'. In conceiving who he is in society and what he is doing there, the artisan discovers himself as the subject of an intelligence common to all, the full exercise of which depends on each person's will. The disciplinary instance of education then becomes the decision of emancipation that renders the father or mother capable of taking the place of 'ignorant schoolmaster' for their child, a place that embodies the unconditional requirement of will: the son will verify the equality

---

23   Letter from Suzanne Voilquin in *La Providence*, 1838, p. 86.

of intelligence in his self-apprenticeship to the extent that the father or mother verify the thoroughness of his effort to learn. The family is thus the site of an awareness in the form of an expansion of self, an extension of each person's 'own business' to the point at which this becomes a full exercise of common reason.

The family deployed in this way does not withdraw into itself; it becomes the point of departure for a different sociability from that of collective fictions and institutional monopolies, the site where an individual is formed for whom being emancipated and emancipating are one and the same thing, experiencing in themselves the powers of reason and life and feeling these as principles of solidarity between individuals. A socialism of emancipation starting from the individual and family sphere, opposed all along the line to a socialist model of education that, by a science of social organization, seeks to repress or use to common advantage the egoistic tendencies of individuals and families. It is notable how this opposition, which crosses the conventional oppositions between doctrines, classes and policies, has its starting-point in a single basic text: the theory of Helvétius on the original equality of intelligences and the all-powerful character of education. By way of Benthamite utilitarianism and Owenist materialism, a tradition was created that interpreted this as a theory of the determining force of circumstances and the social power of education, combating the anarchy of family egoism and obscurantism.

Opposed to this interpretation was a reading of Helvétius in which the power of education was also that of self-education. The impotence of individual will becomes conversely the effort of the individual to win the common title of rational being and make the equality of intelligences an actual fact. The principle of a chain of emancipation opposed to those 'flocks of emancipated'[24] who are held in reins, according to Jacotot, by all the 'good methods' – social, governmental or republican, Saint-Simonian, phrenological or whatever.

Yet certain distinctions need to be made. For Jacotot himself,

---

24 *Journal de l'Emancipation Intellectuelle*, Fourth year, p. 48.

trust in the power of individuals to emancipate themselves was matched by a radical scepticism as to the possibility of a rational society. The same was not true for those who sent their children to the lectures of his disciple Victor Ratier at the Halle aux Draps, or attended these themselves; for these autodidact workers, republican employers, doctors or priests ministering to the poor, lawyers, notaries, grammarians and others who acted here and there as teachers or doctors to their fellow-workers, neighbours, employees or those they administered. People like the communist *canut* Sébastien Commissaire who treated his brothers with Raspail's medicine and taught them the grammar he had newly acquired; the freemason and dyer Beauvisage, a worker who became a master but remained a republican and sought to instruct his employees so that they could become his associates; the carriage manufacturer Hartel who was the providence of Bercy where he served as club president, captain of firemen, mediator in labour conflicts and Raspaillist doctor. All these activists for the social cause saw the new methods as so many demonstrations of the emancipated human spirit that were at one and the same time means available for whoever sought to weave the ties of a new sociability by helping their kind.

Fraternal society

This was the third basic characteristic: the science suited for emancipated individuals was the same science that made them able to help. We have to abandon here the opposition that Proudhon made between justice and charity, or that Marxism and anarchism made between the self-emancipation of the workers and philanthropic paternalism. Just as the theory of the emancipation of the poor was developed as a link between scholarly and popular spaces, so the web of practical socialism was woven by men who – whether bourgeois or proletarians, reformists or revolutionaries – were not afraid to be men of relief and charity. As if to refute simplistic oppositions, a Jacotist pamphlet bore the double title: *Emancipation intellectuelle. Charité.* And Raspail himself, as candidate of the whole socialist far left in the November 1848 elections, did not hesitate to call charity the militant activity that he demanded of those who received the benefits of his medicine and were supposed to spread these. He wanted 'to have in each quarter a good fine soul, who has known more suffering than pleasure, who will have the patience to communicate to others what they have been patiently taught', and to give birth in them to 'tears of sympathy far gentler than the tears of joy'.[25] Communicating to others the benefits of individual emancipation would lead to a new sociability that actualized the relations of solidarity which nature weaves between all living beings. An emancipated science was indissolubly a science of life and a morality of devotion.

This aspect lay at the heart of all the medical polemics. For example, it determined the split of the homoeopaths into two camps. The respectable homoeopaths, led by the former Saint-Simonian priest Léon Simon, thus attacked the 'lay' or 'popular' homoeopaths led by the Saint-Simon proletarian Lafitte and the Fourierist doctor Mure. The latter, who carried out 'popular propagation', placed homoeopathy 'under the protection of skirts', reducing it 'to the harsh extremity of emerging from the temple of medicine to hang out at crossroads and in bars'.[26] The lay faction, on the other hand, prided themselves on breaking 'the circle of the possible' in their dispensaries, where 'the poor classes find for free [. . .] the succour that the high philanthropy of Hahnemann could not always offer them'.[27]

The magnetists, for their part, caught as they were between the reprobation of all serious medicine and the excesses of spiritualism and charlatanism, focused on presenting minimal principles of agreement to a theory and practice of sympathy between sentient beings. These principles were reaffirmed each spring at a banquet in honour of Mesmer. The banquet of 23 May 1850 was particularly significant in this respect. It was held, in fact, at a contradictory

---

25   *Revue Élémentaire de Médecine et de Pharmacie*, 15 February 1848, p. 275.

26   *Journal de la Doctrine Hahnemannienne*, 1840, vol. II, p. 152.

27   Ibid., vol. 1, p. 385.

conjuncture. Magnetism had just experienced two critical years. On the one hand, the revolution of February 1848 had put a sudden halt to its propaganda successes, while the repression and disarray that followed the June days favoured the development of spiritualist escapism, along with clairvoyant charlatanism and fairground sleepwalkers. Other signs, however, gave new hope for the future of a rational magnetism. Though its theory had been abandoned by major figures, it had struck root in the popular masses where its vitalist doctrine had strongly welded with belief in socialism. The victory of the left in the partial elections of April 1850 attested to this. The candidates of socialist democracy, de Flotte and Vidal, were also champions of magnetism.

In this optimistic context, 150 people thronged to the hall magnificently decorated by a restaurateur friend of the magnetist doctrine; and beneath the laurel-crowned bust of the Founder, the director of the *Journal du Magnétisme*, Dr Du Potet, welcomed the repentant returnees from spiritualism and somnambulism. He stressed the division of magnetism into two orders of phenomena, one based on 'completely physical facts that serve as the foundation of science', the other consisting of 'moral effects' of an infinite variety and open to experiment guided by philanthropy. This was in actual fact the contradiction: in order to safeguard magnetism from charlatanism, the 'physical' aspects had to be privileged; yet the moral value of its search for universal sympathy had to be preserved. The sentiment of *humanity* served as a bridge between the two, giving characteristic tone to a meeting that combined Saint-Simonian effusions, talk about nature and sympathy, and an appeal to women. For the first time a woman, representing the 'Trojan Athenaeum of pure and applied mesmerology', spoke in the name of the doctrine. And in so doing she equated the new scientific school, in exemplary fashion, with the new humanitarian church:

> Oh, how fine this religion will be, with its ministers the benefactors of humanity, the living providence of the unfortunate, the dispensers of the inexhaustible treasures of nature, the interpreters of the

Divinity! How rich and venerated this church will be, as the refuge of all those who suffer and hope; this society of believers united together by the bonds formed by sympathy, living from the same life, vivified at the same source, all seated at the banquet that the universal mother of all beings prepares for us and invites us to.[28]

When the president, Dr de Rovère, was prosecuted as a member of Solidarité Républicaine, the Trojan Athenaeum was led to explain once again its scientific and humanitarian mission. It was 'a scientific and popular school [. . .] which people enter and leave with a single thought, that of mutual love and enlightenment'. It was this concern for mutual schooling and support that justified the presence among its activities of a course in somnambulic education. This, in fact, presented 'new investigations that tend to develop a pure and permanent lucidity among people inspired by the desire to be useful to their fellows'.[29] Rational magnetism, in other words, spoke the same language about somnambulist experiment as the rationalist Raspail spoke about magnetism in general:

Let magnetism proclaim itself a work of charity; let it do good without hope for money or reward. Let the possessor of this talisman call on both believers and unbelievers alike, so as to prove that his art is no mere conjuring but rather one of the mysterious benefits of nature . . . In the end, the person who possesses such an influence must experience pleasure not in the manner of Anacreon, attached to a quivering point in space, but rather that of Lucretius, contemplating it in the immensity of the world, as the creative soul of all that is great and beautiful.[30]

The rights of fellow creatures

The paths of both the emancipated autodidact and the humanitarian activist thus saw their firm ground and their adventurous

28   *Journal du Magnétisme*, 25 May 1850, vol. IX, pp. 286–7.
29   Ibid., July 1850, p. 323.
30   *Revue Élémentaire de Médecine et de Pharmacie*, 15 January 1848, p. 251.

course marked by the ambiguity of certain common notions. From one end to the other, it was the sense of the *fellow creature* that served as guide on the road from the known to the 'immense unknown'; it was this that sharpened the curiosity of the flint-searching boy, served as apprenticeship to the ignorant who instructed themselves by Jacotot's method, and authorized the more or less controlled outpourings of the sympathetic sentiment. To advance from the known to the unknown according to the sense of being fellow creatures – this common maxim defined different levels of interpretation. An 'emancipator' such as Jacotot held to an interpretation of common sense close to Cartesian thought and rejected any pantheistic or spiritualistic excess of the fellow-creature idea. An autodidact worker such as Gauny, on the other hand, understood common sense in the manner of Vico, and combined the demand for a rational society with the palingenetic vision of Ballanche. Appealing to Socrates and Diogenes, he was not afraid to occasionally try his own talents in magnetism. As we have seen, the maxim of good sense was movable, in terms of both its point of departure and its destination. On the one hand, the analytic method was immersed in the world of autodidactic apprenticeship in which the starting-point was not the 'first knowable' but rather the 'first known', as given by the chances of social experience. At the other extreme, it was taken in tow by a teleology of universal sympathy and the supra-sensible destiny of souls. The 'unknown' then acquired a determination that it would be somewhat hasty to call occultist (Ballanche's palingenesis had nothing in common with turning tables, and Mesmer's manuscripts on social organization, published by *Le Journal du Magnétisme*, are far closer to Cabanis than to Allan Kardec), but that certainly lay outside the paths of scholarly rationalism – whether conceived after the style of Descartes or that of Bachelard.

Thus the same idea can be realized at several different levels of rationality, susceptible of being combined or separated. Between these levels, the idea of humanity forms the middle term. Between a rationalism of Cartesian common sense and a socialism of universal magnetism, between the this-sidedness of the untrained apprenticeship of the proletarian individual and the beyond of human destiny that the plebs are seen as bearing, there is a middle region where scholarly rationalism and plebeian super-rationalism find themselves in agreement: an idea of the ethical community projected in the very effort towards a stylization of individual life. Across the major thematics of life and language, across the two great concerns of education and association, the question is to realize a certain essence of the speaking being, as an autonomous subject belonging to a society of individuals in solidarity.

3

The Gold of Sacramento: Capital and Labour's Californian Adventures

The aftermath of disappointed revolutions: ships leaving Le Havre are always full in this year of 1850. But are there not two different tracks here, even if on the same trajectory?

'California and Icaria, these are two opposing principles exploding on the same part of the globe'[1] – a palpable antagonism: the greedy egoism of the gold-seekers as against the courageous devotion of those setting off to found their community in the cause of Humanity . . .

Yet to read the accounts left by these travellers, was the gold-seekers' America so different from that of the communitarian pioneers? A country of simple morality with a brotherly welcome and theft unknown: 'We have been received very well by the Americans . . . No egoism at all, but the most generous devotion . . . Nothing is ever locked or hidden . . . the shops remain open at night with their wares displayed . . .'[2]

A new world of equality, where Labour was recognized morally and economically at its just price:

> [T]hose tasks seen as suited to quite disadvantaged men – kitchen service, cleaning, etc. are in fact performed by a fairly large part of our number including those most notable for their intelligence . . . there are people from excellent families who have washed dishes for 8 dollars a day . . . they serve with a cigar in their mouth and

---

1 *Le Populaire*, 11 October 1850.
2 *Le Populaire*, 20 August 1848; *Le Mineur*, July and October 1850.

are quite deaf to the calls of customers! They insist on being called
Mister.[3]

And a land of miracles, into the bargain, where the will to work is
readily rewarded:

> We had scarcely sown the seed in the ground before a few days
> later the plants arose . . . Everything grows as if by magic – steam-
> ships, houses, streets, hotels, etc . . . Everything is prodigious and
> inexplicable, everything proves that you can do anything if you
> desire it.[4]

An America of brotherly workers . . . Nothing resembles the
sermons that blessed the departure of the gold-seekers so much as
the speeches saluting the departure of the Icarians:

> But what guides you in your bold undertaking? Fortune? No, the
> human heart is too great to imagine that . . . You who are all young,
> strong and vigorous, you seek a fortune that has been refused to you
> until today. Would it be then to waste it in material pleasures? In no
> way. Spiritual enjoyments are the only true ones. To comfort
> misfortune, to come to the relief of suffering brothers, that is the goal
> you have set for yourselves in leaving your homeland, your wives
> and your children . . . Those such as us who have seen you set out,
> full of devotion and enthusiasm, will have had to forget in the face of
> that moving scene any egoistic and petty concern for self-interest.[5]

This triumph of devotion was also that of the economic and moral
principle of Association. If there was one line of business in which
this principle, already under attack from reaction, was incontesta-
bly victorious, it was that of the Californian companies:

---

3 *Le Populaire*, 2 September 1847; *Le Mineur*, July 1850; Saint-Amant,
Voyage en Californie et dans l'Orégon, Paris 1854 (a US dollar was worth five
francs).
4 *Le Populaire*, 9 July1848; *Le Mineur*, July 1850.
5 *Le Mineur*, September 1850; *La Fortune*, October 1850.

We had been given as a rallying cry the magic word 'association'! This word was the cornerstone that supported our social edifice . . . the worker needs the capitalist to provide him with the instruments of labour . . . the capitalist needs the worker to put his instruments of labour to work . . . '*The gold-seekers can only succeed through association. Isolation is death.*' Understand these words well, emigrant workers, they are those of one of the leading professors in France.[6]

Let us be fair to these Californian companies. They did not try to hide, in the papers designed for their shareholders, the practical purpose of these vibrant appeals to the spirit of the time, these gains generously shared between capital and labour:

All the hopes of the undertaking rely on the devotion and loyalty of the workers. An immense capital has been committed to this loyalty . . . yet it may happen that on reaching those shores that are so much desired, the leader of the expedition sees the greater part of his travelling companions abandon him . . .[7]

'It may happen . . .' A neat euphemism that those well informed about the Californian situation could readily translate:

The emigrants, setting out at the expense of the shareholders, listen patiently to the verbose speeches addressed to them by the directors, deputy directors, expedition leaders and representatives of the people who serve as representatives of the supervisory board; they drink to their health, they swear loyalty to the commitments made, and repeat at the top of their voices the words of the economist Adolphe Blanqui: '*Isolation kills the gold-seekers. Only association can offer them success.*' But at the end of the crossing, ideas change . . .[8]

6   *La Fortune*, October 1850; *Le Mineur*, July 1850 (quotation from Adolphe Blanqui).
7   *La Fortune*, October 1850.
8   Descubes, *La Vérité sur les compagnies californiennes*, 1850, p. 16.

It was not hard for the workers, in fact, to learn the reasons for Capital's generosity: they had no need for its services. What 'instruments of labour' did it provide, apart from those machines for extracting and washing gold that were obligingly exhibited in Paris, but which everyone in America knew were no use at all? A pickaxe, a bucket and a sieve – that was all the capital the gold-seekers needed. And as for the healthy food, medical care and protection that were promised, didn't everyone know that the climate was highly salubrious, food cheap and crime unknown? The greedy capitalists were victims of the same diabolical logic as the generous Icarians! To attract new recruits they had to extol the charms of the climate, the fertility of the soil, and the easy life under the American sky. But all they attracted in this way were potential deserters, if the description was true, or future rebels, if it was false. The emigrants had therefore to be spurred to disciplined and patient work. But who would go such a way in search of that?

It was in vain, moreover, that the company representatives drew the attention of the incautious to the less idyllic reality of the placers: the difficulty of transport, the battles over claims, the gold that was so easily lost in gambling saloons, and the corpses found the next day of those who had been too lucky there. For workers were not in such a hurry to get to the gold fields. It was not gold fever that made them desert, but rather 'the first contact with menials who earned more in a day by carrying loads at the port than the best workers in Europe did in a week'.[9]

But didn't they already know this when they set off? The promise of employment at high wages was displayed in all the company publications. Fifty francs a day for tinsmiths, locksmiths and lamp-makers, 75 to 100 francs for carpenters, wheelwrights and saddlers, 100 to 125 for bakers, builders and printers – twenty times the average in France. It is true that these figures fell somewhat with each new issue of the papers (a return to truth or the effect of a growing supply of hands?). But even in the years of disillusion, the promise of 25 francs a day for a tinsmith, 30 for a

---

9   *La Fortune*, October 1850.

carpenter, 35 for a builder or 50 (!) for a musician was still enough
to steer men's dreams towards this country where Labour was
king, where the uncertainty of finding gold in the placers was more
than made up for by the certainty of money to be made from the
gold-seekers. The revenge of Labour over Capital (and over
Gold), the highly moral advance of male proletarians accompanied
– should we be surprised? – by a significant promotion of female
labour. With 300 women for 700,000 men, it was understandable
that dressmakers should earn 20 or 25 francs. As for laundry work,
we dare not even think what price this would have fetched if it
were available. But precisely because it was too dear, the emigrants
preferred to throw away their dirty shirts, and all accounts agree in
their obligatory description of streets littered with shirts, stuck in
the mud of the rain and floods . . . The other side of the coin was
that for want of laundresses, rag collectors would make a fortune,
if the abundance there for the taking did not make their trade
useless. As for warehousing, that wasn't even thought of. In this
paradise of political economy, the rise in wages naturally brought
in its wake that of rents. There were houses that supposedly fetched
up to 200,000 francs per year. When the regularity of floods and
fires is taken into account, and of 'removers' who took advantage
of the situation to help themselves to some additional supplements
on top of earnings that were already substantial, it was better to
pitch your tent on the hillside if you wanted to enjoy a cheap life.

If at all possible . . . for how long could one go on paying 90
cents for 'meat' (quantity unclear) and 50 cents for a pound of
bread (already dear), with bakers' boys paid 100 francs a day and
hunters who earned 2,000 francs (as was said of the Marquis de
Pindray, 'the greatest hunter in France and Navarre . . .')?
Fortunately, it was wages in the food industry that statistics show
falling fastest. But as a general rule we have to admit that 'there are
many people trying to earn money and then you cannot always
find work . . .'[10]

You end up then, one day or another, throwing dirty shirts and

---

10   *Le Mineur*, August 1850.

anything else superfluous on the street and heading for the placers of Sacramento where no company shows any remaining sign of life. (In Paris, on the other hand, the courts hear a good deal about them.) But we must be fair: one of the companies, established on the Stanislaus River, is still mentioned, without name, as having courageously persevered: '[I]t was already starting to do well when an American horde of the Mormon sect seized its work after a bloody battle.'[11] If that was the Mormons, what fate awaited the escaped convicts in Australia?

The business was thus confined to 'dreaming the chimera of gold for a longer or shorter while'.[12] An operation not without its charm for those involved, but more painful for the shareholders, whose social condition does not seem to have been much superior to their own (the real financiers would know), and perhaps profitable most of all for a 'French political society' that was purged in this way 'of a large number of brothers and friends who were an embarrassment even when not a danger'.[13]

But perhaps these views are too pessimistic or cynical. There was still business to be done in California. Yet why go there oneself? Better to imitate the inhabitants of Valparaíso who, at the first rumour of Californian gold, clubbed together to have a piece of it:

> A large store was opened, where everyone brought what they had at their disposal: flour in one case, wines and spirits in another, in yet another case furniture; here you had wooden boards, there clocks, others brought hardware, haberdashery, material, clothing, books, etc. Each object was recorded with the name of its owner, and everything sold for more than ten times the price that had been set . . .[14]

The people of Valparaíso, it seems, immediately began again. Why leave them this monopoly on a risk-free voyage? The

---

11   Auget, *Voyage en Californie*, Paris 1854, p. 106.
12   Saint-Amant, op. cit., p. 583.
13   Ibid., p. 443.
14   *La Californie*, 31 January 1850.

Comptoir Californien found the right answer. It didn't send deserters to San Francisco, but simply collected everything that could be sent, from prefabricated houses to books, not to mention furniture ('everything you would want, old or new, mediocre or elegant; when you have a whole country to furnish . . .') and all the clutter from company stores and household attics:

> The arrival of boxes of books was greeted with cries of joy in San Francisco. There were still only a few Spanish books that had come from Valparaíso, and English books, especially Bibles . . . The French book trade, which was in such bad shape at this time, would do well to try this way of offloading its old stock.

No need to travel, the goods do it for you. Was living labour absorbed once again by the dead labour on which it had seemed to take its revenge? True, the Comptoir was also a swindle. 'Silk hats from Paris are sold here for 24 centimes the dozen.'[15] And again, the problems of storage, fires, removals . . . As for doing business, small or large, it was just as well to do it in France. And as for the fraternal ideal and community in the land of liberty, Icarie did not succeed, for reasons that are basically quite similar. Things in America were either too easy or too hard.

> America lends itself marvellously to that deceptive mirage of the dog who abandons its prey for the shadow, until the moment when the sad reality wakes you up in greater despair than ever. Then you take up your worker's chain again as a happy fortune.[16]

In France, fortunately, industry was beginning to move forward rapidly.

---

15 *Le Mineur*, August 1850.
16 Prudent to Beluze, 14 July 1851, Archives Cabet, Amsterdam.

4

Off to the Exhibition: The Worker, His Wife and the Machines

The Exhibition, in our society's imaginary, is a spectacle. A recent play (*En r'venant d'l'Expo*) reminds us of the spectacle of this spectacle: the Exposition Universelle of 1900; the worker – just like the bourgeois – bowled over by the Electricity Fairy, contemplating the wonders of industry, art and science; and, correlatively, set fast – as opposed to the patriotic mythology of the bourgeoisie – in a certain representation of himself and his future: the mythology of *la sociale* and the general strike. If we go back a few decades more here and study the reports of the workers' delegations to the Exposition of 1867, this is not to wax eloquent on the discreet charm of the retro – rather to revolve the stage so as to see the formation of this spectacle, i.e. the moment at which the workers perceive it as a product of their dispossession. The industrial revolution of the Second Empire offered the workers this spectacle of labour becoming foreign to itself; products of workers' industry exhibited as products of the employers and rewarded as such by a jury of non-workers; products unworthy of the 'true principles' of workers' skill, due to speculators who pressed for mass production; the knowledge of the worker broken by the division of labour, reorganized against him in the machine in the hands of the employer. And in this year of 1867, the elite workers of Parisian industry could measure the reality of what a book published that year in Hamburg called the 'separation of the worker from the intellectual forces of production'.

The reports of the workers' delegations – elected by assemblies of each corporation – did not just passively record this dispossession.

They responded to it in two ways. First of all in the 'technical' part of the reports, in which they showed an intellectual grasp of these new machines and cast judgements that were sometimes severe on the products of this divided and mechanized labour, forming a kind of workers' counter-jury as against the jury from which they were excluded. Then in the section devoted to the 'wishes' that the goodness of His Imperial Majesty allowed them to formulate in this special circumstance: wishes that were basically political, since workers' dignity required the suppression of the *livret*[1] and the discriminatory clauses of the labour code, while workers' (trade union) organization required obtaining the freedoms of association and public assembly. Demands for dignity and organization that were to prepare a future to which all the delegations eagerly looked forward: 'association'.

These texts – written in the months following the exhibition and doubtless emboldened by the rise of working-class strength – have a strategic character in several respects. Theoretically, because they are situated at the very point where what accepted doctrine divides into the three distinct levels of economics, politics and ideology joins together: here the verdict on a badly stitched shoe is directly linked with certain political demands and a discourse on the future of the worker. Politically, as they make use of a means of expression granted by the Imperial state and turn it into a weapon of class consciousness: in these reports, and in the deliberations of the Workers' Commission that subsequently met to arrange their publication, we can note the transition from the limitations of corporative thinking – even Bonapartist 'socialism' – to the formation of a new revolutionary working-class ideal. A strategic position, too, because reflection on the new 'agents of production' applied by the capitalists (machinery and women) is located at the meeting point of two powers: class power and domestic power. Some reflection is worthwhile here on the system of powers in play: the power of the capitalist over the

---

1   This worker's identity document introduced by Napoleon in 1803 remained compulsory until 1890. [Tr.]

worker by way of machinery and women's labour; the power of science and technology to be regained by the worker; the power of the working man over his wife.

I. The ambivalent machine

The Exposition Universelle of 1867: the employers invite delegates of the different trades to marvel at the spectacle of machinery. On display, mechanical magic offers the image of a power conjured up by the sorcery of the steam engine: rapid, cheap and effortless production of quality articles will now be possible. The employers seek to cast a spell over the workers – not without malice, as the stone-carver delegates note, when they oppose to the spectacular display of machinery 'the permanent exhibition of moral and material misery' of the workers. The festival of capital, exhibiting 'its' machines, is written against the dramatic background of a working-class defeat; the magic of technological progress resolves without mystery into effects of an employers' power whose new forms of subjection pass by way of mechanization. A spectacle of dispossession, therefore: the machines belong to the employer, the new avatar of capital; the mechanization of production deskills labour by means of its intense division, and tends to deprive the workers of the practical source of their right to dispose of the product of their labour.

The delegates at the Exposition Universelle were mandated by trade associations, which brought together and organized a highly skilled labour force. All of these could see the effects of mechanization as heralding the rapid death of skilled trades. Before founding a right to the product of labour, these trades ensured the worker mastery of a complex know-how embodied in the intelligent skill of the hand working on material. If physical strength was required in a number of trades, only skill could enable its judicious application to a resistant material: it represented the conquest by the worker's intelligence of the strength with which his body was endowed:

It is to man alone that the task has fallen of providing for the needs of his family; it is a duty for him to submit himself to this law of nature, for which he has received the necessary intelligence and bodily strength.[2]

The worker was proud of his strength because its intelligent application was at his command. The skill to which apprenticeship gave access raised his trade to the rank of an art, and was a working-class resource par excellence.

The first effect of mechanization was to depreciate this heritage of the worker by overturning in many ways the relationship to labour. The delegates bitterly note how the quality of articles shows the ill effects of mechanical production, with the careful finishing that signalled a quality article being often lacking. For fabric printers, mechanized work could produce at the same or better quality only those articles that needed low levels of skill; it could not give good results for articles that demanded the full cunning condensed in the tricks of the trade. In respect to the quality of products, as expression of the art of the trade, mechanization represented a very significant loss of the beneficial effects of workers' know-how.

Mechanization was not reducible to the substitution of skilled handiwork by machines: it reorganized the worker's relationship to his labour by intervening in the performance of the labour process in the form of an absolute imperative of output. The machine performed a certain number of operations more rapidly; this technological gain in time was used to define a new social norm of production for the workers, forcing them to work ever more quickly to ensure their wages. Far from re-skilling labour by freeing more time to perfect its execution, mechanization became the paradoxical instrument of deskilling. Monumental masons recorded the destructive impact of the output norm on the exercise of their trade, making any love of their art impossible and vain:

---

2   Engineering workers' report.

Responsibility for the mediocrity into which our country has fallen
should not weigh on the workers alone, for their desire to work
well has had to yield to the necessity of working fast. The first
thing now asked of them is to produce in bulk; good work is only
a secondary concern; because of the immense competition that has
been established, sale prices have sunk so low that the labour put in
has had to be reduced.

Wallpaper printers denounced the new conditions of labour 'that
affect and enervate bodies and lower intelligence', transforming
labour into what the fabric printers called a 'cause of disease': the
workers' representation of productive labour measures how intolerable is labour that has become destructive.

With mechanization, the workers perceived the possibility of
unloading onto machines that part of their labour that demanded
bodily effort: but in practice, this actually intensified effort, as the
chair-makers noted with respect to the bandsaw: 'This tool,
designed to render them great service by relieving them of the
mind-numbing part of their labours, has become nothing more
than a means of struggle used against them.'

The division of labour is indicated as the essential cause of all
the negative effects of mechanization: it dispossesses the worker of
control over his labour and chains him alive to the machine. For
the shoemakers:

When machinery with its thousand iron limbs becomes employed
in the service of industry . . . whereas it should by this very fact
give the worker more time to perfect his labour, the attempt is
made on the contrary to make man himself, by the division of
labour, a kind of machine, depriving him of part of his responsibility and part of his intelligence, and this in order to produce a bit
more, to produce regardless.

Those whom the copper-founders called 'specialized workers', i.e.
performing a divided labour that was mind-numbing in its repeti-
tion, held out to the skilled workers the near image of their own

being, mutilated by the employers' production machine. The following description of the working conditions of these 'specialized workers' was given by workers in leather and skins:

> Those who have seen the devouring activity that prevails in these specialized workshops, where the worker is no longer anything but an automaton functioning ten, eleven or twelve hours per day, with no awareness of the value of the product that he has in his hands, incapable of correcting mistakes made by the first operators, executing his specialized task for better or worse, passing on to others his product, which thus goes successively through ten or twelve hands to its completion in a single day: these, we say, ask themselves what are the consequences of this kind of system for the future of the workers.

In the division of labour that deprives them of machinery's technical benefits, the workers saw a new employers' power being established, aiming at the absolute subjugation of manual work. The ideal of this new power was to dispossess the workers as much as possible of the skilled control of their labour, so as to transform them too into actual 'living machines' (the expression used by the copper-founders), delivering their labour-power defenceless to the insatiable appetite of profit; the employers fantasized a great social machine that would mechanize workers' bodies. The political horizon of the capitalist organization of labour was the subjection of a mass of workers pacified by division, with the goal of forestalling any attempt at organized revolt. Mechanization was thus for the employers an anti-strike weapon: it aroused competition and contradiction between skilled and unskilled labour, and undermined forms of organized resistance in the context of the trade. The division of labour was the employers' war machine, a private machine that captured collective machines that were the work of all; it was the instrument of power of the employers as owners of the machines. The division of labour ensured the absolute reign of the owner, against which the shoemakers challenged: 'Is machinery not also the work of all? Have not millions of workers been involved in this? Is it not contrary to justice and equity that it should become a monopoly for the benefit of a few?'

The employers' monopoly over machinery was an obstacle to the development of a skilled and collective labour-power. If at the Exposition Universelle the employers offered everyone the spectacle of their machines, proposing an imaginary collective appropriation of the magic of progress, in the factory the employer spirited them away, like an owner jealous of his ill-gained property. The hatters described this proprietary madness which deprived the workers of an instrument of labour:

> This machine has no other purpose than to serve the interests of an individual or a company. It is placed in a small dark room, in the backmost part of the premises, and since even this precaution seems insufficient, it is surrounded by wooden boards as if to remove from the regard of the crowd some supposedly holy image, from which a great tribute is drawn one day of the year. Under a double lock, like money and banknotes in the establishment's strongbox, it operates almost invisible to those assigned to its service. Having become a kind of symbol of the passion – or rather, religion – of each for himself, it subsequently escapes the investigations of those who might, by studying it, remove it from its state of inferiority.

If the skilled workers made so many criticisms of mechanization, this was because it proceeded by the division of labour, challenging skilled labour, which was one of the forms of workers' resistance to the arbitrary power of the employer. If they refused to recognize themselves as unskilled workers, this was not simply to defend certain 'privileges' against the arrival on the labour market of a proletarianized mass that would demand its share. The massive use of a deskilled workforce introduced competition into wages, tending to reduce them to a minimum for the greater profit of the employer:

> The same goes for the living machines, in other words the unskilled workers, who often know no more than a tiny part of their trade,

which makes them unfit for any complete and conscientious work, and makes it impossible for them to obtain a remuneration in relationship to the prices established by workers truly worthy of this name in the profession to which they belong.

The fundamental principle of workers' resistance is that of defining a collective right to fair remuneration on the basis of the labour provided and its level of skill. Intellectual and practical control of the labour process goes together with economic and legal control of the product of labour. The defence of skill establishes by right a threshold below which the wage rate is no longer negotiable; the collective practice of this right by the trade removes the price of labour from the employers' arbitrary decision:

At the beginning, the workshop offered workers certain temporary advantages, ones that it obtained above all by the divided labour being able to produce more quickly and favouring unskilled employees. But when these become more numerous (as they constantly are), their wage then falls to the minimum level. Along comes a competitor with the same means of manufacture, and wages fall; the workers are that much less able to resist in that they have become less skilled and the factories more powerful.

On the basis of the division of labour, capitalist mechanization threatens a right by which workers' autonomy is affirmed.

The workers of 1848 claimed labour as a right. The right to labour gives a right to live from the product of one's labour; a minimal right that justifies the claim for a minimum wage, defined in reference to a set of socially defined needs: 'Each individual who works has the right to a wage sufficient to meet his needs.'

Though many of them are far from accepting the presence of women in the workshop, the workers' reports maintain as a principle that each women who works has the right to a wage equivalent to that of the man she replaces, and the cutting-tool workers also demanded for prisoners who work a wage more or less equal to that of free workers. The demand for a minimum wage brings workers together in solidarity into a unified class, practising a right that spells out what may not be alienated by the employer; this consciousness of a right informs workers' perception of the arbitrary power of the employer and justifies the organization of resistance against abuses of his power. The defence of skill tends to maximize this collective right to the product of labour; it is a practical assertion of the worker's right to obtain the maximum for the product of his labour, with a view to the satisfaction of his new needs. This is why the engineering workers refused to accept the claim of an equal wage for all: 'The workers who have demanded this mode of payment are not in keeping with the progressive ideas of the time.'

Love for one's trade, however, should not mystify the practical meaning of the defence of the right to a skilled trade. The engineers were making this argument to oppose those among the workers who criticized mechanization in the name of the 'individual talent' of skilled workers that it would bring to an end; it was not so much individual talent they were defending, as the power that this gave to maximize wages: the worker only acquired his talent with the aim of gaining the highest possible wage.

The workers' reports do not paint the machine as a cold-blooded monster to be destroyed. The age of machine-breaking was over; it was now the capitalist appropriation of machinery, the divided organization of labour, that deprived the worker of his body, his intelligence, his rights and his freedom:

> Suppose for a moment that in order to please all the backward ideas we were to break all the machines, burn all the plans, the designers and the engineers. Should we believe that such acts of vandalism would resolve the situation that individualism and exploitation driven to excess have placed us in?[3]

Is this the sign of a consciousness on the part of the workers that would finally lead them to recognize their true interests and reject

---

3   Ibid.

the infantilism of revolt? It is the development of unskilled work more than anything else that obliges the skilled workers to invent new forms of resistance. Starting from the effect of the employers' power that misappropriates collective work to its own profit, the workers' reports list the possible forms of workers' appropriation of mechanization: break the great private machine of capital by the collective appropriation of the machines, answer the employers' ideology of workers hostile to technical progress with workers' control over mechanization. This initiative on the part of the workers can take the form of a moral appropriation. By conceiving the machines as collective products of wealth-creating labour, the engineering workers do not oppose machinery to labour as dead labour to living, but rather subject it to the workers' morality of labour conceived as the source of life; they refuse therefore to count armaments among the assets of labour: 'The nature of their purpose being too greatly in disagreement with our principles, and too opposed to our feelings of humanity, we did not believe that we had to consider these as industrial products.'

It is in the name of a morality that defines the interests, rights and duties of the working class that the immorality of the employers' power is denounced. This can only be seen as a mystification if we remain blind to the practical effects of resistance to subjugation that this morality justifies. The injustice of the private appropriation of machines makes their collective appropriation legitimate; the immorality of the capitalist division of labour that makes the worker a slave of the machine arouses the class consciousness of a necessary organization of labour by the workers themselves:

> The system that is excellent in its foundation sins at the top, and this great production, accomplished by all, profits only a few. Let us therefore unite our efforts, combine our forces, oppose power to power, and, while respecting the positions acquired, let us gradually substitute for them an economic system more advantageous to all.[4]

4 Shoemakers' report.

Capitalist mechanization corrupts the body, numbs the intelligence, and abandons the unskilled worker to degeneration; the workers' reports imagine what a social and moral use of machines would be. The engineering workers speak of 'the eminently moralizing aspect' of mechanization: by relieving the worker of heavy labour, the machine enables him to devote himself to the part of his task that requires the intelligent application of a high level of skill, and frees time that can be devoted to education: 'Our aim is to have all the material labour performed by machines, and to produce a sufficient number of these so as no longer to have to do more than supervise them for a few hours per day.'

The musical instrument makers see the machines as the means for developing workers' intelligence:

> Let us pursue our studies with care, use our abilities energetically, and assert more than ever that there are still good workers, that they will always be needed, and that at a certain point in time they will be in short supply. For the more that industrial science displaces the strength or skill of the worker by substituting steam, and the more these marvellous processes drive out manual labour, the more the worker's intelligence will be appreciated, if, following the impulse that science gives him, he continues the task that his forebears brought into being.

For the engineering workers, the intensive mechanization of labour opens the perspective of a new type of skill, in the sense of an increased control of the labour process; they thus glimpse a solution to the contradiction that opposed skilled to unskilled workers:

> The day when, by the use of machines, this talent will be rendered superfluous, the worker will gladly stop taking the trouble to acquire it, and learn what he needs to know in the new conditions in which he will find himself placed; he will cultivate his intelligence, employing it so as to be able to direct well the machine that he has to operate.

Mechanization becomes the instrument for a workers' initiative that takes as its goal the socialization and skilling of labour.

On stage at the Exposition was the spectacle of machines, behind the scenes were the workers dispossessed of their labour and their lives. The workers' reports dismantle the employers' power machine in order to recompose a future workers' power in the collective control of machines. The workers' reaction to mechanization clearly traces the limit reached by forms of resistance focused on the defence of rights practised in the context of the traditional solidarity of the trade. Reflection on the effects of the division of labour opened up a future for workers' initiative. There is a remarkable text in which the engineering workers develop on the subject of the machine the fine utopia of machines as bearers of the workers' idea of association:

We also come across it in the countryside, sometimes in the form of a dark steed bearing a white cloud on its head as a pennant; journeying as fast as the wind through the broadest plains and thickest forests; crossing the widest rivers, the deepest gorges; plunging into the sides of mountains; melting alive, as it were, into the heart of the earth, soon reappearing to light after an underground journey of several kilometres, bringing in its wake either materials and goods to quicken trade and make life and movement where all was gloom and silence, or else men themselves that commercial needs summon into these parts, and thus easing relations between the most distant populations – relations that, by spreading the uniformity of ideas, principles, rights and duties, hasten all the more the moment when all peoples, finally understanding one another, will energetically cast off the tutelage imposed on them for centuries, and, definitively shaking off the yoke of capital and ignorance, will finally be able to benefit in the broadest degree from the great advantages that machines offer them.

II. The mirror of man

> What we are opposing, need we say, is not a sex. It is an instrument
> for reducing wages, a lower-priced worker.

This was how the typographers expressed themselves in their
report on the London exhibition of 1862. If they had such a need
to say it, this was because shortly before there had been a celebrated typographers' strike, motivated by the introduction of
women workers at the Paul Dupont printing company. A strike
that was significant in terms of the resolution of the workers and
the radicalism of some of their arguments, for example that of
Jean-Baptiste Coutant:

> They will certainly succeed in finding, if they look hard enough, a
> few declassed women, eternal widows; but they will never find a
> sufficient number to replace the compositors. First of all, you have
> to read, and two-thirds of women are quite illiterate. As for the
> others, their knowledge is so slight that it is useless to mention it.[5]

No assertions of this kind are to be found in the reports of 1867.
This is not simply a matter of the development of ideas, rather that
this line of argument is based on a different logic from that of the
workers' struggle. It is the bourgeois who make use of existing
inequalities to proclaim a lesser right to remuneration (for women,
for less strong or clever workers). From the workers' point of
view, inequality must not be made into a principle: it is always a
consequence. It is the thinking of those at the top that asserts irreducible inferiorities. If woman is eternally inferior, will the worker
not be so too? At the meetings of the Workers' Commission
charged with the publication of the Reports, the pontiffs of
Proudhonism who had come to demonstrate to the delegates the
necessary inferiority of women readily perceived that the workers
were far less 'proudhonien' than most historians suppose:

---

5   *Du salaire des ouvriers compositeurs*, Paris 1861, pp. 23–4.

When Monsieur Dupas demonstrated the physical inferiority of woman compared to man, when he explained that the absence of certain civic virtues on her part was incontestable, that this was so much the better for everyone, and when he logically concluded that they should be kept apart from the workshop, this assertion of inequality produced an irksome impression on the assembly, and, when later a passage from a book written by Madame Flora Tristan was read out, presenting the argument that it would then be highly humiliating for man to have to owe life and suckling to such an inferior being, the assembly, by its attitude, seemed to approve these words.[6]

No argument from inferiority, then. If this existed in fact, it needed to be corrected. We even find a homage to the combativeness of women workers in the report of the musical-instrument makers: these women, who were 'more energetic in this respect than many working men',[7] defeated the government's attempt to extend the constraint of the *livret* to them. Let us note in passing that this resistance had a quite precise significance: the *livret* assimilated women workers to prostitutes. What was exemplary in their resistance was the defence of women's specific dignity.

'What we are opposing is not a sex.' The male workers wanted to reduce the question to a purely economic one: in the workshop, woman existed only as a lower-paid worker. What was at stake here, and placed the typographers in the front line as they had earlier been in the struggle against machinery, was the place of women's labour in an employers' strategy that aimed to break workers' resistance by pressure on wages, and more fundamentally by the threat of deskilling. The supposedly 'economic' question imposed a simple alternative: either women must work without competing with men, or they must remain outside the workshop. The workshop is the place of the male worker, and

6   Declaration by Fribourg, in Tartaret, *Procès-verbaux de la Commission ouvrière de 1867*, pp. 231–2.
7   Musical-instrument makers' report (vol. I), p. 61.

women can be there only on certain conditions. They have a place elsewhere that is reserved for them: the home. A question of power: the distribution of the worker and his wife in the double space of the workshop and the home is the stake in a struggle between bourgeois and proletarians. It is impossible to offer an economic solution without the *moral* question making its appearance.

One particular principle is asserted by almost all: if women have to work, then they have a claim to an equal wage: 'And so when it really is possible, useful and necessary to have women perform work that was previously done by men, then justice, equity and social interest demand that the man's wage should be the basis for the woman's; that equality should be established upwards and not downwards.'[8]

For equal work, an equal wage. This is not a concession that male workers make to women; it is the very logic of their own interest. To accept unequal wages for the same labour would mean accepting a process that would lead to a general decline in wages. To the classic argument of the economists, that women have less in the way of needs, the authors of the reports oppose the old argument of workers' democracy, that of the equality of needs. Some have no hesitation in asserting that women have more needs than men. Once this principle is maintained, the conditions of its application on the labour market remain to be defined. The report of the tinsmiths expresses two main solutions founded on the same principle; woman will only be the equal of man on condition of not being in the same place as him:

> Many people complain that women are doing the work of men, and very few have considered that there are many men doing the work of women. Is it not surprising to see in shops for fashions, haberdashery, millinery, lace, etc., men in their prime passing their time measuring out metres of ribbons and lace? . . . We believe that if women were substituted for these young men whose place is

---

8   Cutting-tool workers' report (vol. II), p. 5.

certainly not to sell cloth, it would already be a step towards solving the problem. Then, if men's wages were sufficient for women to be able to dispense with working outside the home, the question would be settled. For the scarcity of female hands would soon make itself felt, bringing about an increase in their wages, to the benefit of those who have neither father nor husband and live only from the fruit of their labour.[9]

The first solution, then, is a distribution of tasks corresponding to the respective abilities of the two sexes – a distribution that denies it is the arbitrary act of men. This is how the report of the wood-turners, though defining certain trades as specifically female, entrusted a commission made up entirely of women workers with the task of orienting apprentices in those trades 'that are recognized as female situations, such as tailoring, floristry, fashion, etc.'[10] The second solution: to apply the law of supply and demand in the female context, with the conclusion, economically irreproachable but somewhat over-determined ideologically, that the true means to bring about this equality is that only those women should work who have neither father nor spouse. Both economic solutions assert the same moral principle: the solution to the economic *competition* between man and woman is to bring into play their physiological and moral *complementarity*. For men, work on wood and metal; for women, work with the needle and in the home. For, whatever opinion was held about the reality of women's labour, the response to the question 'is woman made for the factory?' was almost unanimous. The tailors assert this with no beating about the bush: 'From the scientific point of view (physiology, health), from the economic point of view, as from the moral point of view, nothing can justify the use of women as agents of production.'[11]

Even supposing that the economic question was settled (organization of the scarcity of working hands), there remains the double

9   Tinsmiths and embossers' report (vol. I), p. 25.
10   Wood-turners' report (vol. III), p. 36.
11   Tailors' report (vol. III), p. 21.

assertion that the factory mutilates the body of the woman – and mother – and exposes her to moral corruption by the proximity of men and the pressure of hierarchy. Woman should not be in man's workshop – not because she is inferior to man, but so as not to be a man. The debates of the Commission Ouvrière on this subject are telling. We see three positions represented here. The two 'extremes' were also represented in the French delegation to the congress of the International Working Men's Association in Lausanne: the doctrinaire Proudhonists (Fribourg, Dupas) arguing the physical and moral inferiority of woman, while Varlin clearly defended female labour as a means of emancipation. The majority of delegates, however, followed a middle course. For them, woman's condition in the workshop is de facto an inferior one. To liberate woman is to find a specific space for her that enables her to be the equal of man. As Dupas put it:

> The more that we are emancipated, the more free will woman be. For woman is a mirror that reflects us, and if we present to her an unemancipated face, this mirror will reflect a slave. We must therefore set ourselves, by improving our customs, to bring woman out of the workshops . . .[12]

And the response of Chabaud, delegate of the tinsmiths: 'I do not have the face of a slave; I am free, quite free, and I believe that we must all do something for the happiness of woman.'[13]

Paradoxically, this 'something' did not differ in practice from the proposals of the Proudhonists. It was a matter of ensuring the presence of woman in the home. The whole difference lay in the underlying principles; in the perception of woman's function in defending the power of the workers vis-à-vis the employers. The definition of specifically female functions did not place women outside the struggle of men waged between employers and workers. It should lead them to an equality that they could never win in

---

12   Tartaret, op. cit., p. 229.
13   Ibid., p. 230.

the workshop. This was the strategy of Boulanger, the engineering workers' delegate:

> Let us ask the government to close the crèches – it will grant this. And then let us work to raise our wages, so that our women can take care of their children, work at home and acquire the rights to equality consecrated by the principles of 1789.[14]

An unconscionable argument, in view of the aspirations that feminist movements have raised for at least a century. From identical premises (i.e. that man is responsible for women's inferiority) he draws the very opposite conclusion. Man's fault here is to have placed woman in a position that was not hers, and in which she was necessarily made inferior. The liberation of woman is then a return to her natural vocation. But however it might appear with hindsight, this line of argument still links up with certain feminist discourses of the time, which sought to bring woman's social role into play and base her equality on the development of the defining aptitudes and qualities of femininity. The liberation of woman is by way of the existence of a reserved domain. In this way, woman is not just a mirror reflecting the degree of freedom that man has been able to acquire. She participates in maintaining a space closed off from the intrusion of the employers and the state: the natural order of the family.

A natural order in which the worker certainly has too great an interest for it to be questioned. What exactly is the meaning of this knot of economic and moral factors? Which of them is fundamental? The defence of workers' jobs, or maintaining a space in which the worker regains his power? An 'economistic' explanation: are not this resolute defence of the family, these paeans too touching to be honest to the sweetness and care of the home, the ideological point of honour of a forced defence of the scarcity of hands on the labour market, the form taken by working-class Malthusianism when it encounters woman as agent of production (a form that is

---

14   Ibid., p. 231.

despite everything paradoxical, when keeping women in the home is supposed to have the effect of ensuring a healthy progeny, who can speedily take their place on the labour market)? It is certain, in any case, that when the male worker did not have to fear female competition he rarely sang the joys of home life. A sad end, settling down to married life for the journeyman who had known the joys of 'friendship' on his *tour de France*![15] Should we see this as the happy result of the bourgeois enterprise of taming the undisciplined worker, settling the nomad? One of the good works that the philanthropy[16] of this time set itself was that of regularizing free sexual unions, and not just Catholic philanthropists, but also republican writers such as Michelet, were seized with a sweet emotion at the sight of the domestic interior that the wife had decorated with cheap Indian prints (thanks to machinery) in order to keep the worker away from the depravation of his bar. If things were in actual fact rather more complex, this is first of all because bourgeois discourse and practice were necessarily divided over this question. The bourgeois were certainly happy to preach morality to the workers, but they were equally interested in exploiting their women. And the philanthropists saw it only as a benefit that infants, instead of the cramped conditions of the family shack and the care of a mother with little understanding of hygiene, should rather enjoy the well-aerated space and enlightened care of the crèche. There is also the fact that conceptions of the benefits of the family were not exactly the same on either side of the class divide. On the bourgeois side, the most important thing was to impose on the worker a regularity that reined in his habits of indiscipline and vagabondage, a responsibility that brought him into the world of foresight, attaching his interests to those of the possessing class. That the worker should love his wife and fuss over his children is certainly touching; that he should be concerned for his future, put money in the savings bank and seek to buy his own house is rather more serious. And it is this serious side that the

---

15   See above, p. 27. [Tr.]
16   A special society, la Société de Saint François-Régis, had this mission.

workers rejected. Le Play and his colleagues who studied the workers note this with a scientific calmness, yet a certain dissatisfaction still shows through: the debauched tailor and the 'good husband' carpenter are joined in a lack of concern for the future, and neither dream of owning their own home. The idea is to see the worker in his house as analogous to the head of a business. But if he happily claims the role of head, this is rather to establish the home as a reserved space, the restoration of a natural order against the disciplinary and commercial order. This insistence on the family expresses the desire to preserve a bit of time and space apart from domination:

> Finally, let him live, and live as a family. The worker who goes off to work before daybreak in winter stops seeing his children; when he comes home in the evening they are in bed. He drinks, eats, sleeps and works. Can this be called living? The exploiter is less tolerant towards this human machine than towards the metal machine. For the former, he accepts no loss of time; for the latter he has to grant this, as it takes its time if this is not given to it.[17]

In the time and space in which labour-power is reproduced, a new power relationship between worker and employer is in play, presenting the threat of a duplication of exploitation. If the woman works, this network of relationships is broken, this organization of a space by means of which the reproduction of labour-power also belongs to the worker:

> Once the household is divided in this way, goodbye to the first joys of marriage! Goodbye to the tender emotions of the family! The children pass into the hands of others; the two spouses grow indifferent to one another; they no longer meet each other except to rest, since they are forced to eat separately.[18]

---

17 Engineering workers' report (vol. II), p. 156.
18 Cabinet-makers' report (vol. I), p. 41.

Sweet emotions: a difference in the imaginary between a space in which the worker still belongs to himself, and a space in which his wife and he are only the reproduction of a labour-power that belongs to the employer. Children who pass into the hands of others like the products of the worker, spouses who become indifferent to each other like commodities; the duplication of the commodity dispossession of the worker; elements of a new strategy of capital, seeking to grip the whole of working-class life in a disciplinary order that is the reproduction of the commodity order: an order of indifference and submission; the world of the crèche, the hospital and the housing estate.

The function of the family, i.e. of the wife, is to see that everything that can escape the order of the employers and their organizations actually does so. The child first of all, who cannot be free if not brought up by a mother's affection. Outside the family there is either the crèche, where, as the painters' delegates note, 'everything is foreseen by discipline', or else the mercenary care of a child-minder. As with everything commercial, death often arrived early.

Then there is health, to be preserved from the disciplinary and mercenary order of the hospital:

> In the hospital there is everything that is needed in the way of medication, dressings, cleanliness; the hospital leaves nothing to be desired in this respect. But as far as delicate care goes, it's a different matter. When you are in charge of the sick by profession, the sick person in your hands becomes a commodity; the care of the nurse or the orderly becomes harsh.

This rejection is more or less general in the workers' declarations of this time, and often accompanied by tales of terror and bitterness: hospital-prison, confined by high walls with visiting allowed only twice a week; hospital-factory, where the worker's body is subject to a second exploitation in the service of doctors, and only returns dead to the family in the form of a commodity that must be paid for on collection. Manipulation of bodies coupled with manipulation of souls by priests and nuns. (Here again, even after death: Tartaret cites cases of a priest imperturbably administering the last rites to people already dead.)

In the crèche, the asylum or the hospital, a power is exercised over the body and soul of the child or the sick person that is in some way symmetrical to that exercised over woman in the workshop where she is subjected to physical sufferings and coarse language. To return the child to its mother, to transform the Assistance Publique so as to replace confinement in hospital by a broad system of care at home – those were the measures needed to re-establish a space of resistance to the bourgeois stranglehold over the totality of workers' lives. The man withdraws the woman from the torture of the workshop, she withdraws the child and the man from the order of the crèche and the hospital. She becomes the organizer of this space of resistance. The care, tenderness and attention that only she can give the man and the child are the domestic complement of the professional skill that the workers defend. If woman must be at home, this is not just to maintain her husband's wage, rather that the function she performs there is part of the defence of the workers' positions in the face of the great offensive of capitalist disappropriation. Woman is both a stake and a hostage in this power relationship.

Defence of the family is also the link attaching work to defence of the employers' order; the chain is broken at its weakest link: the duplicity of the employers' strategy that only hymns the happiness of the family in order to enclose its members separately, that only wants to make the worker an owner so as better to ensure his disappropriation, the loss of this power over his labour and his private life. Nothing is more revealing of this than the attitude of the workers' delegations towards the workers' housing communities – employers or cooperative – in which great ideas of social architects aim to locate the happiness of the worker's family. The engineering workers immediately perceive this project for what it is:

> There are companies or industrial societies that have appeared to do something in the interest of the worker, for example by setting

up shops in which all kinds of goods can be found, soup kitchens, housing communities, churches; which leads one to suppose that they have understood perfectly well how without a life in common, existence is impossible due to the low level of wages. While acknowledging the value of such things, we declare that, as champions of freedom, we prefer to do things for ourselves, and that the only need we have is for liberty . . . Alright, you gentlemen at the head of these companies, these industrial establishments, soon also of food stores and housing estates, not forgetting a little chapel where, under the eye of the master, we shall be obliged to bring our little savings (if we still have any) for Peter's Pence . . .[19]

The copper-founders, for their part, trace the chain of this dispossession of the workers that culminates in their expulsion to the outskirts of town. What is this, if not

reviving in our own day those plebeian quarters that our ancestors called *truanderies*, something like the Ghetto of Catholic Rome. We repeat, you must be lacking in conscience if you want to park the worker outside the heart of social life in this way. Isn't he unhappy enough when he is afflicted by sickness or infirmity and obliged to be shut up in one of those parks of pain known as hospices, whose exterior, we do not know why, is like that of prisons surrounded by high walls that conceal from all eyes the moral and physical sufferings they enclose?[20]

Refusal to be parked in this way, whether under the eye of the master or outside a space that is now reserved for him. The exile of the worker outside of Paris is not just an extra time and fatigue to add to the working day, it is the loss of an equality, a right to circulate in the master's space. The musical-instrument makers, a democratic corporation if ever there was, express most forcefully this rejection of the constitution of two Parises, 'the Paris of turf

---

19   Engineering workers' report (vol. II), pp. 64–5.
20   Copper founders' report (vol. I), p. 20.

and love affairs' as against the Paris of poets, scientists, artists and workers.[21] They alone have no hesitation in their report in demanding a specific political measure to put an end to this division and exile: the election of a Conseil Municipal. They would elect one in March 1871: the Commune, the specific political space that would return the worker to the heart of social life.

The economic form of workers' emancipation is known as association – the only solution to this situation of dependence, in relation to which the defence of women staying at home represents no more than a defence of the status quo, a protection against the extension of bourgeois power over labour to the whole of the workers' life. The family cell appears rather like a substitute for association: a cell of autonomy that rejects the over-obliging care of housing estates and shops established by employers or philanthropic institutions, and asserts on its own terms the principle of 'doing things for ourselves'. But this 'ourselves' is clearly a double one: men decide and women serve. In order for the worker to escape the constraint of the bosses' organization, woman has to agree to see him as her protector.

How would it be in the world of association? The possession by the workers of the instruments of production must be complemented by the organization of cooperation at the level of consumption. What role has woman to play here? The workers envisage her resistance and seek the means to convince her. For the brush-makers, if woman is attached to the routine of marketing, it is for the worker to take the initiative and make purchases at the cooperative, and his wife will gradually accustom herself to this. However slight her involvement, she will make faster progress than the worker. Why is that? The musical-instrument makers supply us with the answer: women's resistance comes from a defective education, but their 'science of calculation' will convince them.

An argument to ponder over. Isn't there some kind of affinity with the argument Lenin would later use with respect to the peasants: they will come over when they see this as being in their

---

21   Musical-instrument makers' report (vol. I), pp. 65–6.

interest. A hierarchy between those who bear the revolution in their head and their heart, and those who must be convinced that it won't harm their purse?

This was certainly not, it would seem, the opinion of the book-binder who was almost alone in 1867 in asserting his trust in women's capacities to emancipate themselves by their own means, and who also drew up a plan for this system of workers' institutions designed to prepare the workers for the operation of a socialist system devoid of hierarchy. Was this idea of a new kind of revolution shot down in the person of Eugène Varlin?

5

A Troublesome Woman[1]

What is involved in reappropriating a lost history? The republication of Suzanne Voilquin's memoirs, with Lydia Elhadad's preface, enables us to take up the questions previously raised in *Les Révoltes Logiques* by Lydia Elhadad and Geneviève Fraisse in connection with Valentin Pelosse's publication of texts by Claire Démar.[2] On that occasion they investigated the effect produced by lost documents from women's history being brought to light by a man. However honest it might be, wasn't a man's commentary forced to reproduce in new guise the oppression it denounced, through the very privilege that his denunciation shared with the viewpoint of the master, the One, the centre? This privilege seemed to them expressed in two ways: by isolating the singularity of a female destiny, separate from the network of words and practices of the Saint-Simonian women, and by focusing interest on the symbolic of male Saint-Simonian power. By showing how Woman as fantasized by Père Enfantin's symbolic repressed actual women, Valentin Pelosse continued to make the action of women depend on the effectiveness of this symbolic mastery, compelling them ultimately to exist only 'in manipulation and recognition'. By referring this symbolic to the reality not only of the oppression of

---

1   On Suzanne Voilquin, *Souvenirs d'une fille du peuple*, presented by Lydia Elhadad, Paris 1978.
2   Cf. Claire Démar, *L'Affranchissement des femmes, textes présentés par Valentin Pelosse*, Paris 1975, and Lydia Elhadad et Geneviève Fraisse, 'L'Affranchissement de notre sexe' in *Les Révoltes Logiques*, no. 2, spring/summer 1976.

women but also of their assertions, he sought to present a particular dissidence on the part of the Saint-Simonian women, thus escaping the dilemma between assimilation and exclusion: a dissidence expressed not only in a series of acts of rupture with male power, both within and outside of the Saint-Simonian family, but also in their own contradictions, and by a choice of plurality against the masculine primacy of the One. In this way the basis was established for a relationship between their acts and the present reality of the women's movement – not a natural communion but a multiform relationship, stimulating an interpellation of the present by the past in two privileged directions: one that sought to make present, in its familiar strangeness, the autonomous positivity of the earlier movement, the other investigating the images and discourses by which this had confronted male political society with a view to seeking an echo here and now, along with questions to return to the present movement and its contradictions.

In the very complexity of the initiatives on which it embarked, this critique of a male discourse on women's history seemed to denote a privileged ground on which a positive response could be given to a more general question: that of the contradictions of the resort to history that followed in the wake of the gauchiste adventure and its crises. How could it be that so many initiatives undertaken to exhume buried documents of rebellion led to discourses about mastery? Could these reversals not be explained by an unavowed solidarity: between the feminist man and the tricks that the male symbolic has always been able to use in order to trap women's desire for liberation? Between the leftist intellectual, and the methodical ingeniousness deployed by his male fellows – philanthropists, ministers, master-thinkers – designed to channel popular energies and turn rejections and resistances to their advantage? The situation of intellectual women then appeared as privileged in relation to the divorce between the oppressed and rebels dispossessed of their history and these intellectual well-wishers seeking to restore other people's history.

To start from the other side, and ask what happens to this privilege in the presentation that Lydia Elhadad has now made of the

Souvenirs of Suzanne Voilquin, is not without raising certain problems. Perhaps it too easily suits the atmosphere of a time in which
demands for a reappropriation of women's history confront the
effects of a false recognition that uses on the one hand, in order to
trivialize the movement, the inflation of speech that assures half of
the sky half of the show, and on the other hand enables the nostalgic, in a worn-out trick, to see this 'triviality' as forging the chains
of a new oppressive order. But perhaps this is also the time for a
rearrangement of the stage. That is in any case what one senses
from reading this text: as if a woman's discourse on women's
history, pressing to the limit the effects of reduction that it ascribed
only yesterday to masculine discourse, by that very fact shattered
the divisions between inside and outside across the whole surface
of gauchiste history and historiography. For the same primacy of
mastery for which Lydia Elhadad criticized Valentin Pelosse is
taken to an extreme in her own analysis. The return from the
symbolic to the real that supposedly gives the Saint-Simonian
women back their identity and makes it possible to relate their
movement to the movement of today seems here to extend the
central place of the master's discourse and radicalize the detour
that connects with the lived experience of the Saint-Simonian
women only by a denunciation of the master that is simultaneously
a fascination with him. Even more so perhaps than Valentin
Pelosse, Lydia Elhadad makes analysis of Enfantin's discourse the
centre of her presentation, the discourse of the male master who
uses the myth of the future Woman to oppress women today, 'old
man's' practices (seduced or abandoned women) being its small
change. And where the story of the Saint-Simonian women and
Suzanne Voilquin's Egyptian adventure come to the fore, we
witness another game of mastery: that of the great manoeuvres of
progressive reason marking out popular spaces here and coloniz-
ing them elsewhere. Suzanne Voilquin's singular trajectory
appears far less here in her relationship to a network of women's
practices and words than in the effects of manipulation and recognition induced by this progressive reason. She thus appears in turn
as a victim of men's lies (whether Saint-Simonian or not) and of

the truth game by which Enfantin ensured his power (reference to the Foucauldian theme of confession); as subject in her relationship to Egypt to the rationalist/progressive discourse of colonization; as driven by her very revolt against the suffering caused by male sexual violence to an overdose of respectability that made her exaggerate the hygienist and moral discourse of the colonizer; and as reabsorbed along with her sisters into the 'socialist realism' of 1848, after abandoning in favour of an ethic of women's public service that radicalism of *La Femme Libre* of 1832, about which moreover we still know so little.

In other words, not very sympathetic. It all happens as if what countered a man's always disturbing interest in these militant women was no longer a communication between two women's movements, but rather a certain lack of interest or disaffection. In the commentator's insistence in listing Suzanne Voilquin's progressive naiveties – her enthusiasm for railways and Haussmann's embellishments, her repugnance towards Oriental promiscuity and lasciviousness, her difficulties in finding her way in unmarked streets without house numbers – we get the same impression felt from outside towards the distance or even aggressiveness of the older and more traditionalist discourse of other women towards their Saint-Simonian sisters. Certainly the discourse of a woman such as Jehan d'Ivray, which with her good sense of an up-to-date woman shows the pitiful results of the naive faith of these exalted young people, or that of Edith Thomas, tirelessly indicating the romantic pathos of Pauline Roland's letters, all proceed from a very different ideological standpoint.[3] Yet when we read Lydia Elhadad stressing Suzanne Voilquin's excess rationality, we get the same impression as from discourses that apologize for the madness of people like Pauline Roland or Caroline Carbonnel; the same ambiguous relationship to heroines seen as too foreign to the spirit of today not to be definitely dangerous to the cause that

---

3   Jehan d'Ivray, *L'Aventure saint-simonienne et les femmes*, Paris 1928; Edith Thomas, *Pauline Roland, socialisme et féminisme au XIXe siècle*, Paris 1956.

invokes them; referred back then to their own time, that of romantic folly or technical reason, objects of a sympathy extended more to the victims of oppression who beat the first paths in a difficult age than to the positive character of their motivations and commitments. In this way, this discourse of a woman on the history of women seems to share the general relationship that intellectual historians – professional or amateur – have with acts of popular memory and rebellion. The heroines and anti-heroines of 'popular memory' share the fate of its heroes and anti-heroes; they all say and do too much for what we want to ask: troublesome in their amphigoric style, their moral norms and their projects of universal regeneration; too crazy for some, too reasonable (and we know what reason is involved) for others; always too much. Hence the constant tendency to put them back in their place in a number of ways: the focus of interest on mastery (for good reason), a sympathy for the victims of oppression that has constantly to excuse the rigidity of their moralism or the naivety of their progressivism, their reduction to the formal role of witnesses or symbols of a dissidence that goes beyond their own discourse. The rather unkind way in which Lydia Elhadad puts Suzanne Voilquin in her place – that of a Parisienne raised in the school of master-thinkers – is strikingly clear here. Reducing the proclaimed sisterhood with the Saint-Simonian women, via the paths of gauchiste disenchantment, to the condescension of the historian's objectivity, she shows us that there is no safe position that can assure against the externality of the object, no collective identity that assures against the risk of knowing exactly what we ourselves invest in this object of study or of love.

Of course some heroes and heroines are more likeable than others. We could set against Suzanne's militant over-seriousness, her rational feminism and her interim conjugal morality, the erotic disorder championed by Joséphine-Félicité in *La Femme Libre*, or the theoretical and practical boldness of Claire Démar. But the zeal that the latter showed far less for the collectivity of women than in an attempt to convert the Republican leaders to Saint-Simonianism, going so far as envisaging that it was worth overcoming her physical

repugnance and pay the price of her person for the sake of winning
one of them over – would that not also fall under the same verdict
that Lydia Elhadad passes on Suzanne?

> An activist determination permeated and invaded everything she
> experienced, in a confusion between private and public spaces.
> The measure of this renunciation is given by the primacy accorded
> to a 'general interest' behind which the individual – the woman,
> Suzanne – hid herself.

It is clear here how this judgement is bound up with the present
state of gauchiste reflection and the experiences to which it relates.
But what solidarity does it leave with those women who – whether
crazy or sane – were activists above all, and made the confusion of
public and private stages not the principle of their effacement but
rather that of their assertion, because the only way they could have
a *different* private life was by way of this appearance on the public
stage? How can we not be struck by the nostalgia with which
Suzanne proclaims, on leaving for Russia, the end of her 'apostolic' life? From this point on, her private life would certainly no
longer be repressed by her public life. But she does not seem to
have experienced any particular joy at the prospect. How can
contemporary discourse on the iniquities of 'public service' and of
denouncing the private sphere account for the action of these
women, compelled and resolved – in order to exist at the level of
their dreams – both to make private space a political question, and
to emerge from this space to fulfil a social function? Does not
showing the radicalism of their dissidence in 1848, retrenched to
the position of a 'socialist realism' and an ethic of 'public service'
that was expressed in the organization of labour, educational
projects, midwives' association, etc., amount to artificially isolating their desire for a break from the concern for moral example and
the projects of social intervention in which they had always been
inscribed? Didn't the challenge that Pauline Roland launched to a
sexual morality that wanted every honest woman to have the father
of her children as husband originate in a desire – crudely asserted

– for sexual enjoyment without hindrance along with the exemplary concern for a *new maternity*. Their distance from a male and bourgeois law was not subsequently recuperated, but rather defined from the start by activist projects of social transformation, in which they saw themselves as mothers, midwives, educators of the human future. And this is indeed what the desire to appropriate their struggle today finds awkward: in the educational projects of Jeanne Deroin in France or Clorinde Rogé in the East, in Suzanne Voilquin's medical and health projects, in the interest that some had in colonization and the advance of indigenous women and others in the rehabilitation of prostitutes or delinquent children, we have learned (or imagine we have learned) to recognize the extension of state surveillance and philanthropic control. Once the demand for female suffrage and the right to work has already been dismissed as illusion, what claims can still be made out of the historic aspirations and struggles of women except in the mode of a principled sympathy with the oppressed? We can better see the fragility of the privilege that these autonomous discourses born in reaction to gauchiste centralism seem to enjoy: scarcely emancipated from the intimidation of Marxism's 'main fronts' and 'objective complicities', they find themselves in a strange relation of companionship with the other great historic discourse that emerged from the shattering of this centralism: that which sought to conduct, in the genealogy of forms of social control binding individuals and micro-powers to the state order, a critique of activist reason; a discourse that recognized the specificity of women's history, but essentially still occupied the sites where this private and activist history encountered the other, more or less imposing the models in which this encounter could be conceived, to reach a point at which women appear as auxiliaries in the domestication of workers, and activist women (and men) as precursors or agents of the state's hold over individuals.[4] We end up perhaps with an effect

---

4   In particular, J. Donzelot, *La Police des familles*, Paris 1977, and D. Rancière, 'Le philanthrope et sa famille', in no. 8/9 of *Les Révoltes logiques*.

of intimidation all the more insidious for being well-disposed, recognizing the form of autonomous histories only in order to deny their contents and offer in exchange for these autonomies without content the exemplary character of their dissidence.

These past revolts that connect with the hopes of the present thus tend to be reduced to a set of formal characteristics, illustrating and authenticating the general discourse of dissidence. Lydia Elhadad, in this way, defines the dissidence of the Saint-Simonian women in terms of a set of formal characteristics that abstract from the activist experience: the choice of women, especially proletarian women, to meet together, the pluralism of women as opposed to masculine centralism, the decision to sign with their forenames, the 'bundle of writings' that make up the *Apostolat des Femmes*. This characterization of dissidence means first of all cutting some awkward corners. A certain number of texts published by *La Femme Libre* hardly seem to be the work of proletarian women; and even those that are do not come from so low on the social scale as Lydia Elhadad suggests. Désirée Véret, for example, was not a common linen maid but belonged to the aristocracy of milliners. And in the diverse bundle of writings that Lydia Elhadad seeks to oppose to the great masculine symphony (however full in these years with the cacophony of the inventors of a thousand new religions, revolutionary methods of education, definitive solutions to the social question, etc.), a dominant voice is soon apparent. *La Tribune des Femmes*, rather than a mosaic of writings from women's experience, appears as the paper of Suzanne, her protégés, protectors and correspondents. But above all, these writings convey positive contents: projects of workers' association, interventions at the Société des Méthodes d'Enseignement, projects for a court of love, literary articles. Reducing this multiplicity to its own demonstration, deemed to relate to an irrepressible feminine exuberance, threatens to introduce a certain solidarity with the male discourse of free speech ('Let those women speak, if they have to . . .'). It is true that they signed their writings with their forenames. But this signature still involves a relationship with the male world that is somewhat more complicated than just a liberation from paternal or conjugal tutelage. Jeanne-Désirée instead of Désirée Véret, Marie-Reine instead of Reine Guindorff – as if father Véret and father Guindorff were not responsible for their daughters bearing such names, calling them by forenames that are rather freighted with connotations? And should we not admire the fact that both crazy Désirée and well-behaved Reine chose to add to a forename marked by paternal desire the name of a redeeming virgin: Jeanne for the Maid of Orleans, Marie for the Saviour's mother? The signature of their dissidence is at the same time that of their commitment to the service of a humanity in need of regeneration.

Their relationship as women among women, then, was only a moment or means in their intervention in the world of men. And it would reduce their lived experience and the project to which it gave rise if this is severed from that love of the other that is always present: the father-lover of Suzanne, Désirée and many others, the man of science (Fourier) to whom Désirée confided her fickle erotic adventures, certain that he would be able to make use of these in founding a phalanstery in which it would be good to live. The supposed distinction between the world of mastery and manipulation on the one hand, the world of a dissidence conceived as separatist on the other, makes it impossible to explore the positive character of that love of the other which – as perhaps in so many other discourses and practices of autonomy – continually inspired the desire to act for oneself. Can we say nothing else about the love which fixed itself on the person and symbol of Enfantin than reducing it to the manipulation of a master? Why should we refuse to see the positive investments made on the other side in this love, in which the relationship of gains and losses was neither so simple nor so one-sided? How can we explain that those worst treated – women and proletarians – were often far more nostalgic than the intellectual leaders from those fine days of 1831 that Sophie Béranger, at that time a young girl in the rue Monsigny, evoked some thirty years, when reduced to the private life of an abandoned woman, mother of an abnormal child and employed for 50 francs a month at the Docks de Lyon:

> What could I tell you that you do not already know? That I love
> you. That is a sickness which took hold of me a long time ago and
> which I do not desire to be cured of . . . the only time in all my life
> that I would like to begin again is that spent in rue Monsigny and
> at Ménilmontant . . .[5]

To investigate the pleasure of a sickness that has nothing in common
with the jouissance of servitude certainly risks ending up reintroduc-
ing a male point of view that excuses Père Enfantin's power in taking
advantage of these proletarian lovers. But to refuse to take it into
account also leads to a vision of women's autonomy that reproduces
an old male point of view: the valorization of 'women among
women' as a birdcage of fleeting fantasies, complicit words, the
unpredictable trajectories of bewitched bodies: an autonomy of
women cosy among themselves, talking, dancing, imagining in the
reclusion of a private space that is suddenly revealed to the voyeur's
gaze. Don't we see this reversal in Lydia Elhadad's text when, having
shared a feminist woman's indignation at the harem dreams of the
'old man' Enfantin and his dallying with Bedouin and Abyssinian
women, she places on Suzanne Voilquin's head the cap of the
Leninist cadre horrified by the debauchery of Oriental bodies:
'bodies bent under effort, bodies naked in the baths, bodies in trance
possessed by the devil, the "lascivious" dances of the *almahs*, the
ecstasy of hashish, etc.', and criticizes her for not understanding

> this reversal of an oppression: if women laugh and chat in their
> places of sequestration like Westerners at the theatre, it is perhaps
> because they also live these as spaces where they find themselves
> among other women, relieved of the male presence.

The conviviality of the harem, the fascination of bent bodies and
Oriental sweat that was at the same time the terror of Suzanne and
the provincial reveries of the young Flaubert and his friends, is
revisited by the contemporary discourse of this new philosophy

---

5   Letter to Enfantin, 23 December 1860.

that assures us that all is well in the sites of oppression, as long as the circulation of certain libidinal flows is allowed free from the jouissance of the master. Perhaps this double image of the harem shows us the point at which the specific study of a women's dissidence reintroduces, in the name of a general discourse on dissidence, the philosophy of the 'old man' against which it set out on the quest for its forgotten sisters, reduced now to being recognized only in the limits and guidelines of the new intellectual discourse on dissidence – mixed, if not just male.

No doubt the exemplary character of this reversal, coinciding as it does with the fate of so much discourse and practice that have seen their assertion of difference lost in an undifferentiated dissident mode, will satisfy those dialectics with an interest in showing the blind alley of a discourse that forgets major priorities and is caught in the trap of its particularity. But the present remarks have a different motivation: the sense that the Saint-Simonian women, by their obstinacy in seeking in the East their path for the West, from the barricades to the classroom, from provocations in private life to the disciplines of collective action, from the paths of their difference to those of their participation, have something else to tell us, something that rightly undermines not only the edifying discourse of recognition but also that dialectic of identifications and misunderstanding that characterizes today's genealogies as much as it did the Marxist classics. Perhaps they actually interest us less by what brings them close to us than by what renders them foreign, far indeed from the frameworks of thought in which we move with either satisfaction or unease: the moralism without compulsion or affectation in which their acts and perceptions were defined; their lack of sensitivity, through attempts and failures, to the crises that periodically overturn the recognized codes of subversion; the irreducibility of their projects to the priorities that press us to know whether they started off as socialists or feminists, to the divisions that induce us to see them as either victims or accomplices; the singularity of these identities whose constancy can never be enclosed in a single identification. It is all very well today to erect statues of Fourier, but his category of ambiguity is still little honoured.

6

The Links of the Chain:
Proletarians and Dictatorships

The workers' movement should not be a satellite turning in the orbit of the government's star, but a nebula inspired by its own movement.

— Verdier, in *La Vie Ouvrière*, 24 September 1919

Thanks to the French Communist Party, the proletarians have now been absolved of the promise or burden of their promised dictatorship.[1] Some may rejoice to see this dictatorship of the proletariat finally buried, after it had become such a weight to carry, and are ready to use to this end arguments that are in themselves rather lightweight – simply quoting, in order to evacuate a concept whose 'scientific' status they emphasized for so long, that 'dictatorship is reminiscent of Chile'. Others wax indignant, or even maintain that this is simply the latest in a long series of 'betrayals' of which the 'revisionist' leaders are guilty. It is possibly more interesting to ask what exactly such treason and revision mean. We are reminded of this by a long-forgotten text from a time when the dictatorship of the proletariat was most acutely topical, when war had put on the agenda, as the scientific organization of labour was also about to do, the integration of the workers' movement into a productive and statist order, susceptible of transcending the very opposition between workers' power and capitalist power. The above quote from Verdier gives us a glimpse

---

1   This is a reference to the PCF's abandonment of the concept of the 'dictatorship of the proletariat' at its 22nd Congress in 1976. [Tr.]

of this; when we speak of 'movement' and 'revolution' this always appeals to a certain kind of astronomy, where the point is to know exactly what is turning under the name of movement, and around what pole it makes its revolution. It is this 'astronomy' and these transformations that first demand our attention. And it is these that we must try to see at work at the time that the Communist Party was founded, precisely for the sake of the dictatorship that it rejects today – also the time, at the end of the First World War and in the wake of the Soviet revolution, that the workers' movement confronted new forms of development of the 'productive forces': the scientific organization of labour and the political organization of class collaboration.

Reinscribed in this time, the question of the dictatorship of the proletariat may initially seem merely one of form: the thesis of dictatorship simply expounds a self-evident situation that more than one anarchist could subscribe to without anxiety in the aftermath of October: the workers' revolution could not limit itself by any law in its task of repressing the class enemy (the difficulty rather arose at the next step, when the question was to identify the said enemy). Commitment to the illegality of dicta-torship, as an extension of the illegality of struggle, was in this sense no more than the consequence of commitment to the legiti-macy of workers' power.[2] And the question 'do we have to maintain the dictatorship as a means for defending workers' power?' was reduced to one of knowing what kind of 'workers' power' was desirable, in what circumstance of class struggle, for the working class; or more precisely for the hegemonic fraction of this class, the fraction that predominantly ensured the repre-sentation of the interests and ideals of the workers in the instances of civil and political society. For the 'betrayal' of the workers' revolutionary ideals cannot be equated with the betrayal of the revolutionary masses by the labour aristocracy. It is certainly possible to say that today's 'Communist' policy represents the

2   This threat of the 'new barbarian' was already the theme of a sensational article in the *Journal des Débats* in the wake of the 1831 insurrection.

interests of a new apparatus bourgeoisie, recruited from the labour aristocracy. But this only pushes the problem back. For the formation of a 'working-class bourgeoisie' is itself a function of the integration of the working class into the industrial state, and the forms of organization and ideals of the proletariat – both revolutionary and reformist – have *always* up till now been defined by a hegemonic fraction of the working class, recruited in its majority from this 'aristocracy'. The supposedly pure and hard party with its 'class against class' line had no more of a base among the assembly-line slaves than does the revisionist party of today. And it was within the technical aristocracy of trades, as opposed to the industrial plebs, that the cultural aristocracy of the revolutionary unions was formed. It is always within the labour aristocracy that a hegemonic fraction is formed, presenting itself as *the* proletariat and asserting the proletarian ability to organize a different social order, on the basis of the skills and values formed in its work and its struggle.

It is very clearly the question of this ability that is in play behind the problem of dictatorship, which initially appears as simply one of form. Behind the public debate there is the question: where do we stand with the old dream of workers' emancipation on which the theories and policies of revolution were founded; the dream of the abolition of wage-labour as the goal and the organization of workers' autonomy as the means, a dream founded on the ideal of free producers able to build a new world with their hands and their intelligence? What transformations within this fundamental aim of the workers' avant-garde could make the dictatorship of the proletariat desirable or undesirable? As a function of what relationships to the mass of the workers, the organization of labour and the apparatuses of the state? A function of what strategies from above and what rejoinders from below?

The triumph of the wage system

Money started to flow even more readily than blood.
                              – Charles Tillon, *La Révolte vient de loin*

How should we act so as to give the movements that will inevitably be unleashed here and there, despite your intentions, that character of strength and nobility, that beauty of conscience in revolt, the revolt of men finally rising up against the deadly reaper of men and midwife of misery and grief?

How should we coordinate these movements, and wipe out these words that demean our wartime unionism: 'Wages! Wages! Wages! Pay! I'll hew coal. Pay! I'll turn shells. Pay! I'll make guns and rifles. Pay! I'll give you my sweat, my labour, my blood, my life. For ten, fifteen or twenty francs I'll hand over my conscience, I'll abdicate my rights, my duties, I'll betray my class.'
                              – Péricat, letter of 2 February 1918

The debates of railwaymen and engineers in the 1920s took place at a time when all these questions came together, when the old ideal of a producers' revolution, threatened with getting lost in the network of new ties that bound the worker into the order of capitalist production and the bourgeois state, encountered the new ideal of the dictatorship of the proletariat. It was the double assault of the war and reconstruction industries that shattered the ideal of syndicalist revolution, not only in its representations (pacifist illusions) but in its very foundation: the freedom of the producers based both on the skill of their labour and on their power *not to produce*, to know no 'general interest' higher than that of the producers. The war industry replaced this freedom of producers who were both indispensable and irresponsible with the servitude of militarized and deskilled work. The great threat that the engineering aristocracy rose up against before the war ('Intelligence is expelled from the workshops and factories. They only want hands without brains and automatons of flesh, adapted to the automatons of iron and steel'[3]), now took on the guise of an irreversible compulsion: Taylorism was established in the engineering workshop, along with female labour. Women were now taken on not simply to replace men but to enchain their future: 'We have struggled enough against piecework and the Taylor system not to introduce it through the back door with women in industry.'[4] The worker mobilized in the rear, however, found himself doubly spurred to produce: by the constant threat of being sent to the front and by the guilt of supposed 'shirking' ('We have to produce, to do all that we can to send the greatest quantity of munitions to our brothers at the front').[5] The reward for this overwork, in the form of (relatively) high wages, brought a reversal in the ethics of the producers. The old ethic said 'Regulate your production by the wage you are paid', and even refused to consider armaments as industrial products.[6] The new slogan would be 'Demand wages corresponding to your production'. In the militarized factory, the bourgeoisie sought to realize its old dream: to produce the worker as over-producer and consumer, chained at both ends of capitalist production. This attempt met with a certain resistance: strikes by women workers, the movement of spring 1918, sabotage and go-slows (in

3　Merrheim, *La Vie Ouvrière*, 5 March 1913.

4　E. Cassin, 'Les Femmes dans l'industrie', *L'Union des Métaux*, September 1916. Cf. Merrheim: 'A factory that I am familiar with, with 20 workers (12 women and 8 Spaniards), displayed the following result: the women initially made 350 hand-grenades a day and were paid 8 francs; the boss paid a bonus of 50 centimes per 100 and the next day they made 700 grenades. The boss then reduced the daily wage to 7 francs but increased the bonus by 25 centimes; the following day they made 1,200 grenades. The boss then reduced the wage by a further 50 centimes, but raised the bonus to 1 franc, and they made 1,700 grenades. The boss then set the daily wage at 5.25 francs and the bonus at 50 centimes. This led to a strike and the workers were sacked. They were replaced by others who worked themselves to death.' Merrheim's talk to the Union des Ouvriers Mécaniciens de la Seine, 26 November 1916 (Archives Nationales, F[7] 13366).

5　As reported in *L'Union des Métaux*, August 1916.

6　Report by the engineering workers at the Exposition Universelle of 1867. See above, p. 73.

particular at the Établissements Militaires in Bourges, where after twelve days' training, two police inspectors reached a level of productivity higher than the regular staff).[7] One theme, however, now haunted even those whose job it was to look out for any signs of resistance to militarized production, the minority trade-union leaders who took a stand against the *union sacrée*: a degeneration of the workers, being simultaneously dispossessed both of individual control of their work and of their collective ideal, a tendency determined *within the struggle itself* by the strategy of the war machine, by the programming it enforced of the use and needs of labour-power. The women workers who struck at the moment when capital could no longer draw anything more from their labour-power and had an interest in replacing it; male workers' bodies bent by overproduction who rebelled in order to demonstrate the increase needed in the reproduction costs of labour-power, tensions of revolt in cadence with the tensions of production. The trade-union elite's obsessive image at the end of the war was that of the worker reduced to a *belly*. Corresponding to this degeneration, it is true, was a new promotion of working-class *brains*: in the representative bodies with equal workers' membership where the Socialist minister of munitions, Albert Thomas, made the union general staff partners with the employers for the greater good of national defence and social peace. It was this double chain of working-class integration, this double servitude of workers' bellies and workers' brains which had respectively become indicators and social partners, that was denounced in 1918 by one of the minority leaders, Georges Dumoulin:

---

7   'On 20 November 1916 two auxiliary police inspectors, Monsieurs Vic and Guilley, the former a bailiff for the justice of the peace and the second representing business, were placed in the "Petits Ateliers" to operate milling machines, with the objective of facilitating their secret surveillance of the workers.' By 2 December, their average output was 30 per cent higher than that of the best of the regular workers.' Report of special commissioner Blanc to the Direction de la Sûrété Générale, January 1917 (AN, F[7] 13376).

The idea is to bind trade unionism to capitalism, to make us part of economic imperialism. In this way our working-class imperialism would amount to industrial barbarism: a tremendous production in order to increase consumption. Taylorized hands and Germanized bellies. Our class thinking and instincts are in danger. I recall the remark of Dr Nicolaï long ago: in order for the Romanians, an aristocratic people, to attain knowledge and moral superiority, they had to have other people work for them as slaves. Let us beware of modern slavery. In a world such as ours, working-class imperialism duplicates the imperialism of individuals, and it would be triplicated by the imperialism of insatiable consumers. Using accidental pretexts, the class struggle is demolished. In the trenches we met up with the bosses, in the factories we 'worked' with the rich, with lawyers and bankers. Exhausted trade unionists took charge of the factory and workers' partnerships flourished on the scrap iron. The number of intermediate occupations, the size of the buffer class, the peasantry and small-scale industry opened perspectives of class understanding. Let us not accept this deformation, this deviation. For us, the class that we combat is not represented by the modest baker who kneads the dough in his cellar with his two assistants; it is the regime that we combat, the capitalist organization as the product of a class, a social state that reduces labour to slavery in order to lead it to barbarism by way of war. This is what we must not allow trade unionism to be harnessed to. This class regime has not changed or modified anything, it is based as it has ever been on the same forces of authority and domination. The state, the church, the army, prisons, continue to form its pillars of error and constraint. Let us reject it and not let ourselves be attached to its chain by gilded links. This chain is prepared: profit-sharing, membership of employers' boards, mixed associations for industrial study, lectures, courses, occupational schools, etc. Once enchained, the best of our number abdicate to it their thoughts and our ideal. Friends of the minority, let us tear ourselves away from this embrace and let the others embark on cohabitation. On this new road to Damascus, they will meet

Samuel Gompers, Karl Legien and Ben Tillett,[8] in the company of businessmen of the international bourgeoisie. We shall approach the workers of all countries with a view to re-establishing the workers' International.[9]

A prophetic text for the future of 'socialism', which however left one thing unforeseen: the swift rallying of its own author to the new order, of which he would become one of the architects – while awaiting something better.

Socialism with French colours

If working-class nationalism is victorious in this country, it is clear that the various measures designed to harness the working class to the capitalist class will find their application.
— Georges Dumoulin, *Ce qu'il faut dire*, 16 June 1917

When we add that the railways must be administered by both producers and consumers, are we asserting a position of class collaboration or one of general interest?
— Léon Jouhaux, secretary-general of the CGT, April 1920

It is already established that the CGT has done nothing that could obstruct the development of our industry, or inflict a sacrifice on the employing class, but that in trade-union circles the establishment of the eight-hour day was viewed as indispensable for spurring on the activity of the industrial world's leaders, who, if this was not forced on them, would not concern themselves vigorously enough with modernizing equipment, a preliminary condition for national renaissance.
— Report of a speech by Laurent, deputy secretary of the CGT, to the Comité National d'Études Sociales et Politiques, 7 April 1919

8   American, German and British trade-union leaders.
9   *Les Syndicalistes français et la guerre*, June 1918.

Once the war was ended, its 'conquests' would be consolidated: the practices of the *union sacrée* were codified in the great idea of workers' participation in national reconstruction, as expressed in the programme of the CGT: maximum production with maximum wages in minimum time (clear recognition of the benefits of intensification of labour); nationalization of key industries; workers' participation in a Conseil Économique and the necessary work of planning; the expected formation of an 'economic council of labour' where the working class would educate itself alongside economists, engineers and technicians who were more skilled than it was, and *therefore* that much more free from bourgeois ideology;[10] in brief, subordination of 'egoistic' and 'corporative' interests to the *collective interest*. The whole thinking of the modern and 'responsible' workers' movement was formed at this time: from the 'scientific and technological revolution' to the 'collectivization of the leading means of production' and 'democratic planning'. But we should not be mistaken: it was still a revolutionary aim that the majority of the CGT maintained in calling on the workers to produce and to go and sit alongside representatives of the state and the employers. The intention in this was to create two conditions for revolution: economic abundance, and the education of a working class that would no longer, when the time came, simply have to substitute for bourgeois institutions symmetrical workers' organizations, forged in the 'collaboration' that was the new path of class struggle. This was how at the end of the war the anarcho-syndicalists caught up in the state apparatus formed the basis of a contemporary 'communism': the workers' movement integrated into the industrial state, thus drawing the pattern for all future 'common programmes': common, we may understand, to the proletariat and the bourgeoisie. This was also how the minister of trade, Clémentel, understood it in an address to industrialists with a vigour matched by appropriate delicacy towards the stubborn

---

10 'We recognize all the same that the education the technicians have received is a more general one, and consequently less bourgeois in the strict sense of the term than the education we received in primary school' – Jouhaux, secretary-general of the CGT, April 1920.

dreams of workers' emancipation. For in the new social order the class struggle, though denied in theory, had still to be given its due, in the readjustment of reciprocal interests and in the imaginary of revolution:

> To the sterile notion of class struggle, a notion 'made in Germany' moreover, we have to substitute the notion of classes collaborating in the common interest. The employers are ready, I am sure, to practise this collaboration, which is indeed a French tradition. On the workers' side you will also find, I can assure you, new dispositions . . . They do not abandon, and you must not ask them to abandon, their theoretical ideas, their dreams of a new social future. You will place yourselves with them on the firm ground of reality, and record as we do the fact that they have ceased to be hostile to machinery and time-saving. You will note, as we do, that their leaders have declared themselves to be concerned above all with increasing production. Economic reorganization, they declare, must be founded on the constant development of national equipment, and aimed at stimulating private initiatives by removing any excuse and any tranquillity for sterile and deadly routine. They have substituted restrictive formulas with a new formula, that of fertile labour, which is both intensive and rewards the maximum production in minimum time with the maximum possible wage and the minimum possible fatigue. What industrialist, with his mind open to our country's future needs, would not subscribe to this programme?
>
> – Speech by Monsieur Clémentel, trade minister, at the installation of Monsieur Ribes-Christophe in the presidency of the Paris chamber of commerce. *Information Ouvrière*, 8 December 1918

Revolution through collaboration

> . . . those who discovered during the war that the collaboration of classes was something useful for revolutionary ends
>
> – Sirolle, CGT congress in Lyon, September 1919

We must reject production and make revolution.

— Griffuelhes, *La Vie Ouvrière*, 13 February 1919

The dictatorship of the proletariat which we speak so much about is dominated by the dictatorship of the country's general economic interests, whose needs have to be met by using the skills and bodies able to cooperate and bring about this result: to produce, for without production we have misery, and through misery a country's demise.

— Merrheim, *La Révolution économique*

How the revolutionary force borne from the rejection of this 'class struggle' of a new type was able to produce a party destined at the end of its trajectory to occupy the same place is a story whose stages we shall not trace here. Only the first steps of this convergence will be indicated, as these were traced by the minority syndicalists: above all those who rallied at the end of the war to the nationalist-productivist order that they had spent the whole conflict denouncing. This rallying of the Merrheims and Dumoulins was in no way a reversal of theory: it proceeded with implacable logic from the principle that they maintained against the *union sacrée*, and on which their adversaries who held to the minority line entirely agreed: the revolution, the ideal of the working-class elite, could not be achieved under the dependence of mass appetites as these had been determined by bourgeois domination. And if the war had corrupted the ambushed workers, bought over by high wages to contribute to its barbarism, the conclusion must be drawn that these were unworthy of making revolution. It was precisely those mobilized in the rear, the engineers and railwaymen, who led the corporative movement between 1918 and 1920.

The minoritarians who took the lead in this movement, and particularly in the rail strike, always emphasized the opposition between the interests of 'bellies' and the revolutionary ideal, but they used the example of the Russian revolution to develop the germ of *idealism* that these movements none the less contained. Sirolle, for example, was ready to make use of 'egoism', and ratcheted up wage demands in order to lead the 'flabby' masses at a meeting where he could make them ashamed of their egoism and speak to them of revolution. A crazy tactic, said Merrheim, for those who would tomorrow have to lead the revolution:

> How could I have heard, at the time of the Paris strikes, at a meeting where I tried to tell the truth to the mass of workers who had been whipped up against me, how could I have heard: 'What, you've already signed up to eight hours of actual work! We don't want to work more than four hours a day!' I say that a state of mind like this condemns us to impotence in our revolutionary action tomorrow, understand me well, and I do not want to find myself impotent tomorrow in this situation, in the face of working masses who do not want to work more than four hours a day.[11]

What we have here is more than the prudence of a future revolutionary leader, it is the sense of the end of a dream: 'Today, indeed, everyone wants money; as for the ideal of liberation – don't deny that they no longer understand or want it'.[12] Even if the aim was to 'rescue the French working class for revolution, from the immorality into which we along with socialism and our ideal have fallen today',[13] its dignity had to be restored by recalling its *responsibility* towards the *collective*, its duty which was to produce and learn to manage for tomorrow:

> Courage means saying and repeating to the masses that each individual is at the same time both consumer and producer, and that the continual development of production is necessary and indispensable . . . Courage means proclaiming out loud that a purely political revolution, such as haunts the minds of the masses, could not resolve the social problem that the war has precipitated, and on which it has imposed its own solution.

---

11 Merrheim, *Congrès de Lyon*, p. 185.
12 Ibid., p. 187.
13 Ibid., p. 183.

> Courage means tirelessly telling them that the revolution that is
> to be made, that has to be made, is the economic revolution, and
> that this is not made in the street, by a delirious and unrestrained
> crowd, destroying for the sheer pleasure and delight of wasting
> and destroying. Telling them that in reality an economic revolu-
> tion draws its sap from labour, and is strengthened, developed
> and achieved by intensified production in both the fields and the
> workshops and factories, through a better application of scien-
> tific procedures and means of production.[14]

This reversal was the culmination of the effects of the war machine.
This did not just discipline bodies to the order of overproduction;
it also produced, in the thinking of the working-class avant-garde,
a prodigious interpretative mechanism that made it possible to see
the workers' efforts to break the chain of overproduction and class
collaboration as the actual manifestation of their enchainment. In
this way, those who were the first to denounce the chain actually
contributed to tightening it, by proposing as antidotes to the egoistic overproduction and collaboration of destructive industry,
overproduction and class collaboration in the service of the 'collective interest' and industrial reconstruction.

Faced with this paradoxical consolidation of working-class nationalism, the trade unionists who remained loyal to the minority line
opposed the Soviet revolution. At this point, however, Merrheim
did not find it hard to go into reverse gear: it was he who, opposing
the school of the factory to the anarchy of the belly, was loyal to
the spirit of the Leninist revolution. For the novelty of this revolution did not lie in its insurrectionary model (political revolution)
but rather in its organization of production (economic revolution):
the organization of soviets whose base was simply 'an association
to defend the political interests of the country, in other words the
general interests of the collective',[15] of economic sections 'working

---

14   Merrheim, *La Révolution économique*, Paris 1919, pp. 5–6.
15   Ibid., p. 20.

in parallel with the occupational trade unions and employers' institutions',[16] of a 'Conseil Supérieur de l'Économie' which Merrheim saw as expressing the CGT's project of a 'national economic council', working together with technicians, 'raising the degree of discipline of the workers, of their skill, speed, intensity of labour and better organization'.[17] The Bolsheviks' merit was to have been able to redress a situation in which

> the workers had chased out of the workshops and factories those who formed the technical managerial section, i.e. the engineers and managers, and found themselves unable to make the factories oper- ate because they did not have the required technical capacities.[18]

At all events, they were able to impose the discipline of production on workers who imagined that 'taking over a store and stripping it was the solution to the social question'.[19] Lenin's theses of 1918 – the necessity of a strategic withdrawal, capitalist participation, appeal to technicians, dictatorship of production and the benefits of Taylorism – authorized the CGT theorist to present his programme as a reversal of the stages of Soviet power: rather than turn back after seizing power to create the rise in production necessary for socialism, assuring instead the development of production in the present context of collaboration and confrontation with the bour- geoisie, and the apprenticeship in management that would make it possible to construct socialism. In Paris as in Moscow, the rescue of socialism meant learning to manage capitalism. Perhaps this was because in both countries the counter-revolution took a new form: that of the forces of anti-production, the 'backward' and hungry masses, greedy to consume but miserly of placing their labour- power in the service of the collective – workers' egoism in one case, peasant barbarism in the other, as in Béla Kun's Hungary where this threatened to strangle the revolution of the proletarian

16 Ibid.
17 Lenin, 'Economic Problems of Soviet Power', cited by Merrheim, p. 23.
18 Merrheim, *La Révolution économique*, p. 15.
19 Ibid., p. 17.

elite. The old image of the anarchic capitalist, wasteful and destructive, was now reversed: as if the masses, having internalized the whole negativity of capitalism, could be bought over by its positive virtues. Beyond the strategic justification of stages, preparations or withdrawals, this involved a complete reconversion of the old ideal. The former ideology of labour versus capital, of the autonomy of the producers, which had authorized Marx's discourse – even in his critical distance from it – was destroyed at the very moment that the era of twentieth-century revolutions was opening. A definitive breach was effected at the very moment when both the revolutionary leaders in Moscow and the trade-union 'traitors' in Paris defined the same *transitional* stage: revolution through class collaboration, and the same *provisional* moral, identifying the workers' proletarian virtue in terms of their responsibility towards the development of the productive forces of their capitalism: either capitalism or barbarism.

Dictatorship for what?

State socialism is the most oppressive machine for the people subjected to it.

– *Manifeste communiste*[20]

We see Bolshevism, as far as we are able to judge it, as a state socialism . . .

– F. Mayoux, *L'Internationale*, 14 June 1919

We are not in the presence of a revolution of morality, but rather one of needs and instincts, which is far more serious and harder to resolve.

– Monmousseau, *La Vie Ouvrière*, 31 March 1922

---

20   This was the manifesto of an ephemeral 'Parti communiste' founded at the end of the First World War, two years before the PCF came into existence. Its paper was *L'Internationale*. [Tr.]

Gilded chains of working-class imperialism, iron chains of Soviet poverty; corruption of abundance and corruption of destitution. The revolutionaries of the CGT minority had no strategy for breaking this chain, but at best a tactical instinct: use solidarity with the besieged Russian revolution to transform corporate struggles into revolutionary ones. The railwaymen's movement was the key example of this. A movement 'off the rails' in the sense that it led nowhere, trapped in this same dilemma about the objective and subjective conditions for revolution. For if they initially recognized in Soviet Russia the old trade-union dream of producers' democracy as against the lies of political democracy, the minority faction were soon confronted by the *atypical* nature of the Russian Revolution. This contradicted the classical image of revolution, based on the concomitant rise of both production and revolutionary consciousness. A 'revolution against *Capital*', Gramsci was to call it. The French revolutionary syndicalists, lacking such literary skill, expressed themselves differently:

> It is clear that the dictatorship exercised by the party implies the centralization of powers as well as of the country's resources with a view to an equitable distribution, since we are forced to recognize that despite Karl Marx's assertion, the proletarian revolution will be above all the action of poverty.[21]

The 'dictatorship of the proletariat' is accepted as a response to this unforeseen situation. It was ultimately Marx's mistake that justified Lenin's position. The purist could doubtless reply that this is a very hasty summary, and that Marx himself upheld such a dictatorship. But it is easy to see how in his case this position was based on a double belief that was now in question: in the revolutionary effects of the contradiction between productive forces and relations of production, and in the capacity of the masses, educated in

---

21 Cotinsouzas, *La Vie Ouvrière*, 4 March 1921. (This was an intervention in a discussion panel on the question of whether the revolutionary unions should join the new Communist Party.)

the conflicts born of this contradiction, to produce a new world – the point at which Marx's dialectical vision linked up with the moral vision of revolutionary syndicalism. 'Backward' and hungry Russia now imposed a new image that would strengthen the sense of a degeneration of the working-class ideal: the revolution was now borne forward not by the capacity of the working masses to manage society, but simply by their inability to subsist. And if revolution was the work of hunger – and not of idealism – this meant that the masses came onto the stage initially under the aspect of bellies to feed – a situation that founds the necessity of dictator-ship and makes this a *party* matter. For the syndicalists of the CGT minority, the greater part of whom rallied to the dictatorship of the proletariat and the Red Trade Union International, were in no way fooled by the reassuring idea that the dictatorship of the proletariat would be the 'dictatorship of the majority', that it would not be a dictatorship 'over the proletariat'. Just like the Bolsheviks on the one hand and the reformists on the other, they were persuaded that those who upheld the revolutionary ideal had to rule over egoistic bellies, and the Russian revolution above all demonstrated the impotence of syndicalism to respond to the tasks of this revolution of needs. This is why in 1922, the railwaymen's leader Monmousseau, who was to bring the newly founded CGTU into the Red Trade Union International, saw Marx's 'mistake' contin-ued in the camp of his new opponents: the pure syndicalists, i.e. the last grouping of those who refused to tie working-class emancipa-tion to the action of state power:

> This is a very clear return of our syndicalism to the conception that, assuming a revolution born in the midst of economic upsurge and development of revolutionary consciousness in the working masses, sees it as crossing all stages at one stroke, abolishing state and government in whatever form, even proletarian and provisional.[22]

---

22   Monmousseau, *La Vie Ouvrière*, 31 March 1922.

Still the same dilemma, both absurd and insoluble: in order for the revolution to advance as dreamed, there would have to be at the same time both an abundance of production and a revolutionizing of the masses. And it is always the same sense of *degeneration* that governs the analysis: the material and moral ability of the producer supported the ideal that sought the least state possible, whereas the new science of good proletarian government was based on the recognized dual incapability of the masses and the union. The latter, for its part, was directly faced with this contradiction. It might well intend not to be a power, to be only the *natural* organization of the workers, but both its reality and its practice gave the lie to these premises. In reality it was an 'affinity group' for the elite of rebelling workers rather than the organized expression of the proletariat; and in the practice of struggle, as Monmosseau recalled at length to the anarchists of 'pure syndicalism', it would not fail to exercise its dictatorship over the masses, forcing the consent of the hesitant, silencing discordant voices and awkward facts: the effective role of vanguard that it performed only by contradicting its concept. But if it had conformed to this concept it would have been only an interest group with no power of revolutionary social transformation. Here the union encounters a contradiction between its *working-class* legitimacy and its *revolutionary* legitimacy. If the revolutionary syndicalists who turned towards Moscow could remain indifferent to the fate of the 'trade-union party' in Russia, and not hear its leader Shlyapnikov ironically congratulate the Bolsheviks on governing 'in the name of a class that no longer exists', this was because they were caught in the same contradiction between their concept and their reality, revolutionary only as an affinity group with no power to lead a revolution once this was no longer that of the ideal but rather one of needs.

The same Monmousseau who maintained in 1919 that 'the dictatorship of the proletariat cannot be crystallized in the statutes of a party, whatever this may be, without constituting a danger by that very fact',[23] in 1922 took the measure of this transformation in a series of articles precisely on the proletarian dictatorship:

---

23 *La Vie Ouvrière*, 31 August 1919.

The Revolution as it appears to us is no longer this pretty girl offering her charms to the worker and the bourgeois, suddenly reconciled, after 48 hours of riots and some eloquent speeches at the Place de la Nation. It now has an uglier face: no longer the girl of the pure idea but the daughter of famine, and this changes the look of things.

We need only lean over a bit to hear the people's instincts rumble, in the mineshafts, on construction sites, on the railways and in the factories, to see the crowd pushed to revolt by hunger and impatience, overthrowing by a supreme effort the artisans of its famine who have long been appointed to it by the elite that speaks in its name.

It is enough to extend to the major social facts the experience that we readily have of small everyday ones, it is enough to take stock of how popular self-consciousness represents the crowd left to its own devices, rushing towards destruction and capable of everything good and everything bad.

For the crowd is capable, in order to prevent war, of getting itself trampled over by Lépine's cops on 30 July 1914, and the next day rushing in an assault wave to the trenches of democracy, after pillaging the 'Maggi' stores.

And yet it is the crowd that makes revolutions, unless these revolutions are mere coups d'état.

In order to speculate on its degree of consciousness, on the continuity of its initiatives and its intelligent efforts, in order to build with it and right away a revolution without a governing principle and without even a provisional power, do we deem this crowd so much changed in the last eight years and since the armistice, able as it has been both spontaneously to build the barricades of the Commune and three months later to crucify Varlin?[24]

The future archetypical proletarians of French Communism clearly did not show any great enthusiasm that the revolution should be the work of the crowd. Their rallying to the dictatorship

---

24   Monmousseau, *La Vie Ouvrière*, 21 April 1922.

of the proletariat was based on the same obsessive image that lay behind Merrheim's rallying to reformism: the image of the destructive crowd ready to crucify the revolution. It was no longer the treason of the leaders that was seen as responsible for the patriotic debacle of 1914; the new leaders rather saw this as the treason of the masses, referred here to its primal scene: the killing of the father of the syndicalist revolution, Eugène Varlin. 'Look at the Paris Commune,' said Engels, 'this was the dictatorship of the proletariat.' Look at the Commune, they now said, *what it lacked was the dictatorship of the proletariat* to defend itself against the bourgeoisie – but also, in the last analysis, against the masses.

The death of Varlin was now remembered in order to justify the burial of the working-class ideal that he was the first to formulate in 1870:

> Unless we wish to refer everything to a centralizing and authoritarian state, which would appoint the directors of factories, workshops and stores, these directors then appointing in turn the so-called foremen, works managers, etc. and thus arriving at a hierarchical organization of labour from top to bottom, in which the worker would no longer be anything but an unconscious cog without freedom or initiative: unless we want this, we are compelled to accept that the workers themselves must have free disposition and possession of their instruments of labour, on condition that they bring their products to exchange at their cost price, so that there is a reciprocity of services between the workers in different specialities.[25]

This dream was crushed, not simply because the new socio-economic system was 'too complex' for this ideal of equal exchange (a 'complexity' that is itself the exercise of a strategy of dispossession), but rather because those who upheld this tradition no longer believed in the capacity of these very masses that they evoked to make a new world. The time had come of processions to the Mur

---

25   'Les Sociétés ouvrières', *La Marseillaise*, 11 March 1870.

des Fédérés, the grand parade of the revolutionary apparatus. We are in the habit of saying that revolutionary syndicalism transmitted its *ouvriérisme* to French Communism. But wasn't it equally the pessimism of the worker elites as to the capacities for self-emancipation of the working masses that Monmousseau, Péricat and the others who joined the new party transmitted? Or rather they transmitted to it the same division between *working-class legitimacy* and *revolutionary legitimacy* that it eventually died from; defence of a revolution that now had its seat elsewhere, in Moscow; defence of workers' interests and of national production; revolutionary dogmatism and class populism. The new Communist force would always be criticized for its sudden changes of line, accused of obedience to orders from Moscow or of conversion to patriotic values. But the very possibility of these turns was undoubtedly already inscribed in its formation, in this duplication of legitimacy with which it originated. A game often played is to try and pinpoint exactly when the PCF started to betray the proletarian revolution. But this begs the question of what proletarian revolution this refers to. Our Communism was born as the bankruptcy administrator of a certain revolution, that of the autonomous working-class ideology of revolution. It was born without being able to propose a new alternative of workers' revolution to the new order of Taylorized industry, and a workers' movement integrated into the state order. The 'dictatorship of the proletariat' was then no more than a substitute for the idea of the autonomous emancipation of working people. Dictatorship of production, dictatorship of the state – these were the realities that now came to impose themselves in different ways on the hegemonic fraction of the working class. Revolutionary dissent was fully invested in internationalism, but this also underwent a change of status: no longer the old ideal of 'free men on free soil', but rather defence of the socialist fatherland. At the end of the internationalist adventure, when this 'socialist fatherland' shows the face of a state capitalism participating in the global imperialist balance of power, we should clearly note that the rejection by the revolutionary minority of the order of 'working-class nationalism' produced by the imperialist war did not forge any new hegemonic ideal of workers' revolution. In the long term, nothing replaced the defunct 'revolution of the producers' that differed from the programme of the majority faction in 1919: transition from the old reign of private interest to a new industrial democracy based on an association of the hegemonic fraction of the workers with the management of the national capital. A new ideal that replaced the abolition of wage labour with the promotion of a wage-earner elite in the service of the interests of the wage earners as a whole.

And perhaps we should be glad that the removal of a mask returns us today to the nakedness of the question raised over fifty years ago by revolutionary syndicalism as it fell apart: what new forces can oppose the nationalist-statist-productivist order of the new industrial barbarism?

7

From Pelloutier to Hitler:
Trade Unionism and Collaboration[1]

I am not one of those tormented by nostalgia for the past.
— George Dumoulin, *La Charte du Travail*

Remember also he who forgets where the road leads.
— Heraclitus

In its issue for 5 June 1943, *L'Atelier,* the 'weekly paper of French labour', commented on the appeal that two activists of the dissolved CGT, Albert Guigui and Georges Buisson, had just made on the radio from London, calling for the re-establishment of an underground CGT. The editorial questioned the reasons that could impel a formerly 'honest' activist to oppose the 'national revolution' of Marshal Pétain and the 'socialist' Europe of Adolf Hitler. Only one reason, in the last analysis: 'because Guigui is a Jew and his racial position was bound to lead him to where he is now . . . because Mme Buisson is a Jewess and made Georges do what he has done.'

No reply to this argument is possible, and it needs no commentary. What however is worth commenting on is the signature at the foot of the text: Georges Dharnes, i.e. – under a pseudonym taken from his place of birth – Georges Dumoulin, a veteran of revolutionary

---

1   Fernand Pelloutier (1867–1901), a journalist who joined the Parti Socialiste in 1892, became secretary of the Fédération des Bourses du Travail in 1895; he co-authored with Aristide Briand the pamphlet *De la Révolution par grève générale*, then moved closer to anarchism before his early death. [Tr.]

syndicalism; the miner who, at the beginning of the century, had struggled against the old reformist union; one of the cadres of the CGT in 1914; friend of Monatte, opponent of the *union sacrée* and author in June 1918 of a pamphlet, *Les Syndicalistes français et la guerre*, that castigated in prophetic terms the subordination of the trade unions to the new industrial barbarism.

There were a number of such figures who represented the great tradition of revolutionary syndicalism on the stage of collaboration, the tradition of the Bourses du Travail and the *sou du soldat*[2], of direct action and autonomous working-class deliberation. Georges Yvetôt, for example, a symbol of the old CGT's antimilitarism, who became president in March 1942 of a Comité Ouvrier de Secours Immédiat (COSI), the occupying power's present to the victims of British bombing, and would be buried with Wehrmacht honours; Charles Dhooghe, whose anarchist outbursts had led to his prosecution several times early in the century, and who welcomed the creation of the Service du Travail Obligatoire in *L'Atelier*; cadres of the 1914 CGT such as Savoie, secretary of the Fédération de l'Alimentation, who became a member of the Conseil National and of the Conseil Supérieur de la Charte; Million, of the Union Départmentale du Rhône, who was given responsibility for labour supply; intellectuals, theorists or fellow-travellers of revolutionary syndicalism such as Hubert Lagardelle, founder of the *Le Mouvement Socialiste*, who became secretary of state for labour in Laval's government in April 1942; or Francis Delaisi, economist for *La Vie Ouvrière*, who tirelessly described the marvels of the National Socialist economy; libertarian teachers such as Maurice Wullens, poet of *Les Humbles*, whose dismissal by the backward nationalists of Vichy only made him more enthusiastic in his glorification of the German peace. Alongside the ex-Communist 'renegades' who populated the parties of collaboration and sometimes reached ministerial office in

---

2   The *sou du soldat* was an anti-militarist campaign, both before and after the First World War, which involved writing letters of support to conscripts, accompanied by a small monetary token. [Tr.]

Vichy, an entire socialist tradition, national in origin and internationalist by vocation, was enrolled in the service of what called
itself by a name formerly claimed also by the left, the 'new order'.
Of course, a list such as this does not prove any direct inheritance.
Only a few passed directly from the path of revolutionary syndicalism or the byways of anarchism to the antechambers of Vichy or
the Propaganda-Staffel. Apart from someone like Lagardelle, who
went by the detour of Mussolinian socialism, the old CGT-ists had
had both time and occasion since 1914 to jettison some illusions.
What cemented the unity of the trade unionists who collaborated
with the Vichy regime was, more than their memories of heroic
days, the reformist and anti-Communist practice of the inter-war
years: the conversion to dialogue and a directed economy, the
legacy of war industry and reconstruction; for some of them, the
seduction of planning or the meetings at Pontigny with enlightened employers; for all of them, the struggle against the CGTU
first of all, followed by that against the Communists in the reuni-
fied CGT. The majority, in the years before the war, had been
together in the right wing of the CGT, the Syndicats tendency
inspired by the man whom Pétain would make his first minister of
labour, René Belin. The new split in 1939 and the anti-Communist
repression gave them back the positions that the Communist trade
unionists had taken away from them at the time of the 1936
reunification.

Yet there was no nostalgia involved, they proclaimed loud and
clear that they had not reneged on anything of their past or that of
the workers' movement. They were never absent in mid-March
and the end of May at the commemoration of the glorious birth
and death of the Commune, and regularly paid homage to their
precursors, Babeuf and Varlin as well as Fourier and Saint-Simon.
They claimed not to reject strikes, which they led while accepting
an order that banned them; or the old CGT edifice while accepting
its dissolution; or the struggle for trade-union independence while
sitting on ministerial boards, committees or social welfare bodies
that the dissolution of the CGT had transformed into new state
functions. Old Dumoulin, at a point when it was becoming

increasingly clear to him that he would shortly have to render accounts, insisted on reasserting this faithfulness:

> We have acted without altering how we see things. We have rebuilt our trade unions and the Unions Départementales without changing anything in our ideas. For four years we took in hand the sacred cause of labour, without changing anything in our thinking about the causes and consequences of the war.[3]

It is this question of change and constancy that we have to dwell on for a moment. Beyond the grudges of some, the ambition or venality of others, something more important was involved: the Vichy state machine's enlistment of a sizeable fraction of the trade-union apparatus. To analyse the origins and forms of this enlistment may lead to an analysis of modern terrorist power rather different from those who investigate the love for a Master or the 'desire' of the masses for fascism. It is perhaps worthwhile to reflect not just on the senility of Vichy or its converse childishness (jingle of decorations and presents from young girls; youth workshops and parades of old soldiers), but rather on its maturity or, if you like, its modernity: its ability to construct, in the shadow of outmoded dreams or indefinitely postponed projects, new forms of consensus or new circuits of power; not just on the excesses of fascist seduction and terrorism (the flames of torchlight retreats, autos-da-fé and crematoria) but on their everyday character – not in the sense in which some people speak of 'ordinary fascism', noting the germs of the great plague in the everyday frustrations of men like Georges Lajoie in the film *Rape of Innocence*, but rather in the sense in which the new power requisitioned the functions and powers needed to ensure the normal operation of a social body, in the sense of the panic that Godard refers to in connection with dreaming of the only true film about the death camps, one that would show us the mad work of administration that the death machine required.[4] By

---

3   'Après quatre années de vie intense', *L'Atelier*, 11 September 1943.
4   Cf. 'Feu sur les carabiniers', *Cahiers du Cinéma*, August 1963.

applying in the most summary fashion the double rule of elimination of obstacles and utilization of skills, by offering the ministry of labour to René Belin, one of the secretaries of the CGT that it was about to dissolve, the Vichy state requisitioned in a new way the trade-union apparatus, its practice and its ideology. As the new minister needed both the help of trade-unionist skills and the force of trade-union pressure, the entire trade-union intermediary found itself solicited, caught up in the double play of its reality and its ideal: the reality being the defence of workers' interests in time of war as in peace, under dictatorship as under democracy, the continuing confrontation with the reason of employers and state that had gradually placed it in the position of arbiter between the interests of the producers and those of national production; the ideal, constantly reasserted, being that of the emancipation of the proletarians and the fraternity of peoples. At a time when the realities of production and supply were glaring in their demands, while the ideals of peace and emancipation were uncertain in their application, trade-union collaboration would ceaselessly swing between a policy of lesser evil and the mystique of the new order.

> What we must forcefully proclaim is that an old world has ended,
> a new world is being born.[5]

The trade unionists who took the course of collaboration with the new state apparatus started off by speaking of realism. The same theme would pervade the four years of collaboration: it was good for trade unions to be present everywhere that workers' interests were at stake. And so the collaborators never stopped accusing those who sat on the fence and refused to engage in trade-union action of treason. One of them attacked a former comrade as follows:

> He has dropped the working class at the very moment when it may
> be experiencing the most dreadful moments in its history . . .

---

5   *Au Travail*, 6 September 1941.

Trade unionism, he himself declared, is above politics. Its role is to
free the workers from their proletarian condition. That remains
true, no matter what the situation.[6]

Trade-union independence could continue to claim proletarian
autonomy. In practice, however, it fashioned itself after the very
opposite, becoming 'trade-union neutrality' in the same manner as
the 'neutrality' of the Vichy state. When Belin signed the dissolution of the CGT, when Pétain banned strikes and lock-outs, these
measures were received by and large as the sanction of a natural
calamity: 'Our old trade-union edifice has collapsed',[7] 'The decree
of dissolution is in reality simply a death certificate.'[8] The CGT and
strikes, just like political parties and the parliamentary game,
belonged to a world that had irreversibly crumbled. Even before
Vichy dissolved the CGT, its fragments, meeting in Toulouse,
themselves signed its death certificate by deleting from its statutes
any reference to the class struggle and the abolition of wage-labour,
and offering to collaborate in the new national 'community'. It was
not just the military rout, the panic of retreat or the scattering in
quest of phantom factories that gave rise to this vision. Little as
Marxism had penetrated their thinking, the trade-union leaders had
learned in its school – or rather from the Bolshevik example – that
revolutions presupposed 'revolutionary situations', produced less
by activist effort than by the collapse of state power and social
decomposition as the result of imperialist war: they had also learned
that the paths of revolutionary reconstruction were not exactly
those of trade-union democracy. The image of catastrophe thus

6   J.-P. Fournier, 'La capitulation', *Au Travail*, 15 May 1943. This
newspaper, founded by Bertin, secretary of the Union Départementale de la
Savoie, was the voice of official trade unionism in the unoccupied zone. It set
out to stick to trade-union affairs and, as distinct from *L'Atelier*, which was
caught up in the Parisian atmosphere of collaboration with the occupiers, not
to concern itself with 'foreign policy'.
7   Leburg (Fédération de la Céramique), *Au Travail*, 1 February 1941.
8   Bardollet (at the engineering unions' conference), *L'Atelier*, 18 December
1943.

implied this double idea of both saving the furniture and building a new world, so that the new power was able to assume a double function: in a free-for-all where social forces were now directly face to face it had to defend workers' interests against employers and a now unfettered administration; and it would be the bearer – conscious or otherwise – of a new era of social revolution.

Two reasons, therefore – whether combined or distinguished – to respond to the appeal of the state. The leaders in Paris, if they believed they had to shout louder than the provincials in the '*zone nono*', came to the same conclusions. In the first issue of *L'Atelier* one of the most lucid of them, Aimé Rey, after rebutting the arguments (politicization, illegal existence) that served to justify the dissolution of the CGT, ended his polemic: 'The dissolution of the CGT can have only one serious and respectable justification: that its organization and structure are unsuited for the mission with which the government intends to entrust the workers' trade unions' (7 December 1940). At a 'trade-union conference' that *L'Atelier* organized shortly afterwards he took the same logic further, concluding a vitriolic attack against Vichy's 'harmful and outrageously reactionary measures' with the following words: 'Precisely because commitments have not been kept, we may be on the eve of a profound and revolutionary change in the country's situation.'[9] In the last analysis, if the state would not support these proposals, it was because it did not see it in its interest to do so. Whether people believed in its revolutionary intentions or not, the diagnosis was the same: a world was dead, a new world was in the process of being born, which would be shaped by those able to exert strongest weight in terms of their presence, their competence and their self-denial. The same slogan could be heard on all sides: 'Get to work!' – *au travail*. 'We are going to do great things,' said the trade unionists that Christian Pineau met at Vichy.[10] A realism that saw both good and bad sides was based on the same fact as this enthusiasm: nothing would be the same as it had been previously.

---

9   *L'Atelier*, 8 February 1941.
10   Christian Pineau, *La Simple Vérité*, Paris 1960, p. 82.

From this starting point, the minimum programme of collaboration, to preserve trade-union operation, and the maximum programme of making a new trade unionism into a basic cell of the new order, would merge in a well-regulated mechanism of power. At the top of the machine was the Marshal. The trade-union collaborators had little to say about his person or his career: neither those who taunted Vichy from Paris, nor those in the unoccupied zone who humbly surrounded him. Few hymns of praise to '*le Chef*', but also few remarks about his past. Only one item in *Au Travail* alludes to trade-union activists' reservations on this subject.[11] If anything could be expected from Pétain in response to the trade-unionists' hopes, this was for three reasons. First of all, the famous 'gift' of his person – the object of a good deal of jest, but not without its echoes in the organic ideology of trade-union secretaries, and more deeply in the history of working-class activism. If the Marshal refused to benefit from the pension that he rightly granted retired workers, this was not without a parallel in the ethic of giving oneself, the devotion that trade unionism had always opposed to the practices of political arrivisme. The Marshal's gift was matched by the devotion of René Belin, appointed to ministerial office at a time when he would have preferred to be relieved of his trade-union functions. The new order could also mean that the exercise of power, the management of the community's affairs, should no longer be the seduction of the masses but rather devotion and sacrifice. To those who accused the collaborationists of selling out, they could show when the time came their empty pockets. This was the theme of many declarations as it became clear that Germany had lost the war. For the majority it was far less the gold of corruption than this very ideology of unrewarded service to the masses that led them into the collaborationist machine, along with what it implied in terms of the demand for power. At a meeting of engineering workers in

11   Referring to a trade-union leader who had refused after some hesitation to join its camp, *Au Travail* wrote: 'We had indicated to him the case of comrades who shared his feelings about people and who fought with us on the trade-union level': 'Le cas Fourgues', *Au Travail*, 15 November 1942.

Lyon, at the end of 1943, the collaborators justified themselves in the following terms:

> We could have played wait-and-see: put our slippers on and concerned ourselves with our personal food supply, cultivated our garden and stayed as white as snow. But we preferred to keep faith with what we said four years ago: whatever happens, we shall never betray the workers.[12]

The word 'treason' was directed at the other camp. The distant past of revolutionary syndicalism and the recent past of reformist trade unionism joined forces in the pious image of a power that was no more than service. Collaborating meant above all service – as in servitude.

But Pétain was not only the symbol of the struggle against 'egoism'. He was also the man who had made peace. If Georges Dumoulin 'worshipped' the person of the Marshal, this was 'because he has spared the lives of a million young Frenchmen.'[13] And the claim of the trade-union collaborators to the heritage of revolutionary syndicalism was based on their struggle against war: 'We were the pacifist minority in the trade unions, the Munich contingent, the section of the workers that sought understanding with Germany in order to repair the injustices of the Versailles treaty.'[14]

Even if this pacifism sometimes had more in common with the prudence of those who were unwilling to die for Danzig than with the radicalism of those unwilling to die for the arms manufacturers, it still gave the collaborators certain credentials: the 1 May issue of *La France au Travail* carried the image of Jaurès alongside that of Pétain, recalling, at a time when the first Resistance bullets were echoing, how he had also been shot as a '*boche*', along with the struggle of the Communists against the Versailles treaty and

---

12   *Au Travail*, 27 November 1943.
13   *Au Travail*, 15 March 1941.
14   *Au Travail*, 11 September 1943.

the anarchists' total rejection of war: Dumoulin had signed the *Paix immédiate* manifesto in 1939, written by the only trade-union leader who had rejected war in 1914, Louis Lecoin. By demanding – and obtaining – the release of Lecoin and other pacifists, the trade-union collaborators not only asserted the brotherhood in arms they maintained with the anarchists, pacifists and various leftists whom they freed from the internment camps and for whom they found jobs with the Secours National, Entraide d'Hiver or the Restaurants Communautaires; they asserted this not in the camp of the state that set up special departments and handed hostages over to the occupier, but rather in the camp of those who still under Vichy paid with their positions for their trade-union and pacifist action: prosecuted workers' delegates or dismissed schoolteachers.

'In a single word: Revolution . . .'

Finally, Pétain was the bearer of a slogan – the '*Révolution nationale*' – that each group active at Vichy hoped to draw in its direction, and whose left interpretation was justified by a few small phrases that the authorized trade-union press – *Au Travail* above all – repeated constantly: 'It is impossible to suppress the class struggle without suppressing the causes that have set classes against one another' (an assertion which no socialist tendency could object to); 'The economy must be organized and controlled'; 'Break the power of the trusts and their corrupting influence'; the assertion that 'the *Ordre nouveau* will not be a moral order', and that it would not be a revenge for 1936; the recognition of workers' 'legitimate' aspirations 'not to sell their labour as a commodity, not to be treated as machines but as living, thinking human beings', the intent to suppress 'the great injustice of our time, the proletarian condition', and so on. Little phrases that were sufficiently well crafted to catch those who wanted to pretend that the revalorization of manual labour meant the emancipation of the workers, and thus set in motion the machine of consent. Not so much in Paris, where the trade unionists who gathered at the *L'Atelier* conference laughed at the false symmetry that simultaneously banned both strikes and lock-outs, the CGT and the bosses' Confédération, and where *L'Atelier* waxed ironic on the 1941 May Day that celebrated at the same time 'St Philippe' [i.e. Pétain] and newly canonized labour. In the southern zone, on the other hand, the friends of *Au Travail* were not going to leave this festival to the reactionaries. Though they blamed 'the conservative and traditionalist working class with its revolutionary verbalism' that 'showed a certain hesitation about participating in May Day', Bertin was caught up by the emotion of this:

Revolutionary First of May

In an earlier age, May Day was less easy. The Chicago martyrs, the innocent victims of Fourmies, the prisoners of Clichy, all you who paid with your lives or your freedom for asserting the necessity of improving the proletarian condition, you can see this year that your sacrifices were not in vain. The truths that you were only wrong to have proclaimed too soon have now triumphed. The plutocracy, the big capitalism that we have struggled against ever since the workers' movement existed, have found a new opponent of substance in Marshal Pétain.[15]

Let revolutionaries laugh only if they are sure that they have never themselves hymned any such slavery!

There was thus evidence at the summit of the state that something like the suppression of proletarian slavery was under way: 'I bring you reasons for living that can be summed up in a single word: revolution . . . Making revolution means suppressing the slavery of the proletariat.'[16] The Marshal's language on social questions certainly has a somewhat strange echo to ears used to socialist vocabulary, but as this was not exactly military speech, trade unionists could readily bridge the gap:

---

15   *Au Travail*, 1 May 1941.
16   Declaration by Lousteau, chief secretary to minister Badouin, *Au Travail*, 4 January 1941.

Our preferences are naturally for words to which we have long been accustomed, and we shall never forget the meaning of our *mouvement syndical*. But the conservative sentiment that sometimes inspires a certain number of workers will not lead to conservatism in words. It may well be then that we shall grow accustomed to talking about 'occupational organizations'.[17]

The workers' movement had certainly matured from the time that it welcomed words from on high like lashes of the whip. Since 1917, especially, the relationship between words and things had been distorted, and in the disorder that heralds upheavals it is only realities that count, or at least signs of commitment. It was above all through social measures and legislation that René Belin sought to position his actions in the heritage of 1936: from the maintenance of paid holidays and collective agreements through to the improvement in social insurance and unemployment benefit, or the strengthening of the labour inspectorate. Measures that were no more than reformist, but which, given the harshness of the time and the rumblings of reaction, indicated that there was still movement in the right direction. The cornerstone of this ensemble, presented as something that the movement of June 1936 had been unable to achieve, was the retirement pension decreed in March 1941, which Bertin greeted as a new dawn of working-class emancipation: 'How happy life is this Saturday morning in the sunny parks of Vichy. Two builders with white moustaches, a little bent over, greeting one another joyfully: "We've got it this time, haven't we!"'[18]

Was this no more than a demagogy at which we need only shrug our shoulders? Perhaps it is worth paying rather more attention to the good-natured terrorism that lies in this rather catchy prose, which reads the bent-over body of an old worker or the clarity of the spring air as the effects of a good and solid government, to these slippages by which populist sympathy with the great suffering and small

17 G. Dumoulin, 'Le démarrage nécessaire', *L'Atelier*, 7 December 1940.
18 'Révolution nationale et sociale', *Au Travail*, 22 March 1941.

joys of the workers melds into the grand poem of state: that of the good life that we owe to the Leader – whether Vichy-style joie de vivre or the exaltation of the new life that Comrade Stalin has made so much better. This illuminated gaze reflects the rays of the new sun of the state on which the revolution now turns; it is a long way since the irony of the anarchists about politicians' phrases:

> I promise you workers' pensions,
> I promise you the end of your miseries.

Serving the revolution now means serving the state. We should not be mistaken about this.

Vichy was overflowing with promises to put an end to workers' miseries. (In one sense everything was mere promises, even the threats that were at the same time appeals for participation.) First of all, the promise of a guaranteed defence of workers' and trade-union rights. At a time when bosses who re-opened their factories carefully sifted the staff they engaged, and reactionary local authorities sought to clean out the Bourses du Travail, the government did precisely what it had do in order to set an example to the employers and officials. Berthelot, as secretary of state for communications, explained to the secretary-general of the PTT that, besides 'professional trouble-makers',

no account should be paid to the former opinions of the staff . . . I particularly warn against the tendency of certain heads of department to get rid of trade-union elements. It is the nature of trade unionism to make demands, and so there is no more reason to attack it than to attack the employers who are by nature conservative. The new order must be established with the agreement of a cleansed trade unionism, relieved of its political influences.[19]

His colleague Peyrouton insisted that 'employees should not be treated less well by the authorities than are employers', and invited

19 *Au Travail*, 4 January 1941.

departmental prefects to punish mayors who displayed 'a blame-worthy partiality against them' – a circular that Bertin commented on as follows: 'The government is not associated with a politics of "social reaction" such as certain short-sighted people like to main-tain. Workers, the government is not as some self-interested parties present it! It wants your collaboration.'[20]

Collaboration, a word that subsequently came to refer above all to collaboration with the occupying power, initially meant class collaboration and collaboration with the state. The revolution to which the new state summoned both employers and workers was one of class collaboration. We should note that this was taken quite seriously by the trade-union side. The former CGTists who organ-ized resistance under the cover of a Comité d'Études Syndicales said the same thing on this point as those involved in collaboration: the class struggle was a fact that workers suffered rather than chose voluntarily, and that they were ready to exchange for genuine collaboration. It is just that there is more to the confrontation between classes than just the distinction between collaboration and struggle. Collaboration also functioned as an antidote to submission and paternalism. When *Au Travail* used as an epigraph for one of its issues the words of the Nantes typographers of 1833 who said to their masters: 'Why should we not meet together to discuss our affairs peaceably?', we can see the constancy of a certain ideological tradition (whether overlaid by a Marxist theoretical grid or the noisy denials of revolutionary syndicalism), of a certain idea of equality between classes. It was in the wake of the revolution of 1830 that this ideal was expressed most clearly, for example in the demand of the striking tailors of 1833 to have 'relations of equality and independ-ence' with the masters: an ideal of sharing and balance between Labour and Capital, each being master of itself but in no position to exercise a tyranny over the other; an assertion that the dignity of the working class and the very recognition of its autonomy lay in not being listened to only when noise from the street disturbed the rest of the powerful, but on each occasion that it had reason to oppose the

---

20 'Justice pour la classe ouvrière', *Au Travail*, 15 February 1941.

present state of things and the discourse of its upholders. This desire to collaborate and discuss on an equal basis can be read clearly enough in the pages of the 1840 *L'Atelier*, whose title was deliberately taken up by the collaborationist trade unionists of 1940, accompanied as it was by the sharpest criticism of employer paternalism and the most resolute defence of workers' autonomy: a paradoxical ideal in relation to Marxist philosophy, but very much a live one with the death of ideologies that were more 'logical' – that of a class position maintained in the suppression of class struggle. The collaborating trade unionists revived this ideology in jointly asserting their desire to collaborate with employers' representatives and their rejection of everything that could destroy workers' autonomy: the suppression of the Unions Départementales, employers' charters, company committees, 'mixed' trade associations combining employers and workers,[21] etc. Collaboration with the bosses did not mean the submission of repentant workers to their goodwill.

> For us at least, social peace is not something we submit to, but something that is agreed.[22]

Naturally, the employers were out to make as much as they could from this collaboration that excluded dependence. After the failed strike of November 1938 and Daladier's decree-laws, the hunt for Communists in 1940, the overwork and repression bound up with the war economy, they embarked on a revenge for 1936. It was not the dissolution of the CGT, the ban on strikes, or their omnipotence in the Comités d'Organisation (responsible for restarting the

---

21 The electrical employer Jules Verger was lauded to the skies in autumn 1936 for his successful resistance to the CGT union of electrical fitters, supported by the whole building industry. He published the lessons of his victory in 1937 in a book titled *Jules Verger, ses ouvriers, sa maîtrise . . . une famille*, in which he offered his recipe for class collaboration: a mixed association of employers and workers to organize the profession. This accolade brought Verger a major role in Vichy, especially in the commission that drew up the Charte du Travail, in which he led the right wing against the trade-union left.

22 *L'Atelier*, 5 April 1941.

production machine) that spurred them to backtrack. The authorized trade-union press was full of reports about their refusal to collaborate: the bosses would not discuss with unions that they were unwilling to recognize, and everywhere sought to impose company welfare committees or workers' delegates of their choice. Not only did they refuse to re-employ trade unionists sacked after the strike of November 1938 who had now rallied to the new order, but they dismissed others for having tried to re-establish, within the existing legality, unions that had been destroyed. *Au Travail* could even cite the case of a chemical factory where twelve activists in succession were sacked for having tried to re-establish their union (13 December 1941). Faced with this ill will, unionists could raise the question: 'We are ready to collaborate. We offer our labour, what are the bosses offering us?'

Nothing apparently. This collaboration had to be *won*. And that is indeed why those who championed it did not feel any humiliation. It was the state as arbiter and rescuer that had to impose social peace on those who refused to conclude this, on a reaction that rumbled throughout the social body: employers, the heads of administrative services, local notables. When the Marshal visited Annecy, he made Bertin the following promise:

Towards the end of the meeting, the Marshal had a direct dialogue with a trade-union leader, with no beating about the bush, which showed how things are in the process of changing in France. The Marshal was again concerned about company unions and welfare committees. 'How are these getting on?' he asked the trade unionist.

'None too well,' the other replied, with a sincere and honest expression.

'Why is that?'

'Because, Monsieur le Maréchal, the bosses don't understand. There are even those who are conducting reprisals against some of our activists.'

The Marshal's expression turned severe: 'We shall force the employers to change their mind. This has to be done.'[23]

---

23 *Au Travail* (after *La Suisse*), 25 October 1941.

But the seduction of the state was not simply because the workers had a need for it; the state also needed them. The force of attraction that Vichy exerted on a section of working-class activists was not just the sum of its social measures and good intentions, it was also its inability to put these into practice. If circulars and instructions had to be constantly repeated, this was because the government's intentions were not being applied. Everywhere activists continued to be dismissed, Unions Locales and Unions Départementales dissolved and Bourses du Travail closed. Nor was there any way of obtaining from the bosses an increase in abnormally low wages, or the indemnities owing their staff for relocation. When worker activists turned to the state for help against employers' resistance, it showed its inadequacy. They had to help the state in order for the state to help them. They had to collaborate with the state so that it could break the resistance of the trusts; they had to collaborate not because this state was a power that bent everything to itself, but rather because it was weak, divided, besieged at its very heart by representatives of the very powers of money on which it had declared war. To the engineering union delegates who met in Limoges, the former Communist engineering worker Marcel Roy, overwhelmed by grievances from the rank and file about a thousand and one irregularities on the part of the bosses, asked 'that delegates should tackle these questions in a more general context, as the difficulties depend on a new order that has to be obtained'.[24]

A modern form of Vichy power, more serious and lasting than the letters to the Marshal, the parades and the pure air of the Chantiers de Jeunesse, was this inability to realize by itself what it said that it wanted, this emptiness drawing in air, obliging the trade unions to be either more or less, to either integrate into the state or disappear, having to exercise this choice in quasi-experimental conditions in which the union, living a provisional existence, was left in a position to judge both its own impotence and the impotence of the state without it. It was not the strength of the state that

---

24   *Au Travail*, 9 July 1941.

made itself accepted and loved, it was its 'weakness' that required aid by way of a new division of functions. No doubt the mass of workers were sceptical in noting that 'too often acts seem to contradict declarations, and immediate results go counter to intentions'.[25] But what was true of the masses was not true of those whose collaboration was demanded: the tenants of a trade-union power who, in this game of promises and threats, strengths and weaknesses of the state, played at double or quits. If the trade unions wished to preserve their little power, they had to take part in the big power.

'*The Charte is a continuous creation*'[26]

In this sense, the story of the Charte du Travail is an edifying one. This charter was not a single law (the law of 4 October 1941 on occupational organizations), but rather an exemplary process of the operation of the Vichy power and the part that trade-union pressure played in it. Fundamentally, the entire labour history of Vichy coincides with the expectation of the Charte and then the expectation of its application. During this whole time, trade unionists spoke of scarcely anything else – what it would be, what they hoped it would not be, the reasons for its delay, the conditions of its application, what was lacking in its text, the corrections that experience would bring it. This grey-on-grey Charte, the text of which was so hard to see, and the realization of which no one would ever see, sums up quite well the main seduction that the Vichy power could offer to trade-union expectation: that of the worst case that is not always certain.

Very soon, by calculated indiscretions on the part of a minister who needed to apply the pressure of his trade-union base, union activists were informed about the twists and turns in the preparation of the Charte, in which René Belin sought to maintain the

25   J. Charvoz (secretary of the Union Locale de Maurienne), 'Que la confiance vienne', *Au Travail*, 4 January 1941.

26   *Le Rouge et le Bleu*, 8 August 1942.

trade-union function against the champions of corporatism and mixed associations. Very soon, they knew that they were under threat:

> The operation would consist in overthrowing our Bourses du Travail, our Unions Départementales and Unions Locales, and only tolerating our industrial Fédérations for the purpose of a technical output objective. The labour dimension would be replaced by little blue flowers, singing children and the bosses' annual party.[27]

This condemnation was unassailable, and the decision it led to unambiguous: 'I want to go to Vichy' was Dumoulin's headline in presenting his candidacy for the commission charged with drawing up this Charte on which the ministers were unable to agree. Two weeks later, the staff of *L'Atelier* published a resounding declaration:

> Let there be no mistake! The French workers will not accept a reactionary Charte du Travail.[28]

The conditions for supporting the Charte were clearly defined here: the maintenance of workers' trade unionism; the rejection of mixed associations and any 'company welfare committees' – these being the Charte's great innovation – that were not on a basis of parity; the defence of workers' freedoms and the assertion of workers' participation in the management of the national economy. The declaration ended with a solemn warning: 'The abolition of the capitalist regime has not been sanctioned in facts. The national community does not exist either organically or in people's minds. Workers' unions, accordingly, must not be destroyed. If this destruction was envisaged, the workers would not tolerate it.'

As far as the content was concerned, this declaration says the

27   Dumoulin, 'Je désire aller à Vichy', *L'Atelier*, 22 March 1941.
28   5 April 1941.

same thing as would be said by the assembly of Fédération secretaries, which included, along with the collaborators, activists
hostile to collaboration or already engaged in the resistance activity of the Comité d'Études Syndicales. And so the divisions that
arose were most frequently not over the content of demands or
economic programmes for the future. The unblocking of wages,
the improvement of food supplies and trade-union independence
were demanded by all. As for the long-term economic programme,
the nationalization of key industries and workers' participation in
economic management, both of which were central for the collaborationists and would likewise be for the resistance, went back to
the same source: the economic plan of Jouhaux's CGT. It was in
practice that things changed: the unionists of *L'Atelier* who added
demands for wage increases were keen that workers did not fall
prey to provocation. What was needed, in this diplomacy that
appeared as the now established truth of the trade-union movement, was that the workers should show their strength so as not to
have to make use of it, that their large-scale presence in the unions
should give the Fédération secretaries, who no longer represented
very much, the power to negotiate new relationships between the
trade unions and the state from a position of strength, to re-balance
the Vichy scales against raving bosses and crazy ideologists. The
more they had decided to play this game, the greater the need to
raise their voices.[29] This extremism of language, therefore, did not
rule out a realistic appreciation. The Labour Charter did at least
have the merit of being designed to give the workers' organizations a recognized legal existence, one that life would be charged
with improving. Better something than nothing. 'The miners,'
their secretary said, 'have always been able to content themselves
with what they were able to win, ready to improve it later on.'[30]
And to the extent that the commission hesitated, this threat was
transformed into promise; the Charte, from which people knew

29   For *L'Atelier*, the question was not just to ensure a mass base for union
negotiation, but, by denouncing the Vichy reactionaries, to support Laval's
return to power desired by the Germans as a demand of the left.
30   Bertron, *Le Rouge et le Bleu*, 15 November 1941.

only too well what to expect, became an object of demand. All the more so as a three-way game developed: the bosses, at the factory or corporation level, set themselves to anticipate the Charte, organizing company committees as they saw fit, or else promulgating, without waiting for the official organization of 'occupational families', corporative charters to their liking. The hairdressers, in the front line in this battle, found the slogan that the situation needed: they demanded 'the real Charte du Travail'. All realists, therefore, soon came to accept the Charte as an 'experimental stage'. As Dumoulin put it, what mattered was 'first of all to live':

> We live in a country where everything is settled with texts, thanks to the natural faculties of flexibility that form the basis of the French character. When a law is unnatural it is isolated and circumvented, as Napoleon did with fortresses, and we advance. If the Charte du Travail, in some of its provisions, is unnatural, its fate will be sealed by the development of life.[31]

When the Charte finally appeared, its good and bad sides were registered. On the good side: the fact of trade unionism continued to be recognized, and especially the Charte's call for the establishment in each occupational branch of single unions that would finally realize the unity of the world of labour; on the bad side, one thing above all was fundamental: 'The Charte does not contain any structural reform attacking the capitalist regime.'[32] On a more down-to-earth level, the Charte, though recognizing trade Fédérations, 'overlooked' the Unions Locales and Départementales, which were sites of class rather than occupational solidarity; it recognized mixed associations with a tripartism of workers, employers and managers; it offered no guarantee of workers' freedoms; it organized in place of the Bourses du Travail so-called 'Maisons Communes' for employers and workers. Finally, there were the company committees, good or bad according to whether

---

31   *L'Atelier*, 6 September 1941.
32   Roger Paul, in *L'Atelier*, 8 November 1941.

their functions did or did not go beyond the context of social welfare and affect the management of the company, whether the workers' delegates were the elected representatives of their comrades or men appointed by the boss. On this subject the Charte spoke imprecisely of appointment 'by agreement with the employer', just as it was also ambiguous in other respects: 'A serious lacuna seems to have escaped the legislators, i.e. the suppression of the Unions Départementales . . .',[33] if not contradictory: 'The creation of mixed organizations risks compromising for the future the idea of the Charte du Travail as initially conceived.'[34] These were also deficiencies that 'life' was supposed to correct. Because the Charte did not say enough, the trade unionists would have to do more. A twofold response was thus almost unanimous:

1. The Charte was disappointing, if not reactionary.
2. Life was stronger than texts, and the value of the Charte would depend on those who applied it.

The minutes of the Fédérations thus assert almost in unison that the workers 'maintain all their reservations', but 'will faithfully attempt the experiment'. Courtois, of the Union Départementale de l'Eure et Loir, expressed the syllogism of collaboration to perfection:

The text of the Charte reminds me of Aesop's dissertations on language; in fact this document is at the same time both good and bad.

It will be what people make of it, either an instrument of social conservatism or a revolutionary weapon.

This alternative dictates the attitude of the trade unionists who want the National Revolution not to be a new disappointment for the workers, and believe that the National Revolution will be a trick if it is not also socialist. But the National Revolution will not

33 Masbatin (Union Départementale de la Vienne), *Au Travail*, 22 November 1941.
34 Fédération des Produits Chimiques et du Papier-Carton, *Au Travail*, 10 January 1942.

be socialist if we refuse to join it; there is even reason to fear that it could be conducted against us.

My position is therefore clear: I accept the Charte as it is; I want faithfully to conduct this experiment.

I am persuaded moreover that life, stronger than the intentions of those who drafted the Charte, will bring modifications in accordance with French mentality and the traditions of working-class unionism.[35]

Here again, the nuances are scarcely perceptible between the statements of the pioneers of collaboration and the statements of those who had decided to limit their participation simply to the defence of the right to exist, such as the secretary of the jewellery Fédération, Sancier:

We shall smooth out the edges without useless curves; our ambition will be to rescue our industries by preserving the labour-power they need, so that people will not die of hunger while working. These are not very optimistic views, but we have paid for defying them.[36]

It was far rather by a certain detachment than by the vehemence of their criticism that the attitude of some former CGT activists signalled their decision not to play the game of the new order. We should not be surprised that those most determined to join in the construction were also the most critical.[37] A delegate from the

35   *L'Atelier*, 15 November 1941.

36   Ibid.

37   It is rather surprising, on the other hand, that certain histories of the Resistance inspired by the PCF present as evidence of opposition to the 'traitor clique of Dumoulin & co.' criticisms of the Charte or lists of demands similar to those put forward by these very traitors, or even weaker ones. In order to show, for current political purposes, that the economic defence of the workers naturally extends to the struggle for democracy and the defence of national independence, they have to maintain that the Resistance was alone in putting forward demands, and conversely that every 'economic' demand was already an act of national Resistance. This leads former leaders

aircraft works at Marignane explained this reasoning very well, in thanking Bertin for his criticism of the Charte:

> Your report has made my task much easier. You did not realize that the Charte du Travail was awaited by the workers with a certain distrust. After reading your report, there is more confidence in the delegates, since from this day on a good number of the workers have come to swell our ranks.[38]

As always, the verdict was divided. If workers were distrustful of the Charte, the delegates' criticism would give them confidence in the delegates and enable the collaborating trade unionists to win them over to a Charte that was corrected in their favour.

For once the text was promulgated, the same game of expectations was repeated. The decrees for its application were awaited, along with the establishment of constitutive commissions in each corporation; and people also waited to know whether the new

---

of working-class Resistance to rather odd arguments: 'Besides, *resisting* meant defending France by resisting the enemy. The workers, however, form part of the national inheritance both as men and as producers; they are even one of the most precious elements of this human inheritance. Defending their existence and that of their children, threatened by restrictions, was thus an act of national defence' (André Tollet, in *Le Mouvement syndical dans la Résistance*, Paris 1975, p. 15). When Tollet and his comrades justified the bruising RAF raids on the Renault factories and elsewhere, they knew very well that the struggle for national liberation and the defence of the workers' existence could divide to the point of being opposed, precisely because the human capital represented by the Renault workers was at that time the capital of the German war industry, which proposed means of its own to ensure the existence of the French workers' children (a famous poster). Collective workers' action formed part of the Resistance not as a defence of the national human and productive inheritance, but as a disorganization of the German war machine and an assertion of the possibility of facing down the all-powerful occupier. It was certainly in this sense that *La Vie Ouvrière* in 1943 called on all workers to follow the example of the striking miners. What was to be exorcised in these retrospectives was the idea that there were several different ways of defending 'workers' interests'.

38   *Au Travail*, 28 February 1942.

secretary of state for labour, Lagardelle, who replaced Belin in April 1942 with the return of Laval, would lean towards a trade-unionist or a corporatist interpretation of the Charte. The employers continued the game of corporative charters and company commit-tees, the rank and file continued to show 'indifference' and 'scepticism'. Hence the need for trade unionists who played the game to develop their action on two levels: that of action at the base, watching over the establishment of welfare committees, denouncing employers' irregularities and seeking in this way to expand the power of workers' control (especially over the question of food supplies): an activity of participation that supplemented current demands over wages, working conditions and safety.[39]

---

39   This activity can be followed in *Au Travail*. As distinct from *L'Atelier*, whose extreme positions on the German question quickly separated it from the life of the Fédérations and Unions, *Au Travail* was based on the activity of a number of trade unions and Unions Locales in the southern zone. It therefore provides useful information on certain conflicts between the collaborating trade unionists and the employers: their refusal to deal with the trade union in the Lyon breweries (15 May 1943); the dismissal of a miners' union delegate who had denounced 'the special actions of the management in the matter of supplies and labour provisions' (15 May 1943); the sacking for 'professional misconduct' of the secretary of the Lyon dough-workers' union who had refused to join an irregularly established social committee (29 May 1943).

Conversely, *Au Travail* welcomed the positive work of enterprise commit-tees that respected the election of workers' delegates by their comrades and practised genuine collaboration: for example the leather industry welfare committee in Romans, which at its first meeting expressed support for a measure that was important both practically and symbolically: an amnesty for the strikers of 30 November 1938 (31 January 1942). The Comité Social of the Bel cheese factory is described in glowing terms: its social workers were visiting 300 homes each month; it had organized support for illness, bonuses for births, assistance to the elderly and mutual aid for prisoners; each worker had been allotted a vegetable garden, and a programme of collective cultiva-tion had produced, among other crops, 40 tonnes of Jerusalem artichokes, 50 tonnes of cabbage and 67 tonnes of potatoes (15 May 1943). Trade-union activity here had gone beyond the context of negotiation and social work: the Union of Aix-les-Bains, for example, sought to solve the question of food supply in a revolutionary fashion: with a view to suppressing middlemen and

But alongside or through this 'economic' action, the major action of this apparatus with no troops was defence of the trade-union function; hence the constant question about trade-union independence, to which federation secretaries, local unions and rank-and-file trade unions were asked week after week to proclaim their attachment. A kind of permanent plebiscite intended to support the dialogue with the state in the absence of pressure from the masses, who scarcely responded to expectations in flocking into the trade unions. This situation, indeed, could lead to the reverse argument: rather than appealing for pressure from the masses the leaders played on their distance, evoking the reserves, hesitations and criticisms expressed in trade-union meetings as evidence of the state of mind of the masses and the increasingly attentive ear with which they listened to Communist propaganda – even the catcalls and heckling that speakers had to put up with, with the conclusion: 'Those in high places would be well advised to either leave us alone or give us back the means of winning over these brothers . . . Some express scepticism, others indifference, even hostility.'[40]

This situation of trade unionism caught between the mobilization of reaction and the disenchantment of the masses called for a strengthening of the bond with the state. We have seen the dialogue 'without half-truths' that Bertin had with the Marshal. The Vichy authorities were keener on this kind of sincere and impromptu dialogue than the liberal and progressive authorities that succeeded them would like us to believe. It was the engineer Berthelot, secretary of state for communications, who 'struck the tone and the words that railwaymen like and understand: "I speak to you as a brother, as a professional man who knows you and loves you." '[41] Laval had the overly ceremonial presidential chair in the conference hall replaced by a more suitable seat in order to explain in all frankness to his

organizing popular unity at rank-and-file level, it set up a supply committee that directly organized the provisioning of factory workers by peasant producers ('Une belle initiative syndicale', 8 May 1943).
40   Georges Trémy, *Au Travail*, 24 January 1942.
41   V. Josse, 'Les cheminots et l'appel de M. Berthelot', *Au Travail*, 20 September 1941.

friends of *Au Travail* the objectives and difficulties of his action. Pétain received the secretary of the dissolved teachers' union without an appointment, and had an astonished official bring in during the meeting the files of the dismissed teachers whom he had come to plead for.[42] This intermittent dialogue helped the rank and file understand better the intentions of the authorities, and also helped convey to them the rank and file's aspirations and problems, so why should it not be institutionalized? Why not make the trade-union instrument the agent of a permanent face-to-face between the acts of the authorities and the aspirations of the masses? Bertin correctly diagnosed what it was that the Vichy authorities lacked: an *organic* bond with the masses that could replace the destroyed institutions and supplement the *sentimental* bond with the person of the Marshal. The Marshal's preferred 'legion of combatants', whose attempts to establish company organizations competing with their own were viewed poorly by trade unionists, could not make the state into a people's state. Only the trade unions offered the site of exchange that was needed between the authorities and the masses:

> This state, which will be forced to wage a battle against the trusts, will experience attacks that we can foresee. If it is to pass through this difficult period, it will genuinely have to be a people's state, in permanent contact with the masses. And it is the trade unions who will assure this permanent contact, the trade unions as transmission belt between the government and the people, telling the government what are the aspirations of the masses, and telling the people what are the decisions of the government, explaining these to them and seeking to have them put into effect.[43]

A transmission belt: Bertin could happily drop this word in the course of the 'week of trade-union studies' that met at Les Sablettes to study the Charte. Yet the section of the trade unions from which he came had been able to take up the flag of revolutionary

---

42   André Delmas, 'Documents pour l'histoire du syndicalisme', *Revue Syndicaliste*, February 1949.
43   *Au Travail*, 13 December 1941.

syndicalism precisely by its express rejection of the Bolshevist theory and practice of the 'transmission belt'. If Bertin was now able to demand aloud this despised function, it was precisely because the struggle against the Communist 'politicization' of trade-union action made possible, in return, a depoliticized representation of the state that was perfected in this representation of a trade unionization of the state function, implying in practice a statization of the trade-union function, expanded to a generalized haggling for the adhesion of the masses to the state.[44]

---

44   This new function of trade-union mediation should also be studied in the field of repression. René Belin and his collaborators constantly emphasized their stubborn efforts to obtain the release of activists whom Daladier and Mandel had interned in concentration camps. A trade unionist close to Belin was specially appointed to sort through these files, but to all appearances he could only save some people by declaring others to be suitable for internment. This trade-union function of sorting good and bad activists was something that the friends of *Au Travail* specifically requested in a letter to Marshal Pétain in which they expressed their concerns in relation to the law of 18 November 1942, setting up a special department for actions promoting communism, anarchy, or social and national subversion:

Why should we conceal the disquiet that reading the law of 18 November aroused in our activists? We have already suggested on a number of occasions that people competent in this matter should get together to define what is meant in practice by communism, anarchism and social and national subversion. We asked that a small glossary be drawn up and sent to all police commissioners and judges. As of now, nothing seems to have been done. Just as on 11 November, there are pell-mell arrests of trade unionists, socialists and dissident communists. Even trade-union action simply to get the existing laws respected is viewed as an 'anarchist tendency' by too many people.

It is completely normal that a government should proclaim the means of its policies. But if the working class risks suffering from these, it is a human duty to advise those responsible before mistakes are committed, pointing out moreover that the emotions existing would perhaps disappear if some clarifications were made. (*Au Travail*, 27 February 1943).

'A little known aspect of Pelloutier's thought'

If the union was a transmission belt, it was also a school. Perhaps there has been too much effort to forget what was done or dreamed of in the Vichy years in terms of training 'the most precious capital', i.e. human beings, managers of the future society: the management schools, study days, reflection groups, economic programmes, demographic studies, etc. from which a good deal of ideas – and people – emerged, bringing the Republics that followed the fruits of a more modern education than is generally admitted.

In this mushrooming of programmes and this need for new elites, trade unionism naturally found a place. Could it not regain – and more than regain – the function of social intervention it had lost with the traditional means of class struggle, as a school of cadres to manage the new planned economy? The efforts in workers' education made by the Institut Supérieur Ouvrier and the Collèges du Travail were continued with the action of the man who was their great inspiration, Georges Lefranc. The trade unionists obtained the reopening of the Collèges du Travail, whose activity is reported in *Au Travail*, and the project was elaborated of a Université du Travail whose students would be proposed by the trade unions, with the object of training what 'the brain factories gravitating around the Panthéon'[45] were unable to train in the way of social cadres. On the other hand, the trade unions' intellectual efforts that had inspired the CGT plan also inspired the study days or study weeks that *Au Travail* organized, and that took up the big ideas of this plan: the establishment of departments that would concern themselves with major economic functions (statistics, company finance, distribution of raw material and labour-power, etc.); nationalization of long-term credit and key industries;

Imprecision was always the vice of this government, and its repressive machinery was no longer capable of distinguishing between its helpers and its enemies. In terms of repression as in economic and social policy, only the know-how of the trade unions could now be the basis of an enlightened despotism.

45 Dumoulin, 'Aurons-nous bientôt une Université du Travail?', *L'Atelier*, 20 November 1943.

control of the independent economic sector; cooperative management of companies.[46] In this educational effort stretching from the general cultural lectures of the Collège du Travail to economic plans for the future, couldn't trade unionism rediscover its most authentic tradition, that of the Bourses du Travail? Charles Spinasse, the economics minister under the Front Populaire, maintained this in his weekly paper:

> The future trade union, as a cultural body with the objective of training elites and preparing them for the work they will have to perform on company committees and cooperative boards, will link up with the old tradition of French trade unionism . . . that we were familiar with before the Communist perversion.[47]

This tradition, which the first issue of *L'Atelier* likewise proclaimed, was paradoxically at first sight 'that of Pelloutier and Keufer', respectively the inspirer of revolutionary syndicalism and the father of reformist trade unionism. In actual fact, the 'new school' of trade unionism went beyond either of these. Its objective was neither to train informed activists nor to train men for a future society free from hierarchy. Nor was it that 'rejection of promotion' which revolutionary syndicalism had emphasized, but rather the training of new elites and managers for a statized economy: the individual advancement of workers (*Au Travail* proposed the establishment of a new school, an 'employers' Saint-Maixent' that would train those elite workers suited to managerial work), the collective advancement of the trade-union elite. The point was precisely not to return to the situation before the 'Leninist perversion', but rather to carry through the trade-union development that the war of 1914–8, followed by reconstruction – whether in capitalist Europe or socialist Russia – had commenced: a trade unionism integrated into the state apparatus, as transmission belt between the demands of state power and those

---

46   These four points sum up the programme adopted at the week of trade-union studies at Saint Colomban, organized by the *Au Travail* team. Cf. *Au Travail*, 'Pour une économie libérée des trusts', 6 September 1941.

47   *Le Rouge et le Bleu*, 13 June 1942.

of the mass of workers, but also a school – a reservoir of managers, whether for the Soviet revolution in Russia or the National revolution in France. This development gave rise to the dream of a trade-union state managing an economy that would no longer be organized for the privileges of capital but rather by the demands of the general interest and the hierarchy of skills: the power of duty and the power of skill were the rational ideas of the *ordre nouveau* that attracted union collaboration: the order of Saint-Simonian 'industrialists' succeeding the age of idle feudalists, an ethic of labour giving an acceptable face to the somewhat ill-sounded trinity *travail-famille-patrie*.[48] This trade union vision of the *ordre nouveau* could certainly find precedents in the history of ideologies and working-class practices. But if it was to claim the direct heritage of revolutionary syndicalism, it had to appeal despite everything to a misunderstood Pelloutier. This is what Georges Lefranc did in a lecture at the Centre des Jeunes Travailleurs, as reported by *Le Rouge et le Bleu* in the following terms:

> Despite his libertarian convictions and his disdain for authority, Pelloutier appears as a powerful inspiration, the very archetype of the 'leader' . . . No doubt Pelloutier's thinking was completely oriented towards class action, but it was also marked by a certain pragmatism. His anti-statism was not irreducible, any more than his anti-militarism, as attested by some of the reflections that he left us. And death struck him in the midst of his development . . . Would he not have recognized that from the crisis of the democratic and liberal state that he condemned there would emerge a stronger state, revolutionary in the full sense of the term, capable of disciplining forces that had arisen outside of it?[49]

---

48   Those trade unionists won over to the *ordre nouveau* sought despite everything to reconcile this trinity with slogans from the working-class heritage. Félicien Nicolas, secretary of the Le Martinet miners, accommodated it with the slogans of the Front Populaire as follows: 'Bread through Labour; Peace in the Family; Liberty in the Fatherland': 'Précisions nécessaires', *Au Travail*, 25 October 1941.
49   *Le Rouge et le Bleu*, 4 April 1942.

A week later, *Le Rouge et le Bleu* returned to this 'development' of Pelloutier's:

> Taking into account certain inadequacies on the part of the workers, he prepared for the collaboration necessary with the state and the employers. This is a little-known aspect of Pelloutier's thought: if there are some people trying to use his name or his example to combat the Charte, others will reply, along with Lefranc, that the Pelloutier of 1898 might well have accepted it.[50]

When it was not a matter of claiming a heritage, however, the champions of trade-union collaboration admitted that it was above all they themselves who had changed. Sometimes the truth peeks through in the garble of declarations of loyalty. Thus Pichon, secretary of the Firmin Union Locale, held that trade-union independence had long been already buried:

> Today we are close to what Waldeck-Rousseau was trying to establish with the agreement of Millerand: the integration of the workers' movement into the state . . . Does it not depend in some way on the fate of the state and its leaders? In such conditions, it is foolish to speak of trade-union independence. The word 'trade unionism' has been kept, but its basis has completely changed.[51]

It had indeed been completely changed: those dreams of union participation in a new economic order, breaking the power of the trusts, were based on a defence of 'trade-union independence' that completely reversed its meaning. The 'single and compulsory trade unions' in which the champions of the new trade unionism pretended to see a recognition – even an advancement – of the movement, reduced trade unionism to the situation against which it had originally arisen, transforming the union card into the

---

50 'Le syndicalisme se penche sur son passé', *Le Rouge et le Bleu*, 11 April 1942.
51 *Au Travail*, 4 April 1942.

workers' *livret*.[52] The originality of this new *livret* was indeed that it was managed by 'workers' representatives'. What 'trade-union independence' meant, therefore, was the independence of the trade-union authorities, the advancement of the union elite bound up with the regimentation of labour: rather like the 'iron heel' that Jack London had described, if somewhat milder in form. The majority of those who acquiesced in this ambiguous defence of trade unionism refused to press things quite so far.

Hence the inconsistency of this dream of the new trade-union order. For trade-union power only means anything if a sufficiently large section of the masses join. In the absence of this, trade-union officials have no other power than what the state lends them. In order to maintain their power, the collaborating trade unionists needed this minimum support. But how could the masses be mobilized around officials whose role was to regiment workers? The dream of the trade-union state was either too ambitious or too modest. A choice had to be made between the negotiation of social consensus and the organization of subjection of labour. The transformation of the National revolution into a Socialist revolution required different means.

'Beyond trade unionism'

There were those, therefore, who sought to transform this disenchanted situation into a new dynamism: trade unionism would never have the means to get the state as it existed to adopt its programme of nationalizations, which alone could advance the socialist revolution. It thus had to go beyond its present form:

> Trade unionism today must therefore realize that it can no longer either defend the workers or transform the regime by acting alone. Better still, the defence of the workers can no longer be conceived without a transformation in the regime – in other words, without the socialist revolution being accomplished. But this revolution is

52   See above, p 65. [Tr.]

impossible without a state that is both authoritarian and popular, and without a revolutionary party.[53]

Those who rose up in 1920 against the Bolshevik subversion of trade unionism and socialist democracy continued to rediscover the ABC of communism.[54] The Vichy people stopped halfway, with their trade-union transmission belt and their programme of nationalizations that they 'respectfully proposed to the Marshal'. In Paris, the activists of the 'Centre Syndicaliste de Propagande' founded by the contributors to *L'Atelier* in the current of Déat's Rassemblement National Populaire were more radical: it was not enough to use the strength of the trade unions to support the Vichy 'left'; the whole Vichy system was rotten and had to be replaced by a people's state.[55] At a 'Conférence Nationale Syndicale' organized by the Centre on 15 November 1941, Professor Zoretti defined the programme of the revolution to be made. Zoretti, who had been the first academic in 1918 to join the Fédération des Instituteurs, was subsequently converted to the merits of planning but remained a pacifist activist and in 1939 signed the manifesto for an 'immediate peace'. Dismissed from his university chair by one

---

53   *Le Rouge et le Bleu*, 13 February 1941.

54   The editor of *Le Rouge et le Bleu*, Spinasse, was himself aware of this, which led him to take his distance from Déat and his plan for a 'single party': 'Marcel Déat takes us back twenty years. The positions he adopts today, to which all his talent is not enough to give a new shine, are those that we opposed at the Tours congress in 1920. They are those that brought Russia into misery and Europe into war' ('La fuite en avant', *Le Rouge et le Bleu*, 1 August 1942).

55   In *L'Atelier*, at least, this discourse never ruled out a 'pure trade-unionist' one. And the denunciation of Vichy reaction that was heard so loud in 1941 became much more lukewarm when Laval returned to power in April 1942 and set up new state bodies to satisfy the appetite of the *L'Atelier* collaborators: the Comité d'Information Ouvrière et Sociale and the Office des Comités Sociaux, where Dumoulin, its appointed inspector, acted as commercial traveller for the same medieval Charte which he had previously ridiculed. Beyond the very clear political games and personal ambitions, however, there was a genuine oscillation between a trade-union view of the *ordre nouveau* and a totalitarian one.

of the ministers of national education who followed at an acceler-
ated pace during the first months of the Vichy regime, Zoretti, who
in 1944 would be responsible for organizing the Université du
Travail, represented very well those trade unionists repressed by
the nationalist and clerical – even royalist – reaction under Vichy,
which brought the forces of collaboration in Paris, and particular
the RNP, the continuity of the great socialist and secular tradition
as well as the martyr's halo. After having saluted the historical
importance of Marxism, he presented his new form of socialism, an
'ultra-Marxism that goes beyond Marxism, that sees the possibility
of grouping the different anti-capitalist forces by means of a return
to the national and the notion of structural reforms'. The economic
objective 'of removing all influence from the trusts by means of
nationalizations' presupposed the establishment of a strong state
'backed by a popular movement in which the workers' element
would guarantee the maximum purity', and internationally the
collaboration of this renovated French socialism with German
National Socialism.[56]

This collaboration with National Socialism was never presented
by the *L'Atelier* people as a harsh reality to which the French had to
bend, but rather as a demand that Vichy reaction refused to satisfy.
Like the defenders of class collaboration, the propagandists of
collaboration with National Socialism presented collaboration as a
victory to be won and played the role of freelance snipers. There was
no shortage of occasions to associate reaction with a rejection of
collaboration.[57] Thus under the headline 'a sad story', *L'Atelier*
reported the story of a white-collar worker, the secretary of his
union, who was persecuted by a Gaullist employer because of his
support for Franco-German rapprochement, as well as protesting
against the poor functioning of the Comité de Secours. 'Do you not
believe,' it concluded, 'that there are other comrades like Robert
who are persecuted without respite for having refused to lend

56   Account in *L'Atelier*, 22 November 1942.
57   Cf. in *La France au Travail* (3 February 1941): 'Collaboration with
Germany in no way horrifies them because Germany defeated us, but rather
because Germany is socialist.'

themselves to Gaullist tricks . . . for having sought to remain activists for the workers' cause?'[58]

L'Atelier never missed an opportunity to tug on this left-wing string, placing the champions of collaboration on the side of the republican, socialist and secular tradition: defence of the municipal councillors elected by universal suffrage when the minister of the interior went on the attack against them: sporadic protests against the excesses of the campaign against freemasons; defence of secularism and the Syndicat des Instituteurs, the spearhead of pacifism as well as of secularism. On 15 March 1941, *L'Atelier* commented on the dismissal of Maurice Wullens: 'At a time when the priest is making a return to the secular school, it is only to be expected that someone like Wullens should be expelled.' *Le Rouge et le Bleu* waxed indignant at the advice that *Candide* gave the new minister: 'All that M. Carcopino needs is a precious collaboration, that of his pupils' parents. The children's exercise books, and still more their conversation, tell a good deal about the way in which they are being taught.'[59] But was it mere accident that these sanctions were applied by men brought up in the tradition of reactionary chauvinism? Marcel Déat's deputy, the philosopher René Château, gave a timely reminder in *L'Oeuvre* that the purging minister Jacques Chevallier had written in the wake of 1918 an unforgettable book on Descartes, opposing healthy French philosophy to the diabolical philosophy of Kant and Hegel. In the same fashion, protests were raised against the Vichy moral order that even banned the performance of Molière's *Tartuffe* in Lyon in 1941. *L'Atelier* was quick to respond to the anti-socialist and anti-union attacks of the far right, particularly defending the memory of Jaurès, the man of socialism and Franco-German reconciliation, against attacks in *Gringoire*, *Candide* and other publications.[60]

---

58   11 March 1942.
59   Cited by *Le Rouge et le Bleu*, 31 January 1942.
60   Jaurès's name had a great symbolic value throughout the Occupation. The collaborationist trade unionists vigorously criticized those local authorities who renamed streets that had been called after him, with a view to currying favour with the authorities, and welcomed Pétain's proclaimed hostility to the very principle of such name-changing.

But it was employer paternalism that particularly attracted *L'Atelier*'s most vehement criticism. Dumoulin excelled in his descriptions of 'employers fond of little concerts and charity fêtes presided over by the director's lady'[61]: an outmoded and feminine characterization of paternalism whose antithesis was the modern décor and virile atmosphere of the German factory. Here as elsewhere the old forces seemed linked with national reaction, and the new forces needed to base themselves on what was novel in Germany. The weakness of the Vichy power, and the impotence of the pure trade unionists – whether Fédération secretaries or the friends of *Au Travail* – were linked with their rejection of the German revolution. It was this discovery of National Socialist modernity that led the collaborators of *L'Atelier* to take the step that separated trade-union indifferentism towards politics, even pacifism, from collaboration with Nazi peace and war.

'Germany as I've seen it'

At the beginning, there were pious generalities about the collaboration of peoples in peace – a peace 'above the storm':

> German victory? English victory? What I would like is for trade unionism to be above all that. Let it be neither Anglophile nor Anglophobe: that doesn't correspond to anything. Let it remain, in conformity with its role, the organ and means of working for the reconciliation of peoples and their collaboration in reconstruction.

This is how Aimé Rey expressed himself at the Conférence Syndicale held on 5 February 1941.[62] Unfortunately, though, the war continued and the German need for labour-power increased. The same style, seeking to obtain this increase gently, was at work in the publication of reports by competent observers on the

---

61 5 April 1941.

62 *L'Atelier*, 8 February 1941.

situation of French workers in Germany. In March 1941, a union delegation led by Dumoulin was invited on a study trip.

Contrary to the old saying, travel may well be less useful for the education of youth than for that of men of mature age, for example these veterans of unionism who had been around a long time, had shed a good deal of naivety, and were able, beyond all ideologies and tall stories, to judge a regime by its 'achievements'. By inviting the patriarchs of British social reformism, the Webbs, to study their achievements, the Soviets did more for the propaganda of the Stalinist order than a thousand Trotskyist or Menshevik pamphlets could undo. Dumoulin and his companions were summoned to play the same role in Germany.[63] They saw there just what someone from the British Labour party might have seen in Stalinist Russia, or a French Gaullist deputy in socialist China: intense activity, workers who had emerged from wretchedness but had not been corrupted by egoistic luxury, clean factories, model social projects; officials who spoke frankly about their problems, plans and achievements, what still wasn't going well but would gradually improve. In the same way they were full of contradictory feelings, admiring the work accomplished, impressed by the mysticism that inspired the working community without themselves sharing it, doubtful as to the possibility of applying in their own country what worked so well over there. This was the case with our Parisians. They did not believe that the organization of the Arbeitsfront, which united everyone in the firm without distinction, was suitable for French workers' traditions. But a certain image remained in their eyes, and the articles that they wrote to inform French workers about the life of their comrades in Germany

---

63   Dumoulin played the role of the man who only believes what he sees with such conviction that he grew rather slapdash with his words: 'Let us leave aside stupidities, wipe out the lies, and take things as they are: food supply is better organized in Germany than in France. There are no queues on the pavements' ('L'Allemagne comme je l'ai vue', *L'Atelier*, 29 March 1941). If he had been less concerned for his truth effect, Dumoulin would doubtless have reflected that there might be a causal connection between food supplies in Germany and France.

reproduce this image indefinitely: those large porcelain-tiled lavatories where water gushed from a basin; those spotless changing-rooms, those spacious and sunny canteens. Here is the account of 'a Paris engineering worker in the factories of the Reich'; not just anyone, as this was Léon Duvernet, one of the founders of the Cercle Syndicaliste Lutte des Classes [class struggle trade-unionist circle] which in the pre-war years had united various components of the far left of the working class: revolutionary syndicalists, expelled Communists, Trotskyists, diverse leftists. In Tuttlingen he met a French workers' delegate from 1936 who shared his amazement with him:

> The canteen, situated on the top floor of the factory, is a large and well-lit hall, with air and light streaming in. Everyone eats well. 'You'll remember,' my comrade told me, 'those sandwiches that we ate on the job in our workshop in France amid the oil and the metal shavings.'[64]

This witness was not lying, moreover, and pointed out that certainly not all factories were like that one. But in telling what he had seen he was singing an old song: these spacious premises with so much air and light are what model employers, philanthropic or concerned for public health, constantly extolled in the previous century as suited to ensuring the regeneration of the poor and social harmony. These dreams of integration through architecture and hygiene were countered by a notion of workers' dignity that did not want to owe anything to benefits from on high. Dumoulin shows us the conversion that had taken place in the development of trade-union thought, and made it susceptible to fascist seduction, in a text in the same issue of *L'Atelier* in which he opposed those who wanted to immediately set up an 'enterprise community' in French factories. The French factory, he says, is in no way prepared for this:

---

64   *L'Atelier*, 5 April 1941.

Compared with the German factory, the French factory in the majority of cases is a pigsty, a box, a grey barracks, lacking any facilities. The French worker goes to his factory or mine with the burning desire to escape from it once his work is finished. The 'enterprise community' presupposes an attachment, attraction and harmony between things and men. It does not presuppose a dark prison, a fortress walled in by warders. It calls for cleanliness, hygiene, safety and dignity at the place of work. We do not have this in France. And so we must build and transform before committing ourselves in a total anticipation that would be purely theoretical, since the context does not exist.

I am also distrustful of a concealed anticipation that would prettify the French factory with little concerts, charity fêtes presided by the director's lady, with sweets for the children, a lottery for housewives, and New Year's bonuses for men in difficulty.[65]

The dignity of the worker and the rejection of paternalism are always mentioned, but now, in the face of a paternalism equated with dirty and outdated factories, it was this workers' dignity, invested in the demand for hygiene, that could appeal from the archaic conditions of liberal capitalism to Hitlerite modernity. Even if Dumoulin, who was aware of representing the people of the mining villages, waxed eloquent on the theme of the liberating value of sunshine and cleanliness, this point of sensitivity to fascist seduction is attested by witnesses that were less solicited: a former member of the Cercle Lutte des Classes remembers the surprise of a Bordigist comrade who had been forced by unemployment to leave for Germany along with a friend:

I saw them when they returned. I wouldn't say that they had become Hitlerites, but though they did not return as enthusiasts, they were at least astonished by working conditions there. In France you had to wash yourself at a pipe punctured with holes where the water came out; there they had sinks with taps and both

---

65 'On n'a pas voulu de moi à Vichy', *L'Atelier*, 5 April 1941.

hot and cold water. It was clean, with tiles on the floor; there was a cupboard in which you put your work clothes, and another cupboard in which you put your town clothes so that they did not get soiled. They worked in a factory were magnesium was machined; this catches fire very easy, so it was forbidden to smoke. But there was a smoking room, and every hour they were able to go out and have a cigarette. That did surprise him.[66]

The cigarette break, as we know, was something of a symbol of workers' freedom in the face of the bosses' devouring of time. This respite time, as well as the cleanliness that meant respect for the worker, indicated a certain tie between the economic demand for decent working conditions and the ideological demand of respect for workers' dignity. We need to remember the feudal oppression that – except in the interval of 1936–8 – often prevailed between the wars in the 'engineering prisons' of France, to make credible this 'freedom' discovered in the Nazi model factory, and understand the operation by which Dumoulin came to reduce the demands for workers' dignity to the modern-ized forms of maintaining labour-power. The other side of this revolution in hygiene was noted by Dumoulin, not without a certain naivety – or perhaps cynicism? – in the lecture he gave on his visit in Bordeaux:

You can see here that what vexed the Frenchman was that he couldn't be completely French. In a German factory, a Frenchman cannot draw graffiti. With all this porcelain, these shining washrooms, you are not allowed to come in with a pencil and write on the walls.[67]

'A fine dream of yesteryear'

The happiness of the German worker that these trade-union dele-gates measured in terms of washrooms was made into a theory by

---

66   Personal communication.
67   *L'Atelier*, 12 April 1941.

Francis Delaisi. This principle was nothing else than the emancipation of labour freed from the tutelage of money by substituting the work-standard for the gold standard. A substitution that had been inaugurated by the clever system of Dr Schacht when, in order to finance the public works needed to absorb the unemployed, he dreamed up a system of credit based not on gold but on living labour:

> Wages must have their own value and their particular standard. Until now it was gold, inert metal, that alone measured availabilities and scarcities, and of which the least that can be said is that it did not take human values into account. From now on it will be human labour . . . This is the sole source of all wealth. It is natural therefore that it should be the common measure of the goods that it has created.[68]

'Was Proudhon a Nazi?', *La France au travail* had already asked.[69] The Proudhonist ideal that creative labour should be able to exchange against creative labour, suppressing the parasitic circuit of gold, Delaisi proposed to realize in a paradoxical way: not this time in mutualist freedom, but in a radicalization of wage-labour and in a statized work and life: this was the German 'revolutionary' practice of the 'full wage':

> In the same way as cost prices include not just the inputs of the machines but also accidents, wear and tear, the amortization of the capital that they cost and their replacement – in just the same way the workers' wage includes not just his food and maintenance (clothing, housing, etc.) but also insurance (sickness, accidents, unemployment), pensions for old age as well as family allowances, even contributions for holidays and sport, etc.[70]

---

68   F. Delaisi, 'L'étalon-travail', *L'Atelier*, 4 April 1942.
69   *La France au travail*, 19 December 1940.
70   *L'Atelier*, 4 April 1942.

This was certainly not the old dream of the republic of workers, but no more was it simply a totalitarian mystique, unrestrained love of the race, the state and the leader; it was rather a reasonable image of National Socialism, one in which the life of the workers, production and the state were united in the mesh of a generalized social security.

But the same problem arises as in any revolution, that of the world market, whose products, fruits of the exploitation of labour, flooded the German domestic market:

> In order to avoid this, the Reich has hit on a simple and bold solu-
> tion: to invite the neighbouring peoples to give their workers and
> employees the same benefits, and lead them to form together a
> wide economic living space, a single domestic market with a single
> currency . . . Continental Europe, by making human labour the
> common measure of the wealth it creates, will thus have freed the
> producer from the yoke of commerce and the competition of
> distant lands . . .
>
> Thanks to the full wage, the conscientious worker, assured that
> his labour will cover his needs, will no longer be under the arbi-
> trary material dependence of another man – the number one
> guarantee for the dignity of the human person.
>
> Thus, by a surprising paradox, the German revolution will
> have brought into everyday reality both the old dream of socialism
> and the most profound aspiration of ancient Christianity.[71]

Should we once again just shrug our shoulders? Wasn't all this discourse about the abolition of gold simply signed by a different kind of gold, the gold of corruption as exchanged for all commodities and ideas? Francis Delaisi was hard up when his trade-union friends offered him the chance of a little writing work. Another testimony, however, invites reflection, that of Christian Pineau, who tells of the meal that he shared with Delaisi on 23 June 1940, in a Charente village where the columns of the German army were

---

71   Christian Pineau, *La Simple Vérité*, p. 72.

just arriving, and where this man, whose intellectual honesty seemed to him beyond question, stood up to say that he would follow the Marshal, as he could no longer accept that Frenchmen should die for the City of London:

> I thought that I had the very same background as he did: a certain peasant upbringing, the same hatred of the power of money. And suddenly, after a few motor vehicles drove through a village, we realized that we did not have the same soul.[72]

It could not be better put: only a trifle is needed, a difference in sensitivity to the new spectacle in the street, for One to divide in two, for the ideas people thought they shared to break apart – the hatred of capitalism, the faith in a planned economy, the desire for a state more capable than the feeble Third Republic of imposing its power on the forces of money; for the path of resistance to present itself to one person, while the other, needing to earn a bit of money, sets in motion a crazy writing machine, able to connect all the old mad dreams and all the reasonable ideas gained in the practice of the workers' movement with the achievements of the Nazi order, so that the workers' dream finds its embodiment in the Hitlerite nightmare. This is his reaction for example when Dr Robert Ley visits Paris, head of the Arbeitsfront and organizer of the 'Strength Through Joy' movement which presided over the happy life and leisure of the German workers:

> People used to laugh, in respectable circles, when we spoke of workers' leisure. As if workers had been created to have leisure . . .
>
> Not a great deal has been achieved in France in this series of ideas, but we can signal all the same such attempts as Albert Doyen's Fêtes du Peuple, the theatre productions of the Centre d'Éducation Ouvrière, and Poulaille's Musée du Soir. These are considerable efforts, given the difficulties they face, but almost nothing in relation to what has been done in Germany.

---

72   *L'Atelier*, 11 July 1942.

> This is why we feel extreme sympathy with what 'Strength Through Joy' has done. It is rather like a fine dream of yesteryear that we can see alive and real in our neighbouring country.[73]

Here again, we see how an old proposition has suffered a change of direction. For the whole point of the revolutionary syndicalist tradition that the Musée du Soir followed, for example, was not to provide labour-power with better conditions for its reproduction, but rather to have workers give themselves an autonomous culture that would be precisely something different from this reproduction, and different again from the culture that justifies the privileges of their masters. What made possible this change was the effect of *ouvriériste* statement, this voice that we have often heard, deliberately sounding a bit rougher than usual to say that these matters of the working class can never be understood at all by people who have studied too much, who haven't known the darkness of pit villages and the struggles of militants in the early days of the workers' movement: the voices of those who, all the better to bury the dreams of yesteryear in their supposed realization, capitalize on the sufferings and sacrifices of others.

Dr Ley, moreover, who called on the workers to 'free themselves from capitalist exploitation',[74] did not come to Paris for any other reason than to reinforce propaganda in favour of that labour deportation initially known as the *relève*, which would later be called the STO. It was this undertaking, which could scarcely still claim to be continuing a trade-union function, and which those Fédération secretaries or groups such as *Au Travail* that had played the game of the *ordre nouveau* preferred not to concern themselves

---

73   *L'Atelier*, 11 July 1942.

74   *Au Travail* greeted the 'moving' *relève* (11 July 1942), and on 8 August published a warning against the detractors of 'the resolve shown by a large part of the working class in coming to the aid of Germany, devoted to serving the legitimate interests of European civilization'. But it later preferred to restrict its interest to more traditional trade-union questions, and the *relève* and subsequent STO seem almost forgotten in the pages of the newspaper.

with,[75] that Dumoulin's Centre Syndicaliste de Propagande had to harness. If the *L'Atelier* people lent themselves to this work without repugnance, it was because their domestic hopes had soon evaporated. Disappointed in their expectation of taking the lead in a re-established trade-union movement, dismissed by their unions or remaining at the head of phantom Fédérations, like Robert Paul, they could not speak in the name of any mass base. If they took part in the application of the Charte, which Laval's return led them to see in a new light, it was not as workers' leaders but as government social officials. Dumoulin, appointed inspector of social committees, travelled the deserts in search of factory committees that neither employers nor workers bothered to establish. Convinced that from the top of the state down to the working-class rank and file, 'woodworms' were sabotaging the Charte, the dream that they needed turned increasingly towards a European socialist revolution. In other words, they turned the rather coarse prose of Gauleiter Sauckel into workers' poetry. For since June 1941, the European revolution was no longer simply a struggle against English Judeo-capitalism, but a struggle against 'its unexpected but natural ally' of Bolshevism:

> Whether union activists like it or not, they are forced to choose. They must opt either for Bolshevism or for the socialist revolution. There is no possible middle term between these two positions.[76]

In this effort, the attempt was naturally made to play on the old working-class chords of solidarity and devotion. But alas! The workers would no longer devote themselves, and in the face of this sad reality the former anarchist Charles Dhooghe approved the establishment of the Service du Travail Obligatoire as a 'work of social justice': 'Finally the state, as emanation of the collective consciousness of a people, has taken charge of questions relating to

75   'Une oeuvre de justice sociale', *L'Atelier*, 26 September 1942.
76   Roger Paul, *L'Atelier*, 9 October 1943.

labour.'[77] And when the STO entered into application at the start of 1943, Rémi de Marmande, also a former fellow-traveller of the revolutionary syndicalists, welcomed this obligation for all – workers and bourgeois alike – that broke the division between manual and mental labour; in this application he saw 'a revolutionary measure', amounting to 'the revenge of Émile':

> 'Man in society is bound to work; rich or poor, weak or strong, every idler is a thief . . . Émile shall learn a trade.'
>
> 'My son learn a trade! My son an artisan? What are you thinking of, sir!'
>
> 'Madam, my thoughts are wiser than yours; you want to make him fit for nothing but a lord . . .'[78]

No doubt, the author notes, this was initially a war measure, 'but the revolutionary measure will necessarily expand and acquire its social significance when peace is restored, in accordance with the creative anticipations of J-J. Rousseau, Fourier, Proudhon and Kropotkin.'

Hitler's executioners found still more theoretical justifiers than their Stalinist colleagues. There is no modern concentration camp system that does not have to acquire the hallmark of emancipated labour, guaranteeing itself 'working-class purity'. Marxism is only one brand among others. It is useless therefore to follow any further the packaging of this all-justifying machine, which, once the repressive apparatus turns fast enough to engage it automatically, can indifferently grind up Marx or Proudhon, Fourier or Jaurès. It is however worth dwelling a bit on this 'workers' dream' that found its exalted reality in the STO and 'Strength Through Joy'.

Behind the justifications that trade-union collaboration gave itself, or the bait that it offered, we see a nightmarish figure of the workers' dream: a workers' nightmare in which monstrous figures of ideals and practices are condensed, systems and images that for

---

77 'Une mesure révolutionnaire', *L'Atelier*, 8 February 1943.
78 Quotation from Rousseau's *Émile*, in *Au Travail*, 3 July 1943.

a century punctuated working-class thought and action: workers' solidarity, in the name of which workers were asked to agree to labour deportation, with the very organization of this sordid trade acting under the signboard of an apotheosis of labour, recognized as the foundation of all wealth at the same time as the cultural and moral foundation of the social order; labour exalted in its materiality, in the great rehabilitation of skilled trades and craftsmanship organized by Vichy or magnified in the modernity of the bright Nazi factory; labour recognized in the 'dignity' it had always demanded by those who requested the representatives of workers to collaborate in the *ordre nouveau*, letting them glimpse the mirage of a world in which the natural rules that govern the selection of working-class cadres, the rules of devotion and skill, would govern the selection of new elites in the service of the collective. Added to this nightmare were caricatures of the contradictory ideologies that had managed to divide working-class activists: the great tradition of trade union apoliticism that became indifference to oppression, the old dream of a union school training free men for the future free society that became a school of young cadres for the statized economy; while the young dream of the Bolshevik revolution, the epic of the Party, the heroic images of victorious Labour and the New Life, found their nerve-grating caricature in the grand gesture of French workers setting out to construct the new life of the 'European revolution' in Nazi Germany. We can also see here how the old plans for workers' emancipation merged with modernistic employers' dreams of reorganized work and new forms of payment. The production cooperative, a residue of the dreams of centuries for abolishing wage-labour, was presented as a cell of the *ordre nouveau*. At the co-operators' congress in Limoges, Victor Josse depicted the co-operative movement as a prefiguration of the Charte du Travail.[79] Workers' participation, the execution of tasks by an autonomous team free to organize its own work and distribute its rewards, had been rekindled between the two wars by Hyacinthe Dubreuil, an engineer and former

---

79   *L'Atelier*, 23 May 1942.

minority syndicalist from 1914-18 who had since come to see Taylorist organization as the new path of workers' emancipation. But Vichy did not reinstate this without competition from elsewhere. To its bold initiatives, such as the suppression of clocking in, there were competing systems such as the 'proportionate wage' championed and put into practice by the great employers' thinker of the RNP, Eugène Schueller, author of *La Révolution de l'économie* as well as the inventor, for the suppression of slums, of system-built houses that also allowed air and light to flood in, to the greater joy of Dumoulin. But interesting effects of the Dubreuil system were experienced in the Ruinet shoe factory, where members of an autonomous team reduced the share of a deaf-mute who worked with them, and replied to the boss who reproached them for this: 'It's clear that it's not your money at stake.'[80]

The retro-modernist nightmare of a working-class fascism drawing support from the trade-union transmission belt, bright factories and housing estates, and workers' participation. Yet this is only an inconsistent image. The fascism sketched by this circulation of working-class fantasies of the new order is something that no one really wanted. The same ideas that suggested it also put a stop to it. Even for the champions of the new order themselves, one working-class value collided with another: for example, the critique of capitalist egoism rebuffed the seductions of participation. Those who did indeed intend to transform trade-union activists into government officials did not want the workers to be transformed into capitalists. And above all, the mass of workers never at any time recognized this 'workers' dream' as their own. The collaborating trade unionists found them opposing a passive resistance to all the seductions of the new workers' order. They might well ask the official trade-union representatives for this service or the other that fell within their remit, but in

---

80   On 25 December 1943 *Au Travail* criticized the Ruinet experiment as follows: 'Didn't M. Ruinet realize that this pitiful state of mind among his workers might be the result of his system? . . . As a capitalist experiment, moreover one in the sense of a more stable and harsher capital, the Ruinet experiment naturally tends to give the workers a capitalist mentality.'

no way did they bother to join the union and supply it with the 'mass base' needed for the grand strategy of trade-union diplomacy. When they were expected at the trade-union offices, they were always elsewhere. Even if this elsewhere was most often the search for food supplies rather than underground action; even when their 'passivity' was waiting for things to change rather than a determined refusal, that was enough to put the machine out of joint, precisely because collaboration does not mean submission but requires action, because it cannot wait on events but has to anticipate and take its chance. In the grand diplomacy of collaboration on which trade-union diplomacy was engaged, the element without which nothing could be done was lacking: the pressure of the masses. This initial absence, this 'indifference' of the masses to the grand projects of national or European reconstruction, was perceived early on by the champions of collaboration, but here again, their experience gave them the means to interpret it. Undoubtedly they increasingly blamed the forces of reaction – employers, technocrats, etc. – that prevented the masses from expecting anything good from the collaboration effort. But the experience of the fresh and joyful war of 1914 had taught them that trade-union activists could not lag behind the masses. Solitude thus became a proof of courage and reason, enabling Dumoulin to proclaim his submission to the Pétainist and Hitlerite order in terms that no one else could have invented:

It is better to disobey

The crowd surrounding me is hoping. It is hoping for a reversal of the facts, a change in the situation, an improvement in the position. It believes that military events will shift things in the direction of their hopes . . .

I would like to share this hope, to join in this belief. But I cannot. I am taking the road of disobedience in setting myself apart from the majority . . . I am for Franco-German collaboration.[81]

---

81   *L'Atelier*, 8 March 1941.

This 'dissidence' was still optimistic. I don't want to play the lone hero, Dumoulin declares. I have to speak to make myself understood and win over the masses. When it became clear that Dumoulin had nothing else to propose to the masses in order to mobilize them except work in Germany or enrolment in the Legion des Volontaires Français, Roger Paul struck a more bitter note in denouncing those comrades who had given up on the possible revolution out of servility towards the mass of workers:

> It is up to the activist to guide the mass of workers, it is he who has to see clearly across and beyond current events, and has to explain them. The iniquities of the capitalist regime invited workers to organize to defend their interests, and imposed on activists a purely *ouvriériste* action, all the more so as the state itself carried out the orders of capitalism. Each time they broke away from this *ouvriériste* action, activists lost the trust of their comrades and found themselves expelled from their positions of responsibility. This is why they were constantly hamstrung in their action by the concern not to lose the trust of their comrades. They formed the habit of being conservative in their own way.
>
> There certainly were innovators and precursors who enabled the trade-union movement to advance. But long years always passed before these were followed by the majority of workers. And these fallow years for the spirit cost a great deal of sacrifice for the innovators and precursors.[82]

Here we can see the end-point of the logic of collaboration: wasn't having failed to convince anyone of your loyalty itself the best proof of that loyalty? At least the result is a good conscience. Let us therefore leave our two 'martyrs' to try and drown the shots of the firing squad with their noise. Let us leave them to weep in August 1944 for their sons who fell for the cause of the Nazi revolution. We shall dwell instead for a moment on another

---

82 'Le syndicalisme et l'action anti-bolchévique', *L'Atelier*, 9 October 1943.

tomb, that of Pierre Arnaud, secretary of the miners' federation in the Loire, a former Communist activist and member of that united opposition that tried to bring about trade union unity around 1930, and whose 'devotion' to the National Revolution was punished in December 1944 by the bullets of the Resistance. In the funeral address of his comrade Thévenon, beneath the rhetoric of homage to the misunderstood pioneers of emancipation, a little more disquiet shows through, perhaps the feeling of having been taken in:

> Pierre Arnaud, you represented for us an idea: the idea of a society in which the formula of one for all and all for one would have been embodied. This idea was pushed to the back of the stage. Brought to the front was the idea of communities governed by hierarchical elites; the direction was towards new forms of exploitation, the consecration of new privileges. It is possible that this may succeed, but the defects of the new regime will not be long to show, and then trade unionism will be reborn. There will be new Varlins, new Griffuelhes, new Pierre Arnauds, and one step further will have been taken on the road of the emancipation of working people.[83]

The rhetoric of a straight line of advance barely conceals the idea that perhaps the cards had been wrongly dealt, and this wasn't a reason to die. But it also raises questions beyond its own scandal or derision. For precisely this eulogy attests to a time when everything had gone wrong in the fine history of the workers' movement, its achievements, its values and its heroes, when the straight line of the activists of yesterday, devoting their lives to the emancipation of their brothers, had been lost in the complex geography of the new relationships between the workers' movement and the state, relationships between the nation and internationalism and the new faces of the revolution; when you could be a sell-out without pocketing a penny or a traitor while devoted to your brothers, because the powers of today strike a

---

83 'Adieu à Pierre Arnaud', *Au Travail*, 22 January 1944.

variety of notes, and finding new opportunities to express devotion might well be a surer means for seducing them.

The fact that there was no longer a straight line of working-class thought and action is evidenced by a resistance to collaboration born out of a rejection of all the 'working-class' values that the champions of the new order put forward. This is the real nature of that 'apathy' and 'indifference' which the workers opposed to the speeches delivered to seduce them: as opposed to the devotion and solidarity that were demanded of them, they rediscovered the virtues of a certain 'egoism' – meaning those of individual with-drawal and an individual regard towards the new environment that engaged new solidarities, freed from the ambiguity of 'objective interests' and undermining the attractions of the officialized work-ers' ideology. Against the hymns to liberating labour, this resistance relearned the subversive virtues of working just to live, as well as those of anti-production – work badly done and sabo-tage. As if the 'workers' nightmare' was opposed by ideas and forms of resistance that proclaimed the need for a different point of view from that of those 'workers' interests' management of which sealed the participation of workers' representatives in the games of the modern state. The history of workers' collaboration and resist-ance casts light on features of the 'normal' course of working-class history that are often poorly recognized: that a mere trifle is needed for the themes that maintain struggle to be identified with those that feed submission; that the idea of class must always be twinned with something else, so as not to be the idea of class collaboration. This is perhaps the role played by the new patriotism that Julian Hapiot or Pierre Georges had learned, not by inaugurating monu-ments to Rouget de l'Isle, but rather by fighting in Spain against the international army of fascism.

8

Good Times, Or, Pleasure at the Barrière

There is nothing new here, except that *The Magic Flute* has been performed eighteen times, with the theatre always full to bursting. It is considered intolerable for anyone to say that they've not seen it. The workers and gardeners all go, even the good people of Sachsenhausen whose children take the parts of lions and monkeys in the opera. Nothing like this has ever been seen here. The theatre is forced to open at four in the afternoon, and despite everything, each time there are several hundred persons unable to find places and obliged to go away

— Frau Hofrat Goethe, 1793 (from J. and B. Massin, *Mozart*)

There is certainly something picturesque about this crowd in their workaday *blouses* who fill the upper tiers of the popular theatres, and perhaps we lose in gaiety and enthusiasm what we gain in individual well-being and general civilization, but this is an advance that is indicated by good taste and seems to be demanded by justice

— Camille Doucet, head of the Theatre division, 'Note to His Excellency the Minister of State', 30 June 1862

Work and goguette: the intoxication of hearts

A decree of 17 November 1849 gave legal existence to a form of entertainment that had existed for only a few years: *cafés-concerts*. This liberal measure, however, brought with it certain restrictions. The day's programme had to be submitted each morning to the commissariat of police. Forbidden, naturally enough, was 'any kind of political or immoral song'; but so too were 'cross-dressing, dancing, fragments of opera, choruses and ensemble pieces, ballet, noisy instruments', as well as the public posting of the programme and 'foreign meetings'. On 12 August 1850, a law of 30 July was followed by a decree laying down the general principle of this supervised freedom:

> In future the directors of theatres, impresarios of spectacles, concerts and *cafés-chantants* in the capital and its suburbs will not be allowed to announce on their posters and programmes the first performance of any dramatic work, any play, individual scene, cantata, ballad, song or ditty – in a word anything that is recited, sung or played in public – without the manuscript or scenario having been approved by the minister of the interior and without this approval having been presented to the commissariat of police of the quarter or the commune in which the establishment is situated.[1]

The police state thus had total control over what could be recited, sung or played: only rarely has repression spoken such an unpolished language as during the legislature of 1849. And yet here as elsewhere, decisions of the state power change their meaning according to whether they are read principally in the sense of what they repress or of what they produce. The monarchical republic of 1850, traumatized by the memory of June 1848, might invent the most meticulous regulations in order to keep tabs on everything that moved or raised a voice, yet the Imperial regime for which it paved the way was just as greedy for spectacles, songs, exhibitions and entertainments of every kind. As well as the obligatory rituals of Imperial parades, something was under way that would survive the defeat of 1870 and see its full development under the Third Republic. In both the everyday world of the cafés-concerts and the exceptional one of great exhibitions, the continuous cleaning-up and embellishment of the city under Haussmann and the

---

1   Archives Nationales (F[21] 1338).

democratization of the Empire's aristocratic pleasures (sports and the racecourse), as also in the popularizing of new cultural inventions (cinema and gramophone), the same movement seems to have been under way, offering popular energies and passions the means, forms and sites of a regulated satisfaction, an optimal use of leisure. A single logic seems to prevail, with the improvisation of the entertainment police following the same curve as the commercial rationalization of popular leisure and culture; until this new culture of the people comes to occupy, in the interstices of working life, a place whose own logic makes the function of surveillance superfluous. (It was at the moment that the cinema and gramophone began to spread that the Commission de Censure des Beaux-Arts gave up the ghost.) It is tempting then to read this complementarity as the deployment of one of those grand strategies of power that are in vogue today, supplementing the rationalization of the exploitation of labour and the factory disciplining of the worker's body with a moralization and organization of leisure. The nature of the object makes it still harder to escape these panoptical totalizations. Popular festivities and their relationship with the state were in fact overdetermined by well-coded systems of images. The progressive and puritanical denunciation of plebs corrupted by circus games organized for them by the powerful was heard for a long time. Today we have visions of the festival as a release of popular energies, resistance to the economic and disciplined reproduction of labour-power, site or moment of a reversal of power in which, whether in simulacrum or derision, the people make themselves the equals or masters of their masters. These visions of a popular resistance to the order of labour, by the diversion of energies into drinking, carnival or vagabondage, are now commonplace. In actual fact matters are rather more complicated. The local bar, which naive historians see as a site of pure release of energy and liberation of popular speech, was equally a place where business was done: if you paid there to drink, it was often to pay for a job, or a job for a relative or friend, to curry favour with the foreman or more long-established workers – or conversely, to gain the goodwill of your workers. The bar did not

overturn the power of the workshop; it was part and parcel of negoti-
ating it. If the employer Denis Poulot joined with activist workers in
condemning it, this was not simply to preserve the labourer's physical
strength and moral dignity, but also because it was involved in an
unorganized negotiation of employment and use of labour-power
that each partner saw as operating to the benefit of his opposite
number. As for the errantry of Paris children, this was often no more
than a slight deviation from seeking or carrying out jobs as delivery
boy or girl, street seller, etc.[2] The respective territories of employer's
power and worker's power, the space of productive discipline and
that of unproductive expenditure, cannot so easily be separated. And
this is the point on which the deliberations of all those who sought to
moralize the workers – philanthropists, missionaries or working-class
activists – focused: the problem lay less in the existence of hideouts of
popular autonomy and indiscipline than in the cross-cutting between
circuits of work and circuits of leisure, in the proliferation of those
trajectories, real or ideal, by which workers moved in the space of the
bourgeois and let their dreams wander there.

Louis Reybaud, more lucid than his colleagues, when he went
to do research in Lyon, was less concerned with the more or less
imaginary orgies and conspiracies of the 'Voraces' than with a
certain calm in the workshops that made the routine of labour the
basis for dreaming.[3] A work that by its very monotony let the mind
of the labourer wander while his body was conscientiously accom-
plishing the task was no longer the antidote to idleness, mother of
all vices. To fix people in their existing state required more than
just those techniques of disciplining the body that certain people
narrowly oppose to the excesses of play and release of energy. The
brothers of Saint Vincent de Paul did not complain that the apprentices in their charge ran around too much, but rather that they did
not exert themselves enough. In the same way as the young
apprentice in the workshop was supposed to raise himself above

2   Cf. A. Cottereau's article in *Autrement* ('Dans la ville des enfants').
3   Louis Reybaud, *Rapport sur la condition matérielle et morale des ouvriers
qui vivent du travail de la soie*, Paris 1860.

the activity of his match-seller or delivery boy friends, semi-industrious and semi-idle, semi-serious and semi-playful, so he owed it to his guardians, by learning to play, to rise above the disordered agitation of their flânerie and practical jokes.[4] 'Pray and play' was the watchword of their missions, but the games that they combined with prayer were not such calm ones as we might believe. All the directors of the Saint Vincent de Paul missions, from the most traditional to the most modernist, were agreed in their contempt for lovers of lotto and dominoes who spent their afternoons sitting down, and gave absolute priority to 'running games'. The virtues they attributed to these might differ: the very austere Abbé Timon-David, for example, director of the project for young workers in Marseille, saw them simply as a way of sending home on Sunday evening youths who were too tired to go out dancing.[5] Maurice Maignen, in charge of Saint Vincent de Paul youth work in Paris, preferred to promote an ethic of light limbs and light hearts, in which the game of prisoner's base was a homologue and complement to confession.[6] But both those who saw tired limbs as a way of removing temptation, and those who sought to lighten hearts to bring them closer to God, shared the same intent: the mission was a place where young people learned play as such, opposed to both industrious errantry and dreamy idling.

As many fantasies can come into play in assessing the dangers of calm waters as in assessing those of carnivalesque orgies. But this provides a better basis for understanding a disquiet that arose less from a counterculture opposing from below the thought and culture of those above, than from the real and imaginary displacements authorized by a cultural space in which meeting-places or passageways between classes proliferated. The *goguette*, for example, was not exactly the place of drunkenness over which some people wax nostalgic. The typographer Supernant, who devoted a series of articles in *L'Atelier* to denouncing it, criticized its poor

4   Cf. *Almanach de l'apprenti*, 1855.
5   Cf. on these organizations' work in Marseille, *Le jeune ouvrier*, 1856.
6   Cf. Le Prévost, *Chroniques du patronage*, Paris 1862.

quality wine rather than its excesses. Nor was it really the site of an autonomous workers' culture. Saucy drinking songs in the working-class *goguette* did not have the same subversive lyrics or savage rhymes as those that echoed at the Caveau, a singing club of 'monarchist' tendency, heir to the sweet life of the days before 1789. And if the workers went there in their *blouses* – as they did to the 'gods' in the theatres – this was in fact less a place of autonomy and working-class communion than a place when you could escape the worker's condition without changing your clothes.

The king of the Belleville *chansonniers*, Gustave Leroy, most forceful in singing the rights of the '*blouses*' in 1848, himself went to Les Amis de la Vigne in evening dress. What idea did he have of worker's dignity, this illegitimate son of a theatre employee who enjoyed the aristocratic education of a Versailles boarding school thanks to the protection of a famous female tightrope walker? Or, if you prefer, what relationship was there between the political enthusiasm of the working class and the cultural emulation of individuals with a view to raising themselves above it? Indeed, the *goguette* served above all as a place of emulation. The 400 *goguettes* in Paris and its surroundings, where people came initially as spectators but might hope to sing and be sung, offered a profusion of underground artistic vocations. It was certainly rare for this to open the door to a genuine artistic career, such as that of the typographer Anatole Lionnet: taken there by a fellow worker who had – unknown to Lionnet – inscribed him for the evening's programme, he was noticed by the déclassé musician who played the piano, Joseph Darcier, who introduced him to the high-society singing evenings of Dr Orfila.[7] Most often success went no further than recognition by others, or by oneself. But that was enough to make the *goguette* less a place of compensatory relief for the productive order or the working-class community, and more an escape and a reverie that had its feedback in the workshop: this was where people made up verses and dreamed of the evening's success, taking advantage of breaks to learn singly or together the

---

7   *Souvenirs des frères Lionnet*, Paris 1886.

rudiments of music and versification, until they could sometimes express themselves better in verse than in prose.[8] And it is not so important that this mutual school of worker-poets did not give rise to a genuinely new expression in its form, or a really radical one in its message. Disorder might well arise less from a distinct working-class culture than from these odd apprenticeships in the common culture: less from a spontaneous culture than from a spontaneous relationship to culture – or, if you like, from a culture in disorder. The worker who, without having learned to spell, tried his hand at making verses to the taste of the day, was perhaps more dangerous for the existing ideological order than the one who sung revolutionary songs. The very possibility that the *goguette* could produce such propagandists as Charles Gille, or activist networks, was by way of this detour, by its aspect of a minoritarian cultural advance, introducing lines of fracture into the class of producers. For it is undoubtedly on the basis of such lines of fracture that a class becomes dangerous, on the basis of lines of escape for those minorities who can no longer tolerate the labour of the workshop, nor yet its manners and talk – in other words, can no longer tolerate *being a worker*. The *goguette* was one of the places that dynamized a class not by unifying it but rather by dividing it, making it produce minorities.

Those crocodile tears that well-intentioned bourgeois wept over the fate of such figures as Jules Mercier or Hégésippe Moreau, workers who died of despair from having sought to be poets without succeeding, sufficiently indicate this sensitive point: the genuinely dangerous classes were perhaps less those savages supposedly undermining the basement of society than the migrants who moved on the boundaries between classes – individuals and groups who developed within themselves abilities that were useless for the improvement of their material life, but suited to make them

---

8   This was the case with Jules Vinçard (*Mémoires épisodiques d'un vieux chansonnier saint-simonien*, Paris 1878). *L'Atelier*, for its part, asked in 1844: 'Which town, even the smallest, which state body, even the least significant, which workshop, even the most obscure, does not have in our day its versifier and writer?'

despise this. Such dreaming minorities in turn gave dreams to the masses who congregated around singers in the street, forgetting in listening to them the errands they were in the middle of, buying the loose sheets that they hawked and taking their choruses back to the workshop. This circulation of working-class songs – which sometimes surprised the authors themselves[9] – formed part of a wider process of acculturation: either workers started to dream of escape on the basis of ballads reaching them from salons that sung of beautiful Andalucian – or Albanian – ladies, proud mountaineers, Neapolitan sailors or the charm of one's native land, or else they reappropriated songs in which the clever poetasters of the Boulevard offered to curious admirers a picturesque image of happy rag-pickers, poor working women or carousers at the *barrières*.[10]

If we add to this all the adjustments and transformations that words and tunes might experience in their travels between the street, the *goguette* and the workshop, it is understandable how this culture in disorder managed to define itself, equally removed from accepted images of culture and counter-culture alike: a spontaneous movement of de-professionalization in the distance taken from one's original trade and the distance abolished with the knowledge of specialists and the culture of music-lovers, the natural proximity of spectacle and action, of 'art' and life, of the mundane and the dream. No doubt those Saint-Simonian workers, quite ignorant of music, who, when a band was to be formed to accompany Enfantin's voyage to Egypt, abandoned everything to learn the trombone in a few months, represent a limiting case. More typical already were the workers of the National Workshops of 1848, who occupied their enforced idleness with their first poetic attempts. 'If you like these, I can do others', one of these new poets wrote in black pencil in the letter with which he sent his first verses to *Le Père Duchêne*.[11] More representative still was the foundryman Victor Renard who rescued himself from the collapse of the

---

9   On the day that Gustave Leroy decided to live from his songs and have La Lionne lithograph them, he printed more than 20,000.

10   Cf. Gourdon de Genouillac, *Les refrains de la rue*, Paris 1879.

11   Archives historiques du Ministère de la guerre (A 3669).

National Workshops by becoming a street singer, or the shoe-
maker Brunet who, rather than take up his sedentary trade on
return from a stint in the navy, became an acrobat and ended up
writing songs, plays and operettas without ever having attended
school.[12] The political refusal of a *goguette* like La Ménagerie,
which constantly moved premises so as to be able to carry on singing freely, or someone like Charles Gille who flouted the repression
to peddle his songs, written by hand, stands in a continuous line
with those individual cultural refusals that attest to a working
population more mobile, less attached to their tools, less sunk in
misery or wallowing in drunkenness than various traditions represent it.

The ambiguous theatre

If the defenders of order would move to ban *goguettes* and subversive singers in the aftermath of 1848, reducing the likes of Charles
Gille and Gustave Leroy to silence, it was still more important for
them to undo the disorder of this cultural network that stretched
from workshop songs to theatre performances, by way of reading
the newspaper at the wine merchant's, gathering around singers
and the thousand other diversions of the street – to repress a
certain dramatization of what was said, sung and done in that
mixed cultural space which saw a confusion of styles, places, practices and classes. This uncertain space in which one never knew
what drama might ensue also attests to working-class participation in the theatre. It was not for nothing that Jean-Claude
Romand, in his model confession of a repentant insurgent, attributed his development of evil passions to his attendance at Paris
theatres, which arose from the fine parties given by an evil serving
woman at a good house, unknown to her mistress and at her
expense. The emotion of the theatre was one of those aristocratic
passions that could turn a tailoring worker into the leader of the

12   Cf. Marc Constantin, *Les cafés-concerts en 1866* (on Renard) and *L'Écho
des concerts*, August 1866 (on Brunet).

silk-workers' uprising in Lyon. The habit, in sum, of being always somewhere that you have nothing to do, of taking an interest in matters that are not your own.[13] Perhaps that was why the brothers of Saint Vincent de Paul only offered the untameable taste of their apprentices for the theatre little skits taken from their everyday experience. The morality of the goal was certainly less important than the abolition of any outlet towards other worlds or other conditions.[14]

At this time, in fact, there was not yet what we call 'popular theatre', i.e. theatre designed for people who do not go to the theatre. For the very good reason that they did go. More or less so, of course, according to the hierarchy that ran from the theatres on the Boulevard du Temple up to the Comédie Française, by way of the Porte Saint-Martin that was the realm of melodrama. But they hardly felt the need of a special theatre for themselves. They only needed to occupy the top tiers of those already existing. This passion was favoured, in the years from 1815 to 1848, by the development of new theatres, corresponding to the slow decay of the Napoleonic organization of theatre privileges. This had codified the separation between 'curiosity' shows (circuses, puppets, mime, tightrope walkers, horse-riding displays, comic characters, etc.) and theatres proper, which were reduced to a total of eight and each required to restrict itself to a specific repertoire: vaudeville in the theatre that bore its name, melodrama at L'Ambigu and two others, and the great dramatic repertoire at the Comédie Française . . .[15] The period from 1815 to 1848, however, saw the proliferation of 'encroachments' on this system, with new privileges granted to riding instructors, soft-drinks sellers, physicians, rope walkers and mimes who were concerned to extend their repertoire. Often, moreover, these dispensed with authorization and gradually transformed their shows into melodramas or

---

13   Jean-Claude Romand, *Confession d'un malheureux*, Paris 1846.
14   Cf. the playlets reproduced in the *Almanach de l'apprenti* and the various collections of Le Prevost.
15   'Each theatre is to be assigned a type of spectacle that it will have to adhere to', decree of 8 June 1806, art. 5.

vaudevilles, stealing even opera choruses from the repertoire of genuine theatres.

The Boulevard du Temple was the privileged site of these fair-ground theatres, which abusively annexed the domain of theatrical culture.[16] And this abuse, which mingled styles and mobilized those privileged by culture against its parasites, brought in its wake another: spectacles of an ill-defined kind were still more prey to those malversations that endangered the theatre: an actor's improvi-sation that addressed the audience, or interventions from the audience demanding topical songs (and when topical meant politi-cal, it is clear what abuses this could lead to), activist initiatives such as the impromptu Saint-Simonian choirs organized by Vinçard in a number of theatres. On 8 February 1831, the prefect of police had posters put up warning that 'no spectator may demand from actors any songs or verses that were not advertised on the day's programme'.[17] The habit of interposing songs in vaudeville or melo-drama performances, the appearance of cafés-concerts from 1845 on, which mingled songs, dances, dramatic extracts and various exhibi-tions, led to a control that was both interminable and ineffective: the songs and choruses interposed in a play might be anodyne, yet they still had the characteristic of stage music of being 'rousing', and however harmless the spoken parts and ditties, they still had a note of confidence or dialogue that addressed the audience too directly, putting them outside the simple role of spectator. As for changes to the programme, these could always produce a significant lapse. Hence the perplexity of the police commissioners who faithfully reported that at a matinee of the Société des Amis de l'Enfance, the actress Rachel had substituted scenes from *Horace* for scenes from *Bérénice*,[18] or that several songs had been sung at the Salle Saint-Jean

16   The Café d'Apollon, for example, started in 1816 to announce vaude-villes and melodramas; in 1830 the Théâtre Lazari went over from puppet shows to live actors, Les Funambules from tightrope walkers to vaudeville, etc. (cf. T. Faucheur, *Histoire du Boulevard du Temple depuis son origine jusqu'à sa demolition*, Paris 1863).
17   Archives Nationales, F^{21} 1045.
18   F^{21} 1338, 18 March 1846.

that were not authorized, including 'Le petit chaperon rouge' ['Little
Red Riding Hood'].[19] But even those theatres that stuck to their
repertoire still offered a dangerous spectacle. We may well be somewhat sceptical in reading declarations of people after 1848 that saw
the 'anarchist' morals of melodramas as one of the sources of the
'demoralization' that had led the working class to its well-known
excesses. Reading them in the way that Marx read *The Mysteries of
Paris*, it is hard to see the revolutionary import of these works, which
described – with the same protective/inquisitive view of Rodolphe
or the sentimental one of Fleur de Marie – a misery represented as
fatalism and a people either chided for its weaknesses or praised for
its honesty. In the theatre of the 1840s, divided between the bourgeois places in the stalls and the places for the '*blouses*' in the gods,
the message was far more ambiguous. What really was it that made
for the melodrama's interest? The spectacle of misery. But how
could the cause of this be indicated without danger? Was it social
injustice? That would be an incitement to revolt. Or private injustice? It was very hard then to avoid bringing in the intervention of
some great lord, minister or magistrate, appointed to vindicate the
people.[20] Or bad conduct? The performance then risked being more
suggestive of this than punishment was useful. Or simply fate? Then
any morality lost its legitimacy. There was for example a play
performed in 1842 by two copyists who had no interest in socialism,
Dumersan and Vander-Bruch: *Les Noceurs ou Travail et goguette*
[*The Carousers, or Work and* Goguette]. This was the story of a good
worker who, having been snubbed by his colleagues, let a debauched
colleague lead him to squander his pay in the drinking dens of the
barrières. His son, seeking to rescue his father's honour, let himself
be accused of his misdemeanours, which led to his own hopes of

---

19   F²¹ 1158, 22 November 1846.
20   In *Marianne*, for example, as performed in October 1850, 'We have
noticed that the authors attributed a miscarriage of justice to the judicial
authorities, leading to the life imprisonment of the play's heroine. Despite
the fact that this involves the judiciary of a foreign country, it is still not
fitting to represent justice in general as subject to error, and consequently to
reduce the respect that is due to its decisions' (F²¹ 1045).

marriage being dashed and his ending up in prison. To be sure, a happy dénouement saw the carouser repentant, the worthy son rewarded and the miscreant punished. And morality seemed to be all the more satisfied in that it was the future worker who gave his predecessor lessons in honesty and temperance. But apart from the always vexing lack of fit between the moral order and the family order, and the doubtful involvement of a young cousin charged with getting drunk together with the unworthy father so as better to keep an eye on him, this hope for a moral regeneration of the working class was contradicted by the model son, who described his father's errors as an obligatory moment in working-class life which he knew he would himself experience one day. It is uncertain what lesson the audience in the 'small places' would draw from this familiarity with morality and immorality. The same goes for F. Duguet's *La Misère*, which attracted the attention of the police in 1850. An initial report recognized in this play the 'maxims of socialism', as all the figures of degeneracy – prostitution, theft, drunkenness – were commented on by the good worker as inevitable consequences of misery. A second inspector, rather better read, recognized the author's moral intentions, but also their ineffectiveness: certainly all the bad actions were punished, but 'the popular classes, with their bad instincts, frenetically cheered these actions or the maxims uttered by various actors, and when punishment arrived this did not bring the result that the author promised, given that the intelligence of most of the spectators was insufficient to enable them to see its application'.[21]

It is certainly hard to preach morality to people who fail to make an analytical connection between crime and punishment. In fact, however, there was something else involved here: a failure of representation, a vision that focused on the image without grasping its function. What this audience had not learned was the distance between image and reality, the art of reading its own image. But that presupposed an atomization of the collective spectator. For the time being, it was the division of places within the theatre itself that governed the reading of the image, and a play

---

21   F[21] 1045.

that established without ambiguity the dismal consequences of workers' immorality would have little benefit for public order if, while arousing the applause of the stalls, it brought 'collisions' with the 'little places'. This division was the source of a disorder expressed in a number of ways: agitation in the queue and pile-ups in the gods, the din of a claque often made up of tailoring workers, with their particular ability to disguise themselves as young play-lovers from the *beau monde*, and disorders of the imagination produced either by the drama or by the actors' prestige.[22] Hence the authorities' unease about any kind of theatre, as a place where 'morality for the people' dissolved in the materiality of the division of the hall, but also as the conduit of a mass theatricality that complemented the reverie of mobile minorities. February and June 1848 revealed something that was perhaps more disturbing than the explosive force of certain operas (*La Muette de Portici* in Brussels or *Nabucco* in Milan): a series of slippages between social reality and theatrical unreality, the capacity of the masses to perform more diligently than any opera chorus the productions by representatives of dangerous minorities (Pujol, in June 1848).

Hence the sense of the repressive measures and acts that the years 1848–50 brought down on public performances. Advance censorship of anything that was recited, sung or played in public sought to reduce the unforeseen element that the police were always too late in sanctioning. At a deeper level, it sought to make any performance space simply the place of execution of a text or a music, a place there-fore where nothing happened, where the singer or actor was reduced to the function of executor and the audience to its function of consumption. The plethora of prohibitions on cafés-concerts (choirs and ensemble pieces, cross-dressing, dancing, ballet, noisy instru-ments, spoken games, etc.) not only aimed to maintain the theatres' monopoly, but above all to remove from the delivery of a song any theatrical element, anything that could be the source of an allusion

---

22 The Lionnet brothers say that they watched Frederick Lemaître in *Ruy Blas* forty-nine times (*Souvenirs des frères Lionnet*, loc. cit.).

or a wink, any incitement of the public to active participation. In September 1852 a decree from the minister of the interior laid down that their repertoire had to be confined to 'little songs and ballads for one or two voices'. The object was to limit the theatre form and its whole chance character. And since the danger of an allusion was omnipresent, nothing could be allowed to escape the vigilance of the state. In 1854 the request for authorization from a certain Théâtre Lafayette gave rise to serious debate. Its director argued in vain that it should certainly be possible to name a theatre after the street on which it was situated. The authorities however made a distinction: streets could be named after the 'glories of national history', but a theatre could not bear the name of a political figure without becoming 'a rallying point, a centre of regrettable demonstrations'. If democracy today allowed a Théâtre Lafayette on rue Lafayette, what could prevent monarchist reaction tomorrow from opening Bossuet, Bourdaloue or Fénelon theatres on their homonymous streets? The superintendent of theatres drew the proper conclusion:

> In my view, the names to be given theatres cannot be left to the free choice of their builders or directors. From the standpoint of moral, political, and religious censorship, they must be subject to the examination and approval of the minister.[23]

And on more than one occasion, His Excellency personally intervened to judge the opportune character of a performance, or the corrections to be made to a verse. A vain attempt, of course, if it were not accompanied by a check to make sure that nothing was sung, said or portrayed that was not in conformity with what the Division des Beaux-Arts intended. It is understandable that the inspectors appointed to this service deserved extra remuneration.[24]

---

23   F²¹ 1157.
24   Cf. a note from the head of the Division des Théâtres of 4 December 1861: 'The inspectors already have a good deal of trouble in carrying out their work by day and night; I would however require them to go sometimes to other suspect theatres and exert a stricter surveillance. It would be right however for them to be allowed carriage expenses.' (F²¹ 1045).

And we can see above all how the principle of state vigilance followed less from any strategic knowledge about disciplining the popular classes, than from a tremendous lack of knowledge as to what might provoke disorder, the impossibility of mastering chance and the unforeseen, which made any site of popular presence – and quite especially all places of performance – a possible place of disturbance.

The prefect and the philosopher

It was naturally useless to hope for theatre or song capable of moralizing the people or inculcating in them proper social doctrines. This however is certainly what the prefect of police was looking for in a confidential letter of 5 April 1850 to the minister of the interior, forwarding him an account of the situation on the front of the eight theatres: 'Here revolutionary plays are performed, there reactionary ones, everywhere immoral ones.'[25] At the Théâtre Français, Ponsard's *Charlotte Corday* only made use of the 'horrible' Marat as a foil, the better to have the 'butcher' Danton's 'moderation' applauded. At the Porte Saint-Martin, *Camille Desmoulins* was taken in the wrong sense by the people, who applauded in it Robespierre's 'bloody maxims'. At the Vaudeville and the Gymnase, 'the cheering was intercepted by royalist tirades'. At the Gaîté, *L'Affaire Lesurques*, which depicted a miscarriage of justice, 'taught the people to suspect magistrates and sovereign decrees'. And we should cast a veil of modesty over the Variétés, where *Les Chercheuses d'or* was 'simply a pretext to represent a few pretty actresses in costumes most advantageous to their figures', or the Théâtre Montansier, where, in *L'Odalisque*, 'a young Lazarist missionary follows on the heels of a lost girl', let alone the Ambigu, where 'a priest, in the house of God, rapes a *bohémienne* almost under the eyes of the audience' – in the prefect's view 'not the way to have religion and its ministers honoured'.

---

25   F²¹1045.

This categorization of Legitimist, 'anarchist' and saucy plays formed a circle for moralizing intentions. It was certainly possible to encourage a theatre that would denounce anarchy. But how could this be done without a 'partisan spirit'? The prefect certainly enjoyed the performance of *Suffrage 1°* at the Vaudeville:

> This is a lively and sharp criticism of the situation, light-hearted and intelligent. Socialism is represented under the old and sulky features of an ancient red Zephyrus who everywhere breathes emaciation, destruction and death . . . Up to that point, all is for the best.

Unfortunately, however, the authors did not stop at that point:

> Then there are Legitimist verses, direct allusions that make a cleverly conceived satire into a partisan play. It is a fine and noble mission for authors to criticize the cretinism of certain minds, flagellate to the quick the men of revolution, and show the phantom of evil doctrines in all its hideous ugliness, but let them not make panegyrics for any particular party. The Empire, the Restoration and the July government all had their raison d'être. Honest people from these times have to forget their particular allegiances and work together to ensure the country's future. We have to unite and not divide.[26]

Suffrage 1° was thus banned. But the government of Napoleon III was soon forced to extend this censorship of Legitimist plays even to Bonapartist works, capable of arousing resentment among those 'honest people' who were partisans of the previous regimes. The same logic would lead to the censorship of anti-Communard songs in the wake of the Commune.[27] In the same way, the works of Erckmann-Chatrian and a good number of patriotic verses deemed susceptible of arousing 'the susceptibilities of the German

26   F^{21}1045.
27   Cf. F^{18} 1681.

ambassador' were proscribed later on under the Third Republic.[28] This diplomatic prudence was accompanied by an evident desire not to give free rein to a patriotism that was still on the side of subversion in the aftermath of 1870. It was impossible, in other words, to imagine an official art for the people. Praises of the existing power always risked creating 'collision' in an audience already divided everywhere that there were cheap and expensive places. The only future solution to the problem of popular culture would be a performance in which there were only proper seats, with no communication between the classes. These aporiae of popular moralization sketched in relief the home entertainment of the future: television, where the absence of the public would make it possible to present the most revolutionary works without risk, whereas the nineteenth-century boulevard audiences could not see the existing order celebrated without risk of disturbance. When the sub-prefect of Lisieux was consulted as to whether it was opportune to perform *Hernani* in his town, he traced a path to the future with his positive response, arguing that 'literature does not exert enough influence on minds in Lisieux for any literary work to be able ever to overexcite passions'.[29] What happy sub-prefectures, already familiar with governing silent majorities!

There was no right politics in the theatre, and so there should not be any politics at all. What was needed was a performance devoid of any extrinsic excitement. But was not an entertainment confined simply to pleasing the senses, with no excitement for the imagination, by that very fact outside of morality? Wasn't a bar with no more singing or politics a bar where people would drink more? (The surveillance of the Empire corresponded to an increase in the number of establishments.)[30] Was it possible to escape political passions and divisions without uniting the public in the cult of depravity? A year after the start of his campaign, the prefect of police noted the following development:

28   F²¹1331.
29   F²¹996.
30   Cf. Levasseur, *Histoire des classes ouvrières de 1789 à 1870*, vol. 2, p. 767.

I have had cause to notice that . . . since plays of a political character no longer attract the public, theatres seem to seek to speculate on scandals of every kind . . . At the present time, the Gymnase with the play *Manon Lescaut*, the Porte Saint-Martin with *Le Vol à la duchesse*, each night offer a spectacle in which morality is unworthily outraged, in which theft, libertinage, adultery and suicide vie for the public's applause.[31]

More significant still was the development in song titles that fell victim to censorship. In 1854 a list was drawn up of those that could not be sung either in the theatres, in concerts or in cafés-concerts. Political titles were particularly prominent: 'L' Aumône du pauvre', 'Le Credo républicain', 'Le Chant du prolétaire', 'Le Christ au peuple', 'Dieu sur terre', 'La Fraternité', 'La Hongrie', 'La Misère', 'L'Ouvrière', 'La Patrouille républicaine', 'Le Pain de l'ouvrier', 'Le Travail plaît à Dieu' (dear to Poulot's heart), 'Le Transporté', etc. loom large.[32] By 1868, however, political songs were hardly censored any more. The censor's scissors had moved on from heroic and sentimental titles to songs such as: 'Commes elles sont toutes', 'Com'on s'marie cheux nous', 'Comme on fait son lit on se couche', 'La dalle en pente', 'Essayez-en, La femme à soldats', 'Je garde ça pour mon mari', 'Je voudrais bien en tâter', 'J'risque le paquet', 'J'n'ose'rai jamais dir'ça d'vant l'monde', 'Et l'zist et l'zest et l'rantanplan' . . .[33]

Virtuous republicans were quick to conclude that the Imperial state supported the vulgar genre in order to root the love of republican virtues out of popular hearts. Yet the care that its officials took in tracking the least bit of sauciness in the texts, and the

31   F[21]1045.
32   'Alms for the Poor', 'The Republican Creed', 'Song of the Proletarian', 'Christ for the People', 'God on Earth, Fraternity', 'Hungary', 'Poverty', 'The Working Woman', 'The Republican Patrol', 'The Worker's Bread', 'Work Is Pleasing to God', 'The Transported Man'. [Tr.]
33   'The Way of All Women', 'Our Kind of Marriage', 'As You Make Your Bed So You Lie On It', 'The Sloping Roof', 'Have a Go', 'A Woman for Soldiers', 'I Keep It For My Husband,' 'I'd Really Like to Try', 'A Risky Business', 'I Wouldn't Dare Tell People', 'This That and the Other'. [Tr.]

least gap between performance and programme, indicates something else. What we can see behind the balance between liberal
and repressive measures is rather a desire to undo the disorder in
an artistic and moral hierarchy of genres. The abolition of theatre
privileges in 1864 was designed to encourage all halls to raise the
level of their repertoire. At the same time, the police who reduced
political passions to pornographic passions defined a genre that
was inferior both artistically and morally, a genre unworthy of
the interest attaching to the defence of freedoms and whose most
stubborn opponents should in all logic recognize that it deserved
additional repression. It was rather in this sense that censorship
and 'immorality' went together, breaking the old familiarity of
aesthetic and political emotion, morality and immorality. This
distancing was supplemented by that of a professionalization
which, before being the occupation of a new niche, was induced
by this very repression, which – as revolutionaries well know –
always professionalizes by the very nature of the techniques that
it imposes, either in order to conform with its predictions or else
to get round them. In the event, administrative procedures, the
calculation of concessions and risks, called for a technical speciality of licensing.[34] But it was not only for reasons of principle that
each year the rejected songs piled up in the boxes of the Division
des Beaux-Arts. It was rather that the demeaning of the vulgar
form risked constituting a new unity, in whose troubled waters
could be seen the formation of other figures of demand and revolt:
a demand for the very spontaneity that the café-concert attributed to the vulgar, or the use of the outspokenness it liked so as
to slip from doubt about the virtues of one's wife to doubt about
the virtues of the government. The first kind included for example the song 'Pas toujours les même' ['Not always the same'],
with the subtitle 'Récriminations panachées d'un soiffard qui n'a
pas son compte' ['Recriminations of a boozer who doesn't get his
share'], listing all the grievances of the worker as against the

---

34   This same mechanism of hierarchical ordering and specialization has
of course played a role recently for 'porn'.

happy fate of the bourgeois, in lines whose ridicule could easily
be turned around:

> You see how the toffs, to make an impression,
> take on two or three lovelies at a time,
> passing from a beauty thin as a board
> to others like the Boeuf Gras.[35]
> And when their darling no longer pleases them
> they find another who is more to their taste;
> while the worker only has his housewife,
> the same soup and the same stew.
> *Spoken:* Oh yes, I've seen enough of that stew!
> One thing that vexes me is how the landlord
> sends round his agent every three months,
> and on the pretext that we're tenants
> each time demands his full rent;
> and the poor worker gives them a wage
> with which they act the great matador.
> It's not enough for them to be a landlord,
> their house has to bring them something as well.
> *Spoken:* Oh yes, I've seen enough of the landlord!
> *Chorus:* A half measure doesn't scare me
> but I'll tell you all the same,
> it's not always the same people
> who'll have all the gravy;
> and when my turn comes
> I'd like to afford a dish.[36]

In this ditty from 1872, whose author clearly has no particular
tenderness for the cause of workers' revolution, how is it not possible to sense the presence of both the real and the imaginary stakes
of spring 1871: from the moratorium on rents to the famous letter

---

35   The Boeuf Gras (Fatted Ox) was traditionally the last meat eaten at
Carnival, before the beginning of Lent.
36   F[18] 1681.

that proclaimed the right of workers over bourgeois women?[37] We
see clearly here how the vulgar genre reconstitutes this level of
uncertainty where derision and demand can always exchange
roles, giving a positive expression to the 'vulgarity' that Rosa
Bordas exalted under the Commune.

The second genre included, for example, another song with
spoken interjections from the year 1872, 'Franc comme l'or'
[Honest as Gold]. The hero, who 'calls a spade a spade', after
making fun of his grocer neighbour who invites him to the baptism
of his latest child 'whom he claims to have had single-handed', and
after refusing to shake the hand of a 'young shrimp' out of fear that
by touching his white skin he would sully his own dirty hands of
an honest worker, ends with a patriotic rhyme that he punctuates
with a spoken commentary stigmatizing the bourgeois traitors as
'cowards who deserted the threatened city'.

> Those people . . . I don't know the name that history will give
> them, but for me, honest as gold, I call a spade a spade and I say
> that these are cowards and traitors who betrayed or sold out the
> country.[38]

The patriotic protestation here is a Communard one, and the
morals of dirty hands that are opposed to the appetite for enjoyment of the 'not always the same's' are combined here in the theme
of the anarchist song that plays simultaneously on the denunciation of the 'clean hands' and the proclamation of national
'recovery'. Once again here, the revolutionary ideal and its derision play a subtle game that makes it possible for anarchists to turn
around several songs composed in order to ridicule them.

Confronted with this game, the successive forms of state power
were not so much complacent as caught in a circle: by censuring

---

37 Cf. J. Rougerie, *Procès des communards*, Paris 1964, p. 197.
38 In 1868, for example *L'Esprit du Jour* denounced 'the garish slang
of fashionable show-offs/the great misconduct, dancing and blow-out',
contrasting the era of the Boeuf Gras and bearded woman to the blessed time
'when our ancestors sung the Marseillaise' (F[18] 1680).

political songs, they supported a vulgar genre that they likewise had to censor so that it did not restore the old ambiguities of popular culture and define new practices of subversion. Hence a spiral of repression, even censoring songs that denounced the very immorality which they censured. Moralizing songs had no more real existence than had politically healthy theatre. In their distant Icaria, the last disciples of the now dead Cabet might well imagine a new role ascribed to entertainment in order to raise the 'moral barometer' of their community, promote a three-point programme 'work, learn, be entertained', and press young girls to use all their charms so as to attract to the ball those recalcitrants who did not want to share their moralizing pleasures.[39] In an ordinary society, this should not even be dreamt of. The best intentioned despaired at the impossibility of raising the 'very low' genre of popular song. Jules Simon, as minister of public instruction in the aftermath of the Commune, confided his discouragement to the prefect of police. He might well blame the 'orgy of song' produced during the Commune, and undertake a new 'pruning' of the repertoire with a view to eliminating 'what had invaded the cafés-concerts and had lowered still further this low genre already so low in itself and so little deserving of interest', and so as to avoid (bad) surprises of execution he had all pieces numbered and required copies of each to be sent to the commissioner. But apart from the fact that it is impossible to be everywhere, and that the most dangerous songs escaped the censorship commission for the simple reason that they were not submitted to it, the evil had more distant roots:

However severe the examination of productions designed for these establishments, however rigid the surveillance of the prefecture of police, the evil lies today in the very existence of these places with their smoking and drinking, where people come together with no idea of morality or art, simply to spend their evening in coarseness.

---

39   Cf. Beluze, *Lettres icariennes*, Paris 1859. F²¹ 1338.

Hence this appeal to the prefect of police's moralizing imagination:

> As for me, if I could suppress them all I would not hesitate for a
> moment. I am constantly preoccupied by the desire to have honest
> and decent music compete with this hateful music. I am looking
> everywhere. Have you not found something on your side?[40]

Little hope, in fact, from this side. The chief of police had a better
understanding of raison d'état than the philosopher-minister, and
as long as public order was maintained, he was ready to dispense
with public instruction. He even proposed, after due examination,
to legalize the recent custom of smoking in the theatres. The author
of *Le Devoir* sought in vain to explain to him that this was not
simply a matter of safety, but of knowing whether it was permis-
sible for anyone who liked to indulge their coarse passions
anywhere that they cared to do so.

Puritans at the barrière

All evidence suggests that Jules Simon should have knocked on
another door – now barred to a man newly enrolled in the great
party of Order: that of the working-class elites with whom he had
rubbed shoulders when he was in opposition to the Empire and an
adviser to workers' societies. It was traditionally among these
minorities that the concern for popular morality had been real,
well beyond the sceptical or hypocritical condescension of bourgeois moralists. The worker songsters who both waxed indignant
at the rubbish of the café-concert and provided a model for singing
of quality, calling workers by hand and brain to forget recent rifts
in order to construct the Republic of Labour and Progress,[41] were
heirs to a working-class cultural tradition that had found its firmest
expression in the workers' newspapers of the July monarchy, and

---

40   F^{21} 1338.
41   Cf. Eugène Baillet's songs 'Le Bataillon de l'avenir' and 'Place aux
déshérités' (F^{18} 1681).

especially *L'Atelier*. Repeated protests against bawdy songs, the Sunday – and Monday – drunkenness at the *barrières* and the wildness of Carnival, could be understood when they came from workers who had recently returned to the religion of *L'Atelier*. But the communists of *La Fraternité* were a match for them on this very ground. And the doctrinaires who wrote these papers were sometimes outbid by their readers. On the celebration of Bastille Day in 1847, a subscriber to *L'Atelier* strongly protested in the name of his comrades against the ignoble dancing at the Carré Marigny that sullied the national festival:

> These dances that cannot be given a name are performed exclusively by men, largely the dregs of society, since even the most degraded women refuse to join them . . .
>
> The labouring class forcefully demands the suppression of these immoral dances, which are not only a sad example given to the youth, but which can also wrongly give a quite bad opinion of the working class, since this actually rejects them quite unequivocally.
>
> We workers therefore demand from the authorities, as guardians of public manners, that they should take the necessary measures so that these dances are suppressed in future and remain so.
>
> Please excuse, gentlemen, the liberty I take in addressing this request to you. But it is in the name of several comrades, all workers, who ask to make known by way of the press the strong desire that they have to see the entertainment in question replaced by another more worthy and above all more moral.[42]

The Carré Marigny, at the foot of the Champs-Élysées, was the place where the first cafés-concerts were established, the place where the first elements of the Fête Impériale were formed; the place, too, where the following spring unemployed workers would come to 'gawp', to the great scandal of the bourgeois and the editors of *L'Atelier*. It is clear that the latter were not speaking

---

42   *L'Atelier*, July 1847.

simply on their own behalf when they adjured the authorities to exercise their power to put an end to the ditties of street singers and the excesses of Carnival – 'so pernicious and dismal'. These pleasures degraded the workers; but perhaps less in relation to pure morality than in relation to the bourgeois who moved in the space of the workers and exercised their gaze upon them. Beyond the virtuous protests and reminders of Christian morality, two fundamental arguments were opposed to the licence of popular festivals and entertainments: the cult of pleasure was an infiltration in the ranks of the people of bourgeois materialism and egoism, dissolving elements that isolated individuals in the quest for an egoistic satisfaction and turned the people away from collective occupation with their affairs, as in the chorus denounced by *L'Atelier*:

> A plague on politics!
> To make a song
> my simple muse
> takes up a Bacchic chorus.
> Long live the gurgle of bottles
> And the sweet kisses of lovely girls . . .[43]

This 'egoistic' debauchery of the worker was borrowed from the bourgeois, and offered in return a spectacle that the latter could use as an argument to justify his oppression:

Our hearts swell when we think that among the reproaches either well-founded or undeserved that the privileged address to us, and by means of which they justify their oppression or their indifference, the most common accusation is generally put like this: 'What can we hope for from the people? Just look at them delivered to their own instincts, their natural aspirations! They are ferocious in their passions, and cynical in their pleasures. Do they know any dividing line between good and bad, just and unjust? And let no one accuse us of prejudice: present ideas have so deplorably

---

43   *L'Atelier*, August 1844.

mingled ranks and distances that we have to speak in full knowledge of the situation! Do we not see them every Sunday, when we
cross one of the *barrières* on our way to the country – or when we
do jury service at the court of assizes, etc.'[44]

Two themes thus knot together in a remarkable way: the definition
of a workers' morality of labour and devotion reflects the desire to
free workers' initiative from bourgeois tutelage. But at the same
time, the image of the worker is asserted as a cornerstone of the
system of dependence to which the proletarians are reduced. The
workers have to reject the egoism of bourgeois pleasures, and
destroy this image of the drunken and debauched worker that
serves as justification for paternalism and moralizing projects. The
required self-discipline then combines a declaration of working-
class independence with a representation of the worker who has to
prove his respectability as social partner in the eyes of the bourgeois. It is in this way, rather than in the abstract demand of
moralization, that the demands of the working-class elite take up a
position parallel to those of the discourse of the state. The common
target of both ideas is this mixed cultural space that was one of
encounter and exchange between bourgeois and proletarians: the
goguette where the worker seeks to raise himself to the rank of
artist or music-lover; the dances and bars of the *barrières* where
young men from good families came to pick up girls of the people;
melodramas and serial novelettes that gave working men dreams
of the life of the great, and working women dreams of the languor
of courtesans. In this half-real and half-fantastic geography of
inter-class exchanges, Carnival held the central place: a festival of
animality (satire, masquerade, and the Boeuf Gras), cross-dressing
(between bourgeois and workers, men and women, human and
animal . . .), a festival to which people of society came slumming
while enjoying the spectacle – both horrifying and reassuring – of
popular vulgarity.[45] The '*descente de La Courtille*', i.e. the return to

---

44   *L'Atelier*, May 1844.
45   Cf. Alain Faure, *Paris, carême-prenant*, Paris 1977.

the Courtille *barrière* of drunken masqueraders, cast out of the
Belleville *ginguettes* on the morning of Ash Wednesday, defined
the peak of intolerability for these theorists of working-class
dignity. In 1854, the typographer Benjamin Gastineau could still
pen an essay about Carnival that dwelt on this vision of horror:

> People thrown out of the *guinguettes* who rush out drunk and stag-
> gering, trampling under foot those who fall; women with police
> caps over their ears, a pipe between their teeth and dressed up in
> sequins, as Pierrettes, as cheeky kids, as fishwives . . . women
> dishevelled, dirty, broken, their gaze numbed by the fatigue of
> vice, with greenish lips, crumpled breasts, and stained clothes . . .[46]

There were also the cries of animals and *arlequins*[47] being thrown
from the windows, to be gathered up by the drunkards and hurled
in the faces of the privileged who had come to the spectacle in their
carriages. This was the key relationship for which the greenish lips
of the broken women of the people were simply a metaphor, this
was the sensitive point: the participation of these society figures,
following the example of the famous Milord l'Arsouille (Lord
Seymour) in sharing the emotion of popular orgies, and with
whom the people maintained a double relationship of exhibitionist
complacency and aggressiveness, reproducing the old relationship
between riches and poverty that working-class political activists
sought to break in favour of a new organization of relationships
between labour and property. Carnival had precisely the same
structure as philanthropy: an exchange of services in which the
poor, by displaying the exposed body of their misery or their
debauchery, paid the offering of the bourgeois-voyeur. The
generic name for this exchange – that which the virtuous editors of
L'Atelier would transmit to the less bashful Karl Marx – was 'prostitution', and the thinking of both converged in denouncing the
same book of popular exhibition/prostitution, *The Mysteries of*

---

46   B. Gastineau, *Le Carnaval*, Paris 1854.
47   Leftovers from restaurants.

Paris. The mixed space of cultural exchange between workers and bourgeois could only be for the worker the site of prostitution. When Benjamin Gastineau cited prostitution and suicide as fatal consequences of Carnival, his discourse was more metaphorical than real. One might rather say 'prostitution or suicide'. In the logic of this thinking, the person who does not prostitute himself as poor could still commit suicide as a worker. This was precisely the case with the carouser and the worker-rhymester. The person who goes fishing for praise from his brothers in the *goguette*, or seeks to forget the hardships of labour by hunting for rhymes, cannot be accused of selling his image to the bourgeois. But his desire to escape from his condition leads him to declass himself in relationship to the work from which he lives and to no longer tolerate the gap between his dreams and the very poverty that these can only increase:

> If they are at work, they have no enthusiasm or application; and if one considers the pitiful lowness of wages today, and how it is at the price of a stubborn perseverance, on the condition of an obstinate use of his time, the worker's only and precious capital, that he can satisfy even his absolute necessities, it is then easy to understand what serious disturbances are necessarily produced in the situation of these people whose minds are constantly bent towards any preoccupation save that of their task.[48]

It did not even need to be said that the worker should not concern himself with versifying; enough simply to note that he could not do so, that any activity that turned his attention from a work hardly sufficiently to live on was suicidal. But the argument cut both ways, and the de facto impossibility conceals an opposition of principles. For didn't the author of this article also devote his evenings to something other than restoring his labour-power, and didn't the articles he had to write, or the meetings of the *L'Atelier* committee he had to prepare, also occupy his daytime thoughts in the

---

48   *L'Atelier*, October 1844.

workshop? And didn't the struggles that his paper supported expose their participants to the risk of losing their livelihood? The mortifying use of free time had thus to be divided in two:

> There are however among the working people men of energy and conviction who, in order to attain improvements and pursue the reforms that the present situation of the labouring classes demands in an immediate and imperious fashion, generally sacrifice a few hours of their day, and nobly brave the crisis that an interruption in their everyday work must cause for them; but what an enormous difference there is between those who, placing themselves at the elevated standpoint of general salvation and emancipation, take some moments from their thirteen hours of toil that they abandon to the cause of all, and those fools whose distractions have no other goal but to satisfy their egoistic and sterile vanity. In a situation where ceaseless application is for the worker more or less a condition of life and death, the moral concerns of the former pertain to devotion, while the preoccupations of the latter amount to suicide.[49]

Everything that goes beyond the application and reproduction of labour-power does indeed appear on the side of death. But that death may be either sacrifice or suicide. The opposition between the carouser and the activist, as antagonistic figures in the working-class minority, was perhaps only so strongly drawn in order to evoke the disturbing awareness of their kinship. To produce a workers' paper, participate in the organization of an association, a republican society or a utopian chapel, to spend one's evenings discussing the best plans for the organization of labour or preparing the means for transforming the political and social order opposed to it – was this really no more than the performance of a duty? Was it not also an advance that brought the worker out of the everyday life of the workshop, raised him above his comrades, and made him an interlocutor of the guardians or reformers of the

---

49   Ibid.

bourgeois order? Did the insistence placed on devotion to the service of his brothers not serve to conceal the idea that some desire to escape or cross over to the other side of the cultural barrier might be involved? Did this concern for a pure class morality not deny the minority consciousness that inspired both the workshop poet and the activist for his class? The author of this article, the typographer Charles Supernant, was himself a repentant carouser, and had formerly mounted the boards of the itinerant troupe of the Seveste brothers. The typographer Benjamin Gastineau, scourge of Carnival, had been Proudhon's collaborator before himself crossing over to the camp of 'men of letters'. And the thinking that they developed was indeed the emanation of those associations of workers who habitually rubbed shoulders with journalists and men of letters. It should be no surprise that those most bitter in defending a pure ethic of the worker-activist were precisely those whose labouring activity placed them constantly at a limit that was not so much a rigid boundary as a place of transition between two classes, themselves composed of hierarchies and minorities. We need only recognize this original twist to the activist worker ideal, this need for the fraction that stands on the border with the other camp to reassure itself of its position by the most intransigent class discourse, to deny the process of *minoritization* that gives it its place by proclaiming its adequacy to a *duty of being a worker*. Their moral indignation in the face of the orgiastic exchanges they saw at the *barrière* of pleasures was less the effect of inculcation by the 'dominant ideology' than the metaphorizing of uncertainty as to their own place, a voluntaristic reflux in the flight that carried minorities of the working class to the other side of the cultural barrier.

The Belleville battalion

A game of hide-and-seek thus began between working-class moralism and raison d'état. For when workers appealed for stricter policing, this was always in the form of denunciation and as an opposition discourse. In 1844, Supernant suspected the authorities of allowing the spread of the rubbish they were supposed to repress, the better to demean the working class. It was this vision that guided republican protest against the Parisian gaiety of the Second Empire, whether in opposing the 'Paris of working people, scholars and artists' to the 'Paris of racecourse and love affairs',[50] or in stigmatizing the degrading entertainments by which the state sought to corrupt the people. The café-concert was the first target of this denunciation. A common front came into being against its rise: the former censors of carousing rubbed shoulders with the old carousers whom they had previously denounced. Nostalgic visions now insisted on the moralizing virtue of the old-style *goguette*, where either wine was not sold at all, or else the intoxication was from music; where families could come, assured that they would hear only music of quality. As against the hierarchy that repression maintained, it was now the concept of quality that defined the combined artistic and moral dignity of the old-style songs. In the pantheon of popular song, artistic and progressive, the austere Supernant found himself side by side with the specialist in ditties, Édouard Hachin, the abominable author of 'Allons Javette, frippe ta cotte' ['Come on Javette, rumple your petticoat'], 'Gertrude n'est pas prude', etc. This popular song, they explained, needed 'always and everywhere its free space'.[51] At one stroke, the bawdiness of the good old days became part of the progressive heritage. This reconciliation was supplemented by another: the Lice Chansonnière, a society of republican singers, saw its old monarchist adversaries of the Caveau develop in its direction. In 1878 they combined their forces to found Le Chanson.

The situation was not a good one. The Republic had followed the Empire without the corruption associated with it seeming to suffer. When the Republic was consolidated after 1877, these representatives of the good old tradition proposed a genre of song worthy of it, exalting labour, progress, education and the reconciliation of classes, one of the best examples being 'Le Bataillon de

---

50   Report of the musical-instrument makers, 1867 Exposition Universelle.
51   *Le Chanson*, June 1878.

Belleville'.[52] But if these songs were in no hurry to support their struggle against the café-concert, was it not that their analysis of Imperial corruption was somewhat inadequate? They themselves sensed, in various incidental remarks, that something had happened that went beyond the classic 'circus games' and explained their reduction to a rearguard role. At the monthly banquet of the Lice, on 1 May 1878, few people showed up, and those attending were distracted by the nearby fireworks and bustle of the Exposition Universelle. At the August banquet of the Caveau there were, according to *Le Chanson*, 'few people and little silence'. Two factors were responsible: 'summer holidays on the one hand, the insistence on talking politics on the other.'

52

We are the people of Belleville;
in order to slander us
the tallest tales are told
and often make us smile.
We can walk with our heads held high;
what does our cohort want?
Sons of the hammer and chisel,
we write on our flag:
'Long live industrial France'.

Peace and glory to humanity!
Our hands break the steel that kills;
liberty on its plinth
takes the plough as its emblem.
Under the three-coloured flag
let's drink to an end of all quarrels;
coiffed with sheaves and flower
the republic invites all hearts
to its fraternal feasts.

Refrain
With arms, head and heart, useful phalanx
march on to progress!
This is where the Belleville battalion
is born, lives and dies.

'Le bataillon de Belleville', words by J. J. Evrard (1878).

Significant examples: if the *goguette* passed away at the moment
when the consolidated Republic shed its refrains of yesteryear, it was
because a certain connection between the gaiety of the festival and
the seriousness of politics had become untied. The cultural space of
the former working-class minorities was now cut across by the division between a political game whose acts and discourses were well
coded, and the deliberate constitution of popular pleasures as entertainment. It should be no surprise that the Exposition Universelle
has a revealing role here. Ever since 1867, the Exposition had been
the site, both symbolic and real, where workers could see both art
and industry detached from their labour. Our carousers, however,
no longer experienced the same working-class unease in the face of
this competition as they had in 1867 when faced with the reality of
labour divided and made foreign to the worker.[53] It was with neither
rancour nor regret that on this 1 May 1878, precisely when one of
their number had just sung Chebroux's 'Fête du travail',[54] they broke
off their meeting to admire the fireworks of this triumph of industry
whose image was now merged for them with that of the Republic of
labour (the 'industrial republic'):

> The chairman of the Lice, intelligently assessing the situation,
> broke off the meeting before the customary time, and all went to
> enjoy the magic sight of a general illumination, finding that the
> tremendous clamour of a people ardent for the peaceful struggles
> of labour and progress was worth the best of songs.[55]

---

53   Cf. 'Off to the Exhibition', above, p. 64ff.

54

> In the hive where the wonders of your works
> will shine tomorrow
> oh workers, dear bees,
> bring new tools.
> To constantly create where men now strive
> let's replace all deadly weapons with the tool;
> place for what produces . . . out with what kills
> a working people is a people rich and strong.
>   – Ernest Chebroux, 'La fête du travail'.

55   *Le Chanson*, June 1878.

As far as the appreciation of industrial harmonies was concerned, our songsters were a match for Toussaint Turelure. Their newspaper, moreover, boasted an advertisement for *La Dentellière*, a joint-stock company for the machine manufacture of genuine hand-made lace. Oddly enough, a certain number of suspicions seem not to have struck them: that an era in which 'genuine' hand-made lace was made by machine quite naturally risked a similar mass production of 'genuine' popular song; that it was precisely the impossibility of distinguishing genuine hand-made lace that gave them the status of (impotent) judges of genuine song; and that perhaps the shameful industry of the café-concert, far more than their old-style handicraft, gave the Industrial Republic a music adequate to it. Was not their crusade for good song a means to avoid raising the question whether this magic spectacle of industry did not have something in common with the 'lowness' of this new industry of leisure and entertainments, the product of a concomitant loss of workers' hand and voice.

It was not that professional skill had represented, as is often said, the necessary centre of a working-class culture. This culture had perhaps been still more the result of de-professionalization. But when this took the form of an imposed deskilling, the escape routes for free time were also redirected. What was lost by hand and brain to the benefit of the materiality of organization and the instruments of labour, was also lost by the voice in favour of singing entertainment. On the one hand there was less singing in the workshop, and less movement between the workshop and the street where singing was done; on the other hand the transformation of the urban space, which in many respects moulded the organization of the city after that of the Exposition, tended to undo the confusion of space in which bourgeois and workers circulated together, workers on errands (or carousing) and perambulating artists, and to bring entertainment back to specified sites.[56] The deskilling of workers and the modernization of

---

56 Jules Vallès, for example, indicates the fate of the popular street singer Théodore Leclerc and his companions: 'Their concert hall used to be the

the city went together with the rationalization of state surveillance in the professionalizing of singing, transforming those no
longer able to sing at work either into stars (a tiny minority) or
spectators (the great majority).

The biographies of the first café-concert artists are of interest
here. Victor Renard, the former foundryman we mentioned
above, had previously sung on his *tour de France*[57] or for his
fellow workers. After his success as a street singer in 1848, he
made a number of tours with his guitar before taking up his trade
again in Reims. Playing in an amateur theatre there, he succeeded
in being noticed by the local dramatic company, which took him
on. From there he moved on to the Paris Opéra, before vocal
problems made him retreat to the intermediate stage of the café-
concert, of which he became one of the leading lights.[58] The
career of Thérésa, the performer – shunned by old performer –
of 'La Femme à barbe' ['The bearded woman'], 'La Vénus du
boeuf gras' ['The Venus of the Boeuf Gras'] or 'Rien n'est sacré
pour un sapeur' ['Nothing is sacred for a fireman'], was more direct
but equally significant. Apprenticed in the fashion trade, she was
dismissed on the grounds that her singing stopped her fellow workers from working. 'It seemed perfectly simple to me,' she remarked,
'that one sung just like one ate, to obey the call of nature.'[59] Sent by
her next employer to take a bill to an artiste, she delayed in order to
listen and found herself sacked once again. After passing through
eighteen jobs in two years, one day she ventured to enter a court-
yard to sing, and thus she begun her career as a professional star
because of being forbidden to sing in the workshop. This professionalization was henceforth accompanied by a cult of the star,

---

Champs-Élysées, where they paid 12 francs 50 a month for their place. This
permission was withdrawn, and now they could only deal with *cafés-chant-
ants*. They were engaged for a season. For a fixed price of . . . they were
contracted to appear and given the benefit of the receipts' (*La Rue*, Paris
1866, p. 133).
57   See p. 27, footnote 2.
58   Cf. Marc-Constantin, *Les cafés-concerts en 1866.*
59   *Mémoires de Thérésa*, p. 14.

maintained by well-orchestrated quarrels and scandals, by each new star writing their memoirs (or having these written), and by the development of an entire specialized press. As Thérésa rightly put it in one of her songs, 'you have to give people something for their money'.

This professionalization was something that those nostalgic for the *goguette* refused to consider as such. Their criticism of Thérésa and her colleagues was made on two levels that gradually became confused: aesthetic defence of quality and moral denunciation of corruption. But the first of these criticisms only had the effect of confirming the hierarchy that we saw was induced by repression itself, isolating the sector of 'quality' singing from the singing of the café-concert that was open to all. The second took over the denunciation of that 'image of the people' which the bourgeois had fabricated in order to impose it on the people themselves: 'Refined people were ecstatic at hearing works that travestied the spirit and form of popular poetry, while the mass of people, with little insight, applauded these caricatures that were handed down from above as faithful portraits.'[60] The very self-evidence of this demonstration was now subject to caution. In *Le Tableau de Paris*, written on his return from exile, Vallès paid tribute to Thérésa, opposing the boldness of the queen of the Imperial café-concert to the timidity of singers under the Republic:

> One day a woman from that direction arrived with virile gestures and voice at a time when men had their mouths sewn up and their arms cut off.
>
>   She cried: 'But you have to give the people something for their money.'
>
>   And the people understood, applauded, and made the fortune and glory of this singer of 'Le Sapeur' who undermined the Empire with a laugh.[61]

---

60   *Le Chanson*, 29 May 1880.
61   *Le Tableau de Paris*, Paris 1932, p. 200.

But Vallès's praise was itself ambiguous. Wasn't the vehemence of the voice he praised precisely made up of the silence of others? Of those, first of all, whom repression had hunted down and sometimes driven to suicide (like Charles Gille); of all those, more widely, who would no longer sing in the streets, the workshops and the *goguettes*, but now went to hear stars and peddle a culture made up of the noise of authoritative voices and the rumour that accompanied them? That was why Jules Vallès, with the populist complicity of a rebel *bachelier*, ended up with an outlook not very different from that of the autodidact workers who defended morality and quality. If he rehabilitated the café-concert, this was strictly in the context of the right of good people to their share in relaxation and compensatory illusion for the harshness of the workshop:

> People like sometimes to leave the domestic hearth, where they don't burn the candle at both ends, and go where there are big gas lights and plenty of gilt. For a few sous you have the luxury of a millionaire before your eyes. And then, however foolish these songs may seem, they help people forget the hard words of the boss or the troubling words of the bank manager. That is at least something gained over the enemy.[62]

The reference to Thérésa in this context, the star of the café-concert in the 1860s, played the same nostalgic function, in these words of the exile returning from banishment in 1880, as the pre-1848 *goguette* did for others – a call to give French song back its lost virility:

> Instead of stupid barcaroles, Bengali chants, savour-less farces, hymns sprinkled with powder to be sung with the air of a dove or a monkey, the new muse would be offered the great wine of the peasants and workers, poetry both sunny and dark, the paradise of nature, the hell of the workshop . . . Come on, old music-hall, you don't have to stand there like a bleating sheep; you have to rebel,

---

62   Ibid., p. 199.

and make revolution like your comrades. Only a traitor could
leave the Gallic skylark of French song in the net of the enemy.[63]

The discourse of the former Communard seems divided in an
exemplary fashion: between a nostalgia for the republican muse, its
songs of workers, peasants and vine-growers being an extension of
the ideology of the *goguettiers*, and a modernism that does justice
to the entrepreneurs and stars who give the people dreams in return
for money. At all events it follows the same displacement, no
longer addressing the workshop poet in his relationship to his
brothers, but rather the artiste in his or her responsibilities towards
their popular audience.

Vallès's rehabilitation thus effects a certain slippage, by way of
which the question of how workers use their free time sits alongside the defence of the consumer. In his estimation, the wine that
warms the heart should replace the pallid milk that the café-concert
poured into its listeners' ears. But this double demand for quality
– on the part of both the producer and the consumer – was one to
which the entrepreneurs of the new entertainments had an answer.
Defenders of the café-concert replied to the political and moralistic
denunciation of those who criticized them for stupefying the
people by claiming for their undertaking a civilizing character
rather similar to that which served as justification for Haussmann's
cuttings. If these destroyed the old dens of immorality and sedi-
tion, the café-concert had the role of purifying the coarseness of
popular pleasures that made up the old-style street entertainment.
Marc-Constantin, a songster won over to this new art form,
rejoiced to see these gradually abandon the 'vulgar and outdated
means' of attracting onlookers that had initially been borrowed
from the tradition of travelling shows: bird-men, one-legged danc-
ers, clown-violinists and various phenomena, all those
'heterogeneous elements' that they had tolerated in the early days
of their existence steadily disappeared from it. A contributing
factor to this elevation was also the comfort of the new halls, which

63   Ibid., p. 201.

discouraged coarseness of speech and gesture. In the same way, the tradition of taking a collection was abandoned, lingering only in 'the sleazy Paris cafés-concerts, the nomadic fairground troupes, the squalid casinos of sea ports and garrison towns'. Struggling against all these manifestations of bad taste, the cafés-concerts would manage to wipe out their 'original stain' and confer on working-class pleasures the 'dignity' that their austere representatives themselves demanded. Could they not also oppose to these recriminations the additional proof of labouring dignity represented by the formation in 1865 of a mutual aid society of café-concert singers?[64]

---

64   Marc-Constantin, *Les cafés-concerts en 1866*. We can see here how, to the same argument about 'circus games', the promoters of new entertainments could oppose the educational and civilizing character of their enterprise. This continued, in sum, a certain policy of the spectacle and performance that combined two things in one: purging the coarseness of popular manners, but also dissipating the confusion of mixed and unclassifiable genres, practices and spectacles. This commercial 'moralization' could thus link up with the more concerted policy that presided over the individualization of sport as a specific form of performance and leisure activity. The beginnings of this popularization of sport, when Jules Simon, having perhaps discovered the philosopher's stone of moral entertainment, stretched out a hand to the ex-Communard Paschal Grousset and the Marquis de Coubertin, were possible on the basis of an aristocratic purification of popular gestures. The paradigm of this purification was French boxing, as effected by masters such as the Lecour brothers, who removed it from stevedores and pimps to make it the pleasure of nobles and men of letters: 'M. Charles Lecour has brought this struggle of crooks, the boxing of the Court of Miracles, to an art, he has raised it with a single blow to the level of English boxing. Revised and corrected by him, these ignoble gestures have acquired elegance and grace.' This certificate of nobility was awarded in 1847 by one of Lecour's best clients, Théophile Gautier. But Lecour, a singer of sentimental ballads, still belonged to the mixed culture, just like Bruneau, a slaughterhouse worker, who also sung ballads alongside his boxing activity, or August Massé who sung Pierre Dupont's songs with 25-kilo weights in his hands (Charlemont, *Le boxe français*, Paris 1899). It was this kind of exhibition that sporting dignity would henceforth reject, as it also rejected cycle races organized in a fairground context, etc. This was the meaning of the struggle for amateurism.

A seat at the Châtelet

At a time when this moralizing republican discourse was led to withdraw to the ground of 'quality', the entrepreneurs of entertainments and promoters of the new city could counter it with another 'morality'. To the aristocratic morality of working-class cultural minorities, they opposed the practical purging of the coarseness of popular manners that the nobility of the new streets and the elegance and comfort of the new places of popular entertainment would necessarily produce. But was this raising of manners anything more in fact than the improvement in the context of life or leisure, was it more effective than all previous regulatory and moralizing efforts? The *barrières*, which had resisted past anathemas, would not resist the integration of outlying communes into the city.

The idea of profiting from the embellishments of the capital to undo the disorganized confusion of the old popular cultural space was expressed in two different directions: the stimulus to an architectural repression that expelled the unwanted population along with their rickety buildings; and the quest for means to make the pleasures of the working-class population more comfortable, and therefore more civilized. Evidence of the first is the petition drawn up, on the eve of the 1855 Exposition, by landlords from the Château d'Eau quarter, who brought up to date, in a perspective of the Exposition city, the old aesthetic protest against the coarseness of popular pleasures:

A considerable number of the most eminent inhabitants of the 5th and 6th arrondissements met together on 18 December last to protest against the deplorable state of the land situated on the rue de Bondy between no. 2 and the rue de la Douane behind the Château d'Eau, facing the Boulevard Saint-Martin. The alignment of the rue de Bondy and the new Boulevard du Nord has seen an accumulation of dingy cobblers' shops, fried-potato sellers, etc. on a jumble of stalls that are not lit up at night, a café-concert closed off by a piece of sordid cloth where an exhibition of giants is held, a public dancehall on the first floor, parts of which are smashed in, with an indescribable appearance and threatening ruin on all sides. This state of affairs has dishonoured the quarter for seven years, attracting immorality and compromising safety.

But now that this place will become a link between three boulevards, the Boulevard du Temple, the Boulevard Saint-Martin and the Boulevard du Nord, created by the initiative of His Majesty the Emperor, it is impossible to let this situation continue, paralysing the profitable building industry, since this site is naturally designed by its magnificent position to receive major constructions that will cast light and prosperity on the quarter. The exposition universelle will open Paris to France and abroad, and the authorities cannot tolerate that people who come to admire the Château d'Eau will find as backdrop to this fine monument the unworthy spectacle of these huts.[65]

This is an exemplary text in the formation of modern 'public opinion'. In a wonderful short-circuit, the former disorder of the popular street, its little shops and precarious buildings, not really constructed and not really closed, is opposed by both material and moral safety, national prestige and the interests of the construction business – which are also, as everyone knows, the interests of the workers themselves. Wide streets, solid buildings and artistic perspectives also mean a balanced distribution of populations, hence the concern that shines clearly through at the end of the petition, attacking the project for a saloon with thirty billiard tables:

There already exists the Café du Hameau, the café-concert Boulevard du Temple, opposite the dramatic theatres, and several much smaller dancehalls. The quarter thus supports more than its legitimate share in the way of these kinds of popular establishment, and it would not be right to aggravate this state of affairs, or prudent to attract the entire bohemian population of Paris to a single point.[66]

---

65   F^{21} 1157.
66   Ibid.

This repressive version of the transformation of Parisian streets and pleasures was opposed, however, by a positive conception, which Haussmann himself promoted when he had the two theatres on the Place du Châtelet built. As well as improvements in heating, lighting and ventilation, he proposed to add a revolutionary measure: the numbering and selling of all places without a supplement. Up to that time, in almost all theatres only the good places were numbered, and seats were sold at a supplementary price. Hence a double discomfort for the 'working classes' who occupied the un-numbered places above: a queue of three or four hours in bad weather, and a throng of spectators forced to stand pressed behind the first-class seats to see something of the show. Haussmann's good idea, however, was not a response either to a concern on the part of the theatre directors or to a demand from the workers. The head of the theatre division, Camille Doucet, made it clear that both parties seemed to be satisfied with the system:

> The supporters of the present system reply that pleasure already begins at an earlier stage; that the queue is its first element, that waiting adds to it and that the gaiety expressed there is the best argument against those who want to suppress it. The directors, for their part, see it as a living advertisement for the theatres; the crowd attracts a crowd, and success is proclaimed even by its victims.[67]

In one sense, this popular patience and gaiety should have gratified the authorities. It ruled out demonstrations of impatience that might lead on to more serious demonstrations. But it was precisely this way of integrating the non-pleasure of waiting and the disorder of the queue into the arrangement of pleasures that was suspect; this ability to waste time, and even take pleasure from it, was no longer in vogue:

> The authorities have to take a higher point of view. The queue is itself something disorganized; if the people joyfully accept it and sometimes find a certain pleasure in it, it is no less true that in every

---

67   F²¹ 1045.

respect it would be better that they were not forced into it. They could easily be doing something more useful, for example continuing their work. That would be more rewarding and more healthy.

There is no reply to this argument: someone who can spend three or four hours standing at the door of a theatre would spend this time more usefully in working. A good organization of pleasures should not allow them, along with the trouble of waiting, that of themselves calculating their pleasures and pains. That was precisely Haussmann's intention: to enable each person to have their own numbered place, giving them that luxury which at the moment only the privileged could obtain against payment; and to suppress at the same time the disorder of the galleries, bound up with the existence of places that were unnumbered and invisible:

> From the moment that people pay, it is necessary for each to have their place; it is right that each person can sit down in order to decently enjoy the show, and that workers are no longer piled up pell-mell, men and women together, as at the free spectacles.
>
> All the galleries will have seats, each spectator will be in their place, as is already the case at the two circuses and the Hippodrome.[68]

It is remarkable how this argument reproduces the classical discourse of philanthropists about housing – even in its fantasies of sexual promiscuity. What Haussmann proposed to do for popular leisure activities corresponded exactly to the same problem that his contemporary Godin expressed as the principle of his 'Familistère' at Guise: to give the workers *the equivalent of riches*. That meant in particular to give them, by the stimulant of comfort, the taste for a reserved place. In all the discussion around this project, the theatre seat functioned as a metaphor for property, and the desire to have workers sitting comfortably at a show encountered precisely the same problems as the Fourierist inventors of social palaces or the philanthropists who initiated the law on slum clearance. Both of

---

68   Ibid.

them came up against the requirements of property: it was impossible to make a profit on capital from building comfortable housing at low rent on urban land; impossible therefore to require from landlords who had difficulty collecting modest rents the works that a strict application of the law would demand.[69] The prefect of police indicated the same obstacle: the intention was to turn all the places into numbered seats, but 'if a place is capable of being sold, it is indispensable that the spectator should be able to reach it readily; he has to be able to remain seated during the whole of the show, to see the stage and hear the actors.' If applied to the four main theatres on the Boulevard, this measure would have the effect of abolishing '750 to 780 cheap places where the workers could see and hear while standing, but which could not be numbered or divided, as they had no individual existence.'[70] The suppression of restricted-view places and the space gained for circulation, added to the abolition of additional prices for seats, made it impossible for the directors to turn a profit any more. And even supposing that the ingeniousness of architects found a solution, the practical problem risked turning into a philosophical one. If the workers were given the taste for cleanliness and comfort, would this not risk making them only too fond of these, and see them put haphazardly into practice the old principles of the bourgeois philosophy of property:

> How could the places sold be kept? It is already hard enough to do this with the stall seats and places of this kind: how would it be in the third and fourth tiers where only uneducated people generally go? These people will never understand that the best place does not belong to the first occupant.[71]

The prefect, moreover, despairing of a regulatory solution to the problem of queues, could hit on no better solution than to have these protected by covered galleries (another Fourierist fantasy),

---

69   Cf. Danièlle Rancière, in *Politiques de l'habitat*, Paris 1977.
70   Ibid.
71   Ibid.

only calling forth the objection that these would necessarily encroach on the usable space of the theatre and be a further drain on profitability. As with working-class housing, it was a problem of squaring the circle.

Not that this view of the problem was mistaken. It went without saying that the bourgeois order would be better assured if it could guarantee each worker at modest cost a comfortable home and leisure activity.[72] But the prefects of police, ever-present defenders of this order, knew what the prospective view of philanthropists and the retrospective view of genealogists both tended to ignore: that no regulatory or architectural disposition could confer the principle of sufficient reason on strategies that sought to assure the subordination or integration of working people in the system of domination or exploitation. Low-price comfort can be neither invented nor decreed. To provide the workers with this, without damaging the immediate interests of property, would need a transformation in the conditions of production, accelerating the division of labour and mechanization so as to win the acceptance of those workers who saw the promise of their enrichment as consumers on the basis of their impoverishment as producers simply a trick.[73]

And so, as far as leisure was concerned, it was far more the spontaneity of industrial initiative that would slowly find the solutions

---

72   This prospect did not yet meet with unanimous approval from the possessing classes, more than one of their number still agreeing with the sensible words of the philanthropist in Georges Darien's novel of 1897: 'The miners of the Loire basin almost all own the little house and garden that you refer to; they live well and do not do without much. Monsieur, there are no beings more insatiable and more tyrannical towards their employers . . . The miners of the Nord departments, on the other hand, live in unsanitary slums, eat rotten potatoes, squat in the most abject destitution – and yet they do not complain, or in so timid a fashion that it is ridiculous' (*Le Voleur*, Paris 1987, p. 203).

73   Cf. the discussions on this theme at the time of the Expositions, and particularly the report of the shoemakers to the Exposition of 1862, in which denunciation of cheap production – even for the working-class consumer – and the defence of 'principled shoemaking' expand into a hymn to eternal beauty.

that moralists, town planners, ministers and philanthropists had sought in their imagination. What finally put an end to the 'orgy of song' was on the one hand the industry of the café-concert followed by that of records, which fixed it in its status as a commodity, and on the other hand the transformation of rhythms of work. And if Haussmann contributed to solving the problem of workers in the theatre, it was above all by sending workers to live outside the space where they had formerly circulated. As working hours became more constraining, and the distance between work and home greater, the problem of coexistence between workers and bourgeois in the theatre would resolve itself automatically – by the simple disappearance of the workers. Around 1900, this desertion was already well under way, amplified by a phenomenon of specialization that offered the workers more comfortable places of entertainment[74] and transformed the theatrical repertoire, which became that much more personal and psychological as its audience was socially restricted – by this very fact still further accentuating this restriction. The state, registering this phenomenon, projected four major popular theatres oriented towards the outlying quarters, with a historical, mythical and social repertoire ('the general major scientific and social ideas, in the guise of the most captivating graces of intellect and poetry'),[75] adapted to popular needs and desires. The age of 'popular theatre' could now begin. Artists and directors could bend their efforts to bringing the people the treasures of culture, putting themselves in the service of their struggles, or teaching their children the language of theatre, while dreaming of a time when theatre had been 'popular' because the various moments of the people's life (employment, work, trade, reading the newspaper, the words of protest or the gestures of demonstration) were spontaneously theatrical.

---

74 'The shabby gods of the Théâtre de Belleville are no longer considered fit for Saturday night. Instead you go down to the café terrace on the corner of the Faubourg du Temple and the Avenue Parmentier, where for four sous a head you can drink, smoke, look around, see movement and hear noise' (R. Bizet, 'L'Âge du zinc', *Le Touche à Tout*, February 1911).
75 'Les Théâtres populaires', *La Cité*, 6 April 1907.

'Le Temps de cerises'

We can compare two different regards on entertainments simultaneously transformed into myths, separated by a distance of sixty years.

In 1854, Victor Fournel, historian of Parisian street life and amusements, described the spectacle of the *quais*: where the strains of the 'melancholy charlatan' or ruined former band-leader mingled with the declamations and performances of sellers of indelible ink, ointment to make hair grow or stain-removing soap. One of the latter accosted a member of the Academy coming out of the Institut de France, to test the excellence of his product on the latter's suit. The way the honourable scholar was put to rout shows the power of a popular culture that was still an element of everyday life and labour. Victor Fournel, continuing his stroll, marvelled at the crowd who congregated and vibrated around this open-air theatre, the criers and musicians, the participation of spectators that he explained as the result of an active relationship to culture, and to music in particular:

> The people are fundamentally music-lovers ... Every street seller, no matter how surly and stubborn, at least owns an accordion that has been preciously handed down and preserved as the palladium of the household; every concierge in a good building has a piano for her daughter, a distinguished pupil at the Conservatoire; a number of workers shake off their tiredness by playing the clarinet or flute for hours on end. And so we see what an immense circle generally extends around the least of singers.[76]

No doubt this vision was somewhat idyllic, with the bourgeois journalist complacently offering his readership the spectacle of a plebs finding in its own culture the compensatory power of laughing at its masters; but the hyperbole was only possible on the real foundation of a popular relationship to music, as attested to by many others as well. Sixty years later, Lucien Descave, a writer attentive to the

---

76   Victor Fournel, *Ce qu'on voit dans les rues de Paris*, Paris 1858, p. 87.

transformations of popular life, wrote a play titled *Philémon, vieux de la vieille* [Old Soldier Philemon]. His hero Colomès, a former jewellery worker exiled after the Commune, evoked the time when song was not yet separated from daily occupation:

> The division of labour and the development of machinery had not reduced the worker to a new slavery, as it has done now. He could still salute the work of his ten fingers with a song. The noise of a machine did not drown out his voice. Do I want to sing when faced with a steel monster that is incessantly cutting or piercing holes? Just try to put words to that kind of music! The movement of flywheels and connecting rods would make it stick in your throat.[77]

Colomès-Philémon is taking up here the polemic of the old *goguettiers* against the stupidity of the new ditties. And he likes to recall the scene he made on his return from exile in a Châtillon *guinguette*, hearing young people singing the new hit 'Joséphine, elle est malade'. To 'shut them up', he stood up to declaim Pierre Dupont's song of the Commune, 'Les Temps de cerises':

> I was like the flag-bearer of popular song, real song, good song, the best song! I would have let myself be killed for it! Their Joséphine was no longer ill, she was dead! Her interpreters listened to me stupefied. After the final verse they gave me an ovation, rushed up and demanded something else . . . of the same kind![78]

This success proved, for Colomès, that the people were sensitive to beauty, and it was possible to oppose the cretinizing enterprise of those who claimed to be on their level. But one Sunday, when Philémon and his wife were 'hanging around at the crossroads' and 'humming a cavatina suited to that fine day', a different adversary came on the scene:

---

77   *Philémon vieux de la vieille*, p. 87.
78   Ibid., p. 118.

All of a sudden, from an invisible mouth, there came a rheumy and puppet-like voice, a caricature of a voice that burped out a kind of announcement that was unintelligible at the distance where I was standing. Then the popular chorus 'Viens poupoule!' [Come Here, Ducky!] started bubbling on a lively and sizzling fire, without offering us the grace of a verse.

But that was not all. The song of the streets was immediately followed by a polka with piston solo, a monologue, the aria from *Faust*: 'Gloire immortelle . . .' and a hunting fanfare, all this presented on a stage with a metal gutter rather like a dentist's bowl.

To end up, a military and dramatic medley brought to our ears the 'Charge' and the 'Marseillaise', accompanied by the burst of a fusillade, the shouts of the troops running to the assault, and finally sounds of 'Cease fire! To the flag! March!' etc.[79]

At a dizzying speed, Philémon and his friend saw the spreading invasion of the gramophone:

At other windows there appeared other vomitories – horns, trumpeting, discharge tubes, storage tanks that alternately spread the refuse of the café-concert, confused military fanfares, and the toilet waters of comic opera. It was the bar and the fairground *en famille*, the assault on silence by the most tyrannical of noises. The ogre seemed to swallow discs and spew them out, like the fairground game where a wooden frog spews out coins.[80]

It was no longer possible, the narrator makes clear, to silence the voice of 'progress' as in the Châtillon *guinguette*:

'You had the advantage over the young people taken by surprise and convinced of their error . . . but I defy you to silence this sovereign mechanism.'

'Don't be so sure,' the hero replied, 'it's one more result of

---

79   Ibid., p. 114.
80   Ibid., p. 115.

machinery taken to the extreme! After having supplanted human hands, it still remained subject to the voice . . . the human voice! Now this is held captive and filtered through a muffler.'[81]

Certainly, both the disenchanted discourse ascribed to the former Communard, and the marvelling discourse of the journalist of 1854, forged myths simply by their selection of images. The workshops, streets and shacks of 1854 did not exactly offer the backdrop of singing bohemia that Victor Fournel described. Conversely, the streets of 1913 were not devoid of singers and street cries; and self-taught workers were not without resources for escaping or subverting the new techniques of cultural diffusion. What should rather hold our attention here is the very formation of this representation, half-real and half-fantastical, of song as a 'thing of the past', the shift in perspective that these judgements – whether positive or negative – imply on worlds either enchanted or disenchanted. The transition from milling around on the street to the invasion of the home is significant, for example. On this point, the nostalgic discourse of the old Communard defines the place of the gramophone in a way that is similar in the end to that of those who praised it. In the panoply of new cultural inventions, the gramophone, even if its importance as entertainment was less great than that of the cinema, perhaps better introduced what would be the great twentieth-century revolution in the industry – and politics – of leisure: the master's voice at home. Moreover, even if they fulfilled different roles in pedagogic or advertising discourse – the concert at home or the democratic spectacle of the future – both gramophone and cinema were most often understood under the same notion, that of the pedagogic instrument with a universal calling. 'The cinema', Pathé declared, 'will be the theatre, the newspaper and the school of tomorrow.' In response to which was the gramophone's ambition to be the absolute teacher, 'the instrument that combines and performs everything'. Authoritative instruments suited to effecting the purging of popular pleasures that

---

81   Ibid., p. 119.

well-meaning politicians had set as their purpose and that the entertainment entrepreneurs flattered themselves they were realizing.

The cinema followed the same trajectory as theatre or sport,
with its origins in the travelling show. After having itself sacrificed
to 'human torsos' and other fairground monstrosities, it had
achieved all the attributes of the new respectability: between 1905
and 1910 it settled down to a sedentary existence, with comfort and
luxury fulfilling Haussmann's impossible dream, and established
good relations with municipal and police authorities concerned to
avoid new 'impulsive effects' of this embryonic spectacle. It could
now also assert its pedagogic vocation. It was not hard for the
gramophone to demonstrate that it delivered the best teaching: the
model performance of the star artist. To the listener symbolized by
the famous dog, it brought 'his master's voice'. The successors of
the typographer tenors of an earlier age would no longer have to
murder the *bel canto* arias that the illustrious Caruso had recorded
for them. The cinema, in its own way, produced a similar type of
effect. Not something incomparable, but an entertainment closed
in on itself and not repeatable. Perhaps more than the 'aura' of the
unique work,[82] the new means of technical reproduction did away
with the possibility of appropriation, of unauthorized reproduction. They supplied the technical means for realizing the pious
dreams of the repression of 1850: a spectacle at which the spectators were simply consumers – precisely because they no longer
had any connection with its production. Out of all the pilot inventions of consumer culture, the gramophone was the most
exemplary, in as much as it established passivity at home right
from the start. It is curious, moreover, to see how the theme of the
home acquired fantastical insistence in the advertising material of
the Compagnie du Gramophone. In the form of stories or poems,
the various uses of the marvellous instrument always end up being
identified with the role of organizer, guardian or representative of
the home. Here is its evocation of a warm summer evening:

---

82   Cf. Walter Benjamin, 'The Work of Art in the Age of Mechanical
Reproducibility'.

From an upper storey the Gramophone is playing and everyone listens to it. Those who had not heard of it imagine that a high-quality musical and artistic soirée is in progress. And the whole life of the building is suspended, in order to listen. Maids forget to wash dishes, children refuse to go to bed, delighted to hear such lovely sounds . . . In the distance you hear the confused murmur of other Gramophones. I tell you truly, the piano falls silent, replaced by this instrument that is so complete, that combines and performs everything . . . And in this way the triumph of the Gramophone is displayed to all . . .[83]

Despite the air of incitement to idleness and disobedience, what holds pride of place here is the function of silence. But this paradise needs guarding, and the dog then shows its other side:

> It's over: the bandits are about to break down the door,
> the children are frightened, the wife almost dead.
> But a sound suddenly rises and echoes in the air,
> another; a real concert makes the three brigands flee
> believing the building is full of fine artists . . .
> The saviour was that divine Gramophone![84]

Guardian of the home, the gramophone ends up being the home itself, transportable to the depths of the desert where the house poet imagines a burdened Arab making his way under the burning sun:

In the Desert

> The pensive traveller, full of sadness,
> his soul fatalistic and resigned,
> feels his heart entered by nostalgia:
> his homeland so far off and the road so long!

---

83   *Gramophone Nouvelles*, August 1904.
84   Ibid., March 1904.

And yet he smiles, for among his luggage
is a box – what a mysterious gift!
Its songs that strike the heart of the wildest men
will put joy and hope back in his eyes!

In the midst of the desert the divine Gramophone
delightfully conjures up the dear absent homeland,
clearly repeating with a resounding echo
all the well-loved songs, and making the present less hard.
And the delighted Arab, on his distant course,
scorns all the troubles that he might well face,
since the Gramophone with its superhuman voice
brings the song of his hearth into the bitter desert.[85]

Let us leave the poets of the gramophone with their pan-acoustic
fantasies. What strikes us as more important is how the new form of
entertainment is announced here, different from the contrast that
gave rise to the panoptic imagination. The latter, in fact, opposed to
the antique stage, as centre of attention of the popular collectivity,
the circular regard of the central observer over isolated individuals.
The formation of modern public opinion, on the other hand, seems
to have passed by way of a third figure: the central spectacle viewed
separately by each individual. In its naive advertising, the Compagnie
du Gramophone well said what television would be: the transformation of the broadcaster of the entertainment into an element of
furniture. For it was not so much individuals as state power that had
to be domesticated in order for the entertainment of the future to
function, one that would bring the whole world into the home and
let only its own production escape: the spectacle without replica,
confined in the space of the home: in no way the instrument of
'stupefication' or levelling down that certain people have described,
but rather the summit and complement of a hierarchy of leisure
activities giving each person the spectacle that suits them: the universal simulacrum in place of a thousand games of social theatricality.

---

85   Ibid., June 1904.

Was the time of cherries then at an end? In 1900, Jean-Baptiste Clément took part in a congress of singers held in the context of the Exposition Universelle – yet again the same revealing presence. The preoccupation of those attending was still the same: how to struggle against 'the growing invasion of the dramatic stage by the sickening products of pseudo-songsters who, without a care for literature, art or morality, for the respect due to the public and for their own dignity, write with the dung and mud in which they are happy to wallow'.[86] *Barrières* and prostitution: the former Communard inexorably meets up with the obsessions of Senator Corbon. But more radical than he, the president of the Caveau Stephanois let it be understood that the great struggle of morality against immorality, of quality against inanity, only made sense against the background of the exclusion of the people:

> There is no more need for songs, since they no longer sing; they hum negligently without thinking. They hum what they hear in the cafés-concerts . . . Let us admit it, the people no longer sing . . . This is why the place of true song is more than ever to be found in literature, in the manner of other poems, prestigious Iliads . . . In its happy days song was to be sung; it has become, with the creation of monologue, song to be read.[87]

It was the feeling that the people no longer sung that exacerbated the opposition between true and false singers, yet at the same time rendered this derisory, dividing verse between the two poles of literature and sexual excitation. Against the background of this exclusion two tasks presented themselves. First of all, an education of the people that required the mobilization of all pedagogic and cultural forces:

> The minister of public instruction must give every facility to teachers during the period of adult classes in order to organize

---

86   Exposition Universelle de 1900, Compte-rendu des travaux du Congrès de la chanson.

87   Ibid.

sessions of singing at which the most popular and most moral
songs will be taught . . . Societies of popular instruction (the Ligue
de l'Enseignement, the Association Philotechnique, etc.) should
encourage and promote by way of reward these moral and patriotic songs . . . and the Académie Française kindly reserve one or
several prizes to recompense the authors of the most moral songs.[88]

In order to establish a lasting place for song, 'it has to be brought
into the education of the people. A choice of the best songs should
be revised every five years, and made available to primary
schools.'[89] The other task was the combined defence of the material and moral interests of singers and the interests of the public
that song was to instruct. This task would be assured by an association able to defend the interests of its members and impose these
on the directors of cafés-concerts, with the aid of the state, to make
room for quality song. If the specifically moralizing concern is left
aside, as with the advances of commodity culture this tended to
disappear completely under the demand of quality, we can recognize the major preoccupation in which undertakings of popular
culture would now exist: where the people no longer sing and no
longer go to the theatre, the state has to intervene more and more
in order to assure the quality of popular spectacles and assure
popular spectators for quality spectacles. State pedagogy and the
trade union organization of artistes who deserve this name has to
rescue the popular audience from commodity vulgarity.

The union soon gave signs of prosperity. On 26 February
1903, a certain A. Bargas wrote to the head of the Division des
Beaux-Arts to explain his problem. In order to have his songs
sung on stage, he wanted to join the Syndicat. But in order to be
a member of the Syndicat you had to be a member of SACEM;
and to be a member of SACEM you had to have six published
songs; to find a publisher, moreover, a minimum celebrity
acquired on stage was needed . . . And to show that he was the

---

88   Ibid.
89   Ibid.

victim of a new monopoly, this unfortunate author sent the text of an article that had been published in the trade-union newspaper, insisting on the need to preserve the trade of song against the intrusion of non-member amateurs:

> The trade of songster is encumbered by people who are not what one may call professionals. These are people who obstruct progress because their temporary intrusion in a prosperous organization impedes free progress. A delay is produced and the profession, which is a hard one . . . becomes still more so, since those who are genuinely active have to struggle against others who are not. It was just and necessary that serious singers, for whom song is their trade, should combine and organize. They do not exclude any bias, but before accepting someone they insist on making sure of all the guarantees. By so doing, singers will keep their place and defend their livelihood threatened by these intruders who block the path.[90]

This marked the end of a certain development. It was no longer a question of regretting the popular choruses of the past, nor even of defending the right of popular consumers to quality or decency. Nor yet of complaining that people no longer sung, but rather that too many people did so. The new barriers completely reversed the game that had been played at the old *barrières*: the amateur singer was no longer blamed for forgetting his work, but rather for encroaching on that of others. Let each person work and struggle in their own speciality! But this enclosure that rigidified the play of yesterday's cultural minorities, by no longer referring each person to the overall character of a worker's duty but rather to the specific character of his production, was complemented by a new and radical confusion: professional and activist were here two interchangeable terms. To produce and to struggle became one and the same thing.

To be sure, this was simply a norm – which as always could be got round or twisted. The ambiguous play of cultural promotion

---

90 *Le Nouvelliste des Concerts*, 30 January 1903 (F[21] 1331).

and class consciousness, however, did not disappear. We need only look at the biographies of several members of future workers' parties to understand that the role of working-class activism in cultural promotion was not dead. The new forms (pedagogic, commercial, professional . . .) of occupying free time, of training individuals and bringing culture to the masses, opened the field of new contradictions between the lines of cultural escape and class consciousness and organization.

Acknowledgements

Following the request of Alain Fabbiani, who took the initiative
for the present volume, I have collected here all the articles that I
published from 1975 to 1981 in *Les Révoltes Logiques*, with the
single exception of 'Le Chemin du retour', published in issue
14/15, a revised version of which makes up the first part of my
book *Short Voyages to the Land of the People* (Palo Alto, 2003). All
the other articles are reprinted unchanged, including the two texts
written jointly with Danielle Rancière and Patrick Vauday. Two
of them, however, The Links of the Chain and The Unthinkable
Revolution , have been reworked to make them intelligible outside
the context of articles to which the former served as introduction
and the second offered a response. I take the opportunity here to
recall that *Les Révoltes Logiques* was not a magazine that published
these articles among others, but rather the expression of a collective of work and discussion.

Rather than keeping to chronological order, I have preferred a
thematic sequence with a view to illuminating the overall course of
these pieces, and showing both the diversify and articulation of
research topics and issues under discussion. The present edition
also includes two texts that appeared in the volumes *L'Empire du
sociologue* (1984) and *Esthétiques du people* (1985), published by the
Révoltes Logiques collective after the suspension of the journal, as
well as the text 'Heretical Knowledge and Popular Emancipation'
initially published in the collection *Les Sauvages dans la cité*
(Seysell 1985).

Chapter 1 is the transcript of a presentation for a doctoral thesis on *La Formation de la pensée ouvrière en France: le prolétaire et son double*. This was subsequently published in 1981 under the title *La Nuit des prolétaires* (English edition: *The Nights of Labor*, Philadelphia 1989, forthcoming 2012 in a new Verso edition with the title *Proletarian Nights*).

Index